I08814639

Moments In Time

JEFF PORCARO STORIES

by Robyn Flans

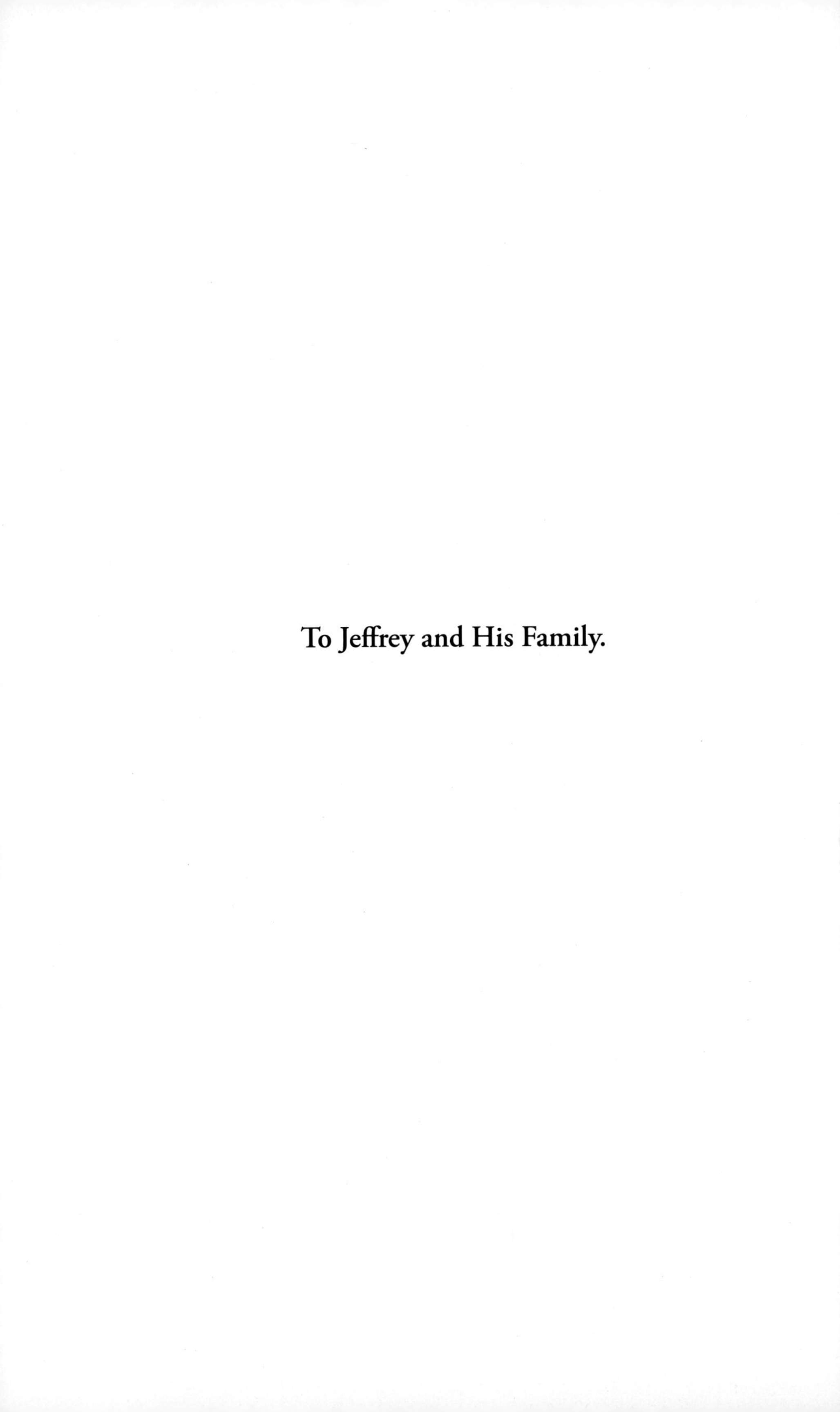

To Jeffrey and His Family.

Moments In Time

JEFF PORCARO STORIES

by Robyn Flans

Edited by Joe Bergamini
Produced by Rob Wallis
Book and Cover Design by Michael Hoff
Cover photo courtesy of Barney Hurley
All photos used by permission.

Jeff Porcaro Discography provided by the website Jeff Porcaro Session Tracks
Maintained by Mary Oxborrow
View the full discography with future updates at frontiernet.net/~cybraria/

HUDSON MUSIC®

CONTENTS

THANK-YOU'S

Forever to Taylor and Jamie, my twins, my inspirations, my heart of hearts, the loves of my life, who give my life purpose.

To the Porcaro family for the never-ending support, especially Steve who lets me bother him all the time!

To the Toto boys, who have always been there for me during this emotional ride.

To Gary Katz, the greatest gift Jeffrey left to me!

To Barney Hurley, for whom I am so grateful! He has championed this cause and assisted me in collecting photos, as well as procuring interviews, every step of the way.

To Andy Leeds for sharing his personal never-before-seen photos.

Always to Jim Keltner for letting me bug him.

To Randy Goodrum for his special contribution, and Steve Forman for sharing his poem which Mercy Baron so kindly sent to me.

Again to Karen Kent and her entire family for a loving friendship that included financial support that kept a roof over my head at times when it almost caved in.

To Ed Eblen for always coming up with the next idea.

To my dear forever friend Bruce Wandmayer, who coincidentally was born the same day as Jeffrey and bought my first book for so many friends, and whose presence on this planet I will miss for the rest of my days.

To Jason Wall, who has changed my life.

And always to Rob Wallis, for his support and enthusiasm, and for bringing both books to fruition, in addition to Joe Bergamini and the entire team at Hudson Music, whom I couldn't do this without!

Gary Katz (seated), Walter Becker (left) and Donald Fagen (right) at the Village Recorders, Los Angeles, California, during Steely Dan sessions, circa 1973. (Photo by Roger Nichols, courtesy of the Roger Nichols Estate)

FOREWORD

I think of Jeffrey a lot!

I met Jeffrey along with David Paich as they walked into a barn deep in the San Fernando Valley, at Cherokee Ranch Studio, where there was a miniature noose hanging from the doorway as you entered. This prompted Jeffrey's first words to me: "Damn, this is a tough room!" We were beginning to record Steely Dan's third album, *Pretzel Logic*, and once again we were having more than our usual share of difficulties—which is to say, a whole lot. We had been trying to get a basic track for the song "Night by Night" and having no success or luck. Either would have been more than ok with us. Denny Dias, one of the band's guitarists, said he knew these two young and great musicians, which, as it turned out, were Jeff and David. Collectively, we were all more than hoping Jeffrey and David would play it more "steady in time," something that was the very most important aspect of a track to Donald. All I was thinking was, "Geez, I hope these guys can play this, otherwise we're going to lose the song."

At the time, obviously, I had no idea that Jeffrey and I would become as close professionally and personally as we did. I remember that first night, beers were in hands, and joints were being passed as Donald played the song down for Jeff and David to learn. Fortunately, it was a great evening, getting a wonderful track, and it was the beginning of a long-lasting friendship I hold close, to this minute.

Our friendship evolved quickly as a result of the time we spent together in the various rooms we were most comfortable in: studios. During those days, we spent time getting to know each other as we did—not knowing he walked into Cherokee Ranch that night already a dyed-in-the-wool Steely fan. He and Denny had developed a friendship when Denny came to L.A. from New York, joining Steely as the other guitarist along with Skunk Baxter. Jeff would finish a date across town and come to the studio where we were working, walk in, let out a "yo" and fall asleep on the couch, usually under the console while we were working—and of course, commenting (in his sleep) on the mix from below. We all loved having him in the room. Not many just walked into a Steely session and plopped down. It was totally cool with Jeffrey, because it was "Paco," as I called him. There was never a word about his being in the room, from anyone, anytime!

As time went by, Jeff and I formed a close friendship, and timing being what it is, Steely was in somewhat of a transition from being exclusively a five-member band to feeling more open to working with other musicians as well. It was a natural course of events, and so the timing of it all was perfect.

I still cannot believe when Jeffrey broke his right hand while playing midnight volleyball at Cher's home—the night before we were going to be recording! He walked in the studio with a sizable cast on his right hand saying, "It's cool, I can play," but it was easy to see that Donald was more than concerned about the situation. With Jeffrey being his cocky self, he went into the drum booth as the other musicians were getting ready, and after starting to play and having great difficulty, he threw his sticks against the wall and said, "Fuck this, get Purdie," and walked out. At this point Donald was more than upset that Jeffrey had just left, leaving us and the other musicians looking at each other. Donald said we should end the session, but I said no, not only to calm Donald down, but to buy some time and give myself a few minutes to try and work it out. "No, no Fagen, he'll walk around the block, and he'll be back" —which is exactly what happened. Jeffrey walked back in fifteen minutes later and said, as was his custom, "Yo, let's play!" Thirty minutes later we had a great track of "Black Friday."

Jeffrey's talent as a musician was equal to his professionalism and willingness to make something work, no matter what it took, not just for Steely, but for everyone. Admittedly, I, along with the artists I worked with, were demanding of the musicians, for sure, which

Jeffrey not only accepted, but in his way, welcomed as a musical challenge, which I appreciated as the producer and admired as a friend. Jeffrey was the ultimate "team player": someone you could always count on to go the extra two miles, after hours of playing, which I was (more times than not) apt to ask for.

My most rewarding production and studio experience with Jeffrey took place in New York, recording the title track for Steely Dan's *Gaucho* album. There was an understanding between Donald and Walter that if we couldn't get a track as we all wanted, in a reasonable (or more likely, somewhat unreasonable) amount of time, Fagen would say, "Let's stop. These are the best musicians in the world, and if they can't play it the way we like and want it, there must be something wrong with the song." We lost songs I loved over the years because of this, and I could smell it was about to happen again, only this time to one of my favorite songs: "Gaucho." As we were recording and not quite getting the track as we wanted, I heard Fagen say to Walter, "It's not quite right and it's not going to happen. Let's go," which made me nuts. "No, no. Not this time Fagen. We are *not* going to lose this song." Walking toward the door and smirking, he said, "Walter, let's go, and If you guys get something you like, call and let us know. I'll be home," as they walked out of the control room. As they walked out, everyone else slowly (maybe not so slowly) followed, except for Jeffrey and another close friend, bassist extraordinaire Chuck Rainey. Donald and Walter's walking out only added fuel to Jeff and Chuck's well-deserved egos. We were all determined to get a track and make them have to come back to the studio in the wee hours of the night—and see them eat the large portion of crow we were going to prepare for them. Along with Elliot Scheiner and Roger "The Immortal" Nichols, Jeff and Rainey played it, literally, bar by

Gary Katz at A&R Studios during the *Gaucho* recording sessions. (Photo by Roger Nichols, courtesy of the Roger Nichols Estate)

bar into the wee hours, and after Roger's many magical edits, we had a track we loved. I was more than glad to call Fagen between 4 and 5 a.m. and, with a smirk, wake him and say, "You need to come back, we have a track," which, amazingly, they did—half-heartedly and more than half asleep. They listened only once, and Fagen said, "Nice job, sounds good," and left. Jeffrey was as proud as I was, and we left together—smugly!

Anytime I picked up the phone or saw Jeffrey or ran into him, anytime I was with him, it was cool, and in some inexplicable way, calming. I'd come home at night and my wife would say, "You have a message," knowing full well who it was, but she knew I liked hearing his one word greeting: "Yo." One of Jeffrey's most endearing qualities was his unending loyalty; always there when you needed him. There were a few others like that, but Jeffrey was my friend and part of the band—no matter which band. And he was always himself – a pain in the ass or not, he was always himself.

I think about Jeffrey often. I'll drive up to Woodstock (which I do often), where we spent good times and made records together. I'll think about him when a track we did comes on. People here and there will come up and talk about something that had to do with Jeffrey. Little things will cross my mind and make me laugh, and I wish I could call him and say, "Yo. What are you up to?"

Gary Katz

PREFACE

When my book *It's About Time: Jeff Porcaro, The Man and His Music* was released in September 2020, I was quite honestly surprised by the overwhelming outpouring of response. I expected excitement, but not quite to the emotional degree that occurred. I received countless messages from people all over the world about how important that book was to them; how long they had waited, and how they didn't want to finish it because they didn't want it to end. I'm still getting messages from people telling me they are on their second and third readings of the book and how grateful they are. Often they mention the discography; I'm grateful to Mary Oxborrow for allowing us to use her original, upon which Joe Bergamini could expand.

All the messages, posts and comments made me wonder if there was more to do. Some wrote to me and told me they wished they had known I was writing a book because they had a story about Jeff. Hmmmm… It got me thinking.

And then I met Jeff's youngest son, Nico, at Joe Porcaro's memorial service. When he told me how much the book meant to him, I knew I had to do another one. I understood that my dedication in the first book—to Jeffrey and His Family—really was what it was about. I had meant to write the book for Jeffrey, to leave his legacy behind for his sister, brother, and most importantly, his children. It had really impacted Nico. It was my responsibility to continue to do this.

Plus, if I were honest with myself, I was not ready to let go.

After working eight years on the first book, I was feeling a sort of post-partum blues once it was done and out in the world. Somehow continuing to work on Jeffrey's behalf makes me feel close to him and helps me manage the large void he has left in my own life.

In the process of working on this book and continuing to speak with people in his life, I was able to uncover some more interesting stories and even correct a few errors unwittingly told in the last book. I even found some inaccuracies in the discography while speaking to some of the additional artists for this book; we have corrected those.

I was able to dig deeper into some of the accounts of those infamous Jeffrey episodes and perhaps finally get to the truth. Then again, we all must remember that sometimes, even people who were present at the same event might recall the story differently from someone else all these years later. I ran into quite a bit of that. In some cases, I had to go with the old "majority rules" principle and leave out the one person who had an extremely conflicting version. Sometimes I included all the different recollections with that qualifier.

While doing some more exploring I found additional hidden musical gems like the quirky and whimsical Kenny Loggins cut "Some Kitties Don't Care." I wanted desperately to have Loggins weigh in, but after months of trying, it turned out that he didn't recall the recording of the track. Still, I mention it because Jeff's nuanced playing makes it worth taking a listen. As I was proofreading Jeff's discography one last time, I took a listen to Clover's *Sound City Sessions* and lo and behold, discovered that John McFee, who would go on to be in the Doobies, was at the core of that band—and Huey

Lewis was its vocalist. Another treasure definitely worth checking out! In some cases, with a song I might have overlooked in Jeffrey's catalog, if the artist was gone, I found someone to talk about Porcaro's contribution, like with *Tonight!* by the Four Tops. Hearing Levi Stubbs singing on top of Jeffrey's feel was magic!

Even I was astounded at the sheer abundance of players who recounted how Jeff was responsible (as Myron Grombacher put it) for not only getting them through the door but kicking them through the goal posts and teaching them about paying it forward. By his actions, Jeffrey taught so many individuals lessons—in their craft, in their demeanor, and in their behavior. The impact of his too-brief life is nothing short of profound.

I am grateful for the many reviews of *It's About Time* on Amazon, about 98% of which were glowing. The other 2% will surely be the same people who won't care for this book because there is no discussion of Jeffrey's death, and it consists only of a bunch of stories, obviously from those who admire him. Again, like the last book, it is not all Pollyanna. Jeffrey was Jeffrey, and like the rest of us mere mortals, he had flaws. Although he took his work very seriously, he had his own way of doing things that, for some, took a little getting used to. The people I spoke with were forthcoming about the pleasure, the quirks, the lessons, the irritants, the generosity, the kindness, the hilarity, and the silliness that was Jeff Porcaro in all the music and occasions they experienced with him. This book is not a biography—the last one was. This is a collection of memories from people who were privileged to share space with Jeffrey in those *Moments in Time.*

Robyn Flans

ODE TO JEFF

Words and Music by Randy Goodrum and Larry Williams

HE CAME FROM SOMEWHERE WITH HIS AMAZING BAG OF TRICKS
HE REACHED INSIDE AND FOUND SOME MAGIC STICKS
AND WHEN HE PLAYED EV'RYONE'S HEAD TURNED HIS DIRECTION
THEY SAT AT ATTENTION

HE JOINED A BAND MADE UP OF SOME KATS HE MET AT SCHOOL
TIME WOULD TELL HIS STORY WITH ITS ENDING WAY TOO SOON

GEORGY PORGY, NINETY-NINE, LIDO SHUFFLE, HOLD THE LINE
GOD BLESS THE DRUMS ON AFRICA
JO JO, LOWDOWN, HEY MISS SUN, ON ROSANNA, HE'S THE ONE
THAT MADE THE GROOVE THAT'S NEVER BEEN OUTDONE

HIS MAGIC POCKET KEPT TOTO STRAIGHT AND TRUE
HIS KICK AND SNARE BECAME THE GOLDEN RULE
THE WAY HE LAID IT DOWN, HIST'RY WILL SAY, APPROACHES PERFECTION,
HE WAS THE HEART OF THE SECTION

HIS TWELVE-EIGHT SHUFFLE WAS A NEW WAY TO BREAK **THESE CHAINS**
AND DON'T FORGET TO CHECK OUT **PAMELA** AND **I'LL BE OVER YOU**

IN THE BLINK OF AN EYE HE JUST DISAPPEARED
WAY BEFORE HIS TIME HERE WAS THROUGH
ARCHIVED TO LAST THROUGH THE AGES
CAPTURED, THE NOTES THAT HE PLAYED ON

GEORGY PORGY, NINETY-NINE, LIDO SHUFFLE, HOLD THE LINE
GOD BLESS THE DRUMS ON AFRICA

Paul Young and Jeff. (Courtesy of Paul Young)

SUMMER 1992: SO YOUNG

PAUL YOUNG picked up the phone. It was producer Don Was on the other end. "I have some bad news for you," he began and proceeded to tell Young that Jeff Porcaro had just passed away.

Young, best known for 1985's number-one hit "Every Time You Go Away," was stunned. Jeff had just been in the studio with the two of them two weeks ago working on Young's album *The Crossing.* When he got that call, they were in the middle of overdubs and had to take time off because the news hit like a ton of bricks. Several of the musicians were Jeff's close friends and were shaken to the core. Everyone wanted to attend his funeral, including Was and Young. "I remember his children were there and they were coloring," Young recalls. "At the end of the funeral, they rolled up their colorings and put them in the coffin with Jeff—with drumsticks."

Young says that Jim Keltner's eulogy meant a lot to him, because he was still getting to know Jeffrey, and Keltner really "filled in the blanks" for him that day.

Producer **DON WAS** (who has worked with everyone including Bob Dylan, Ringo Starr and the Rolling Stones) first mentioned Porcaro to Young a year earlier, while Young was in Los Angeles to write and gather material for the album. Later, when Young and Was met to talk about musicians to use on the album, Was brought Porcaro's name into the conversation. "He was saying he would use Jeff on this song and that song, and another drummer for another couple of tracks and another drummer," Young recounts. "At the end of it, just before we started, he said, 'You know, I've been thinking about this. I think Jeff's the guy to play on all of these songs.' So Jeff was there for all of the studio sessions that we did. 'It Will Be You' came in at the eleventh hour, along with two that the English record label wanted. I didn't think the record needed those, but I went along with it." (It was only after Jeff was gone that the record company rejected a couple of the songs and wanted some additional tracks recorded. Two other drummers, Ed Greene and Peter Van Hooke, were called in for those tracks.)

Was explains that back in those days there was money to spend and the luxury to experiment in the studio, "so we would try to cast the musicians for each song," he says. In fact, he points out the amazing level of players on *The Crossing,* such as Billy Preston, Larry Knechtel, Dean Parks, and Pino Palladino—and says he believes it was the only time Porcaro got to record with legendary Reggie Young.

Unfortunately, Porcaro didn't come on to Was' radar until about 1990 because of preconceived notions he had of the drummer. By then there was little time left to work with him. "The big picture regarding Jeff was that I was stunned that he could do anything. For a number of years, I didn't call him for sessions because I heard him on some slick records and thought, 'Well, that's what he does,' and it wasn't appropriate for the kind of records I was making," Was explains. "The first time I worked with him was when we did Bonnie Raitt's 'Luck of the Draw.'" (More about that later.)

Young met the band at Ocean Way Recording Studios. Pino Palladino, Young's regular bass player, had told Young that Jeff was his favorite drummer with whom to play. Young, of course, knew of him. During the session, Young was doing guide vocals with the musicians. "When we would go into the control room to check back with what was being done, that's when it became apparent what a great drummer he was," Young says. "He'd be so delicate and yet he could really play

Lenny Castro (percussion), Paul Young, Reggie Young (guitar), James "Hutch" Hutchinson (bass, Bonnie Raitt), Benmont Tench (Hammond organ, Tom Petty & The Heartbreakers), Don Was (producer), Jeff Porcaro, Larry Knechtel (piano). (Courtesy of Paul Young)

hard as well."

The track "Souls Unknown" was rejected by the record company, to Young's dismay. "I loved it, it was out there," declares Young. "I was singing in a darker, lower side of my voice, which is why the record company didn't like it. It was perfect for a vampire movie—in fact, I was trying to get it into Interview for a Vampire, which they were filming at the time. I was looking for management and I went to see Peter Asher. He liked most of the stuff I played for him, but when I put on 'Souls Unknown,' I saw confusion go right across his face. If you want to hear how Jeff can do something really delicate, there's the track 'Follow On,' and the other side of that is 'Souls Unknown,' which showed up on my box set *Tomb of Memories*."

Also on the box set is another Porcaro track not on *The Crossing*: a Texas swing version of "Cold Sweat." Reflecting on some of the other tracks, Young says he loves "Won't Look Back" because of Jeff's understated playing. He also brings up the jazz-flavored "Half a Step Away." "I wanted it to have a feeling of walking into a '60s jazz club on Sunset—and that was another thing he could play. He's known as a rock drummer, but he absolutely nailed that one as well. That's probably one where Don was thinking it could be done by someone else, but then realized, 'Ah Jeff can do that one too; he'll nail it.' He plays that so delicately as well."

Mark Pinder, the drummer from Young's earlier albums, who at that point was assisting Young's manager, was thrilled to hang out at the studio and watch Porcaro. According to Young, Pinder says that Jeff told him that he sometimes got a tingling in his arms when he played. "Mark who is quite a conscientious guy, quite a spiritual guy, said, 'Have you ever had a health check?'" Young remembers. "Jeff said no, and Mark said, 'You should have one.'"

Young was so impressed with Jeff that he mentions Porcaro's "perfect time" in his liner notes. While tracking the slow song "Follow On," Was pressed the talkback and said, "Jeff, we're so close to the take we want. If you could just take it down one or two BPM's." "There were no click tracks," Young reminds. "Jeff was tapping his hi-hat with his foot. While he was doing this, he got a pouch out of his shirt, a cigarette paper, put some tobacco or something in it—all the time keeping time with his left foot—and said, 'About this tempo, Don?' 'Yeah, that's it, it's just under what you had before.' 'Ok.' I saw him lick the paper, roll it with one hand, pick up the drumsticks whilst he was going, 'one, two, three...,' put the cigarette in his mouth, light it, put the drumsticks in both hands and go bam, and start the song so softly."

Was says for three weeks after Jeff's funeral, they were working on the album and while playing back the songs, they could hear Jeff counting them in. "It tore us up," Was says. Looking back, Young says that next to his first album, which broke him as an artist, *The Crossing* has become his favorite album in terms of being a pleasure to make. "Jeff played a large part in that," he says.

FELIX CAVALIERE

Before '92's *The Crossing,* Don Was produced **FELIX CAVALIERE**'s *Dreams in Motion* (although it was not released until 1994). This would be Cavaliere's fifth solo record after the demise of The Rascals—the legendary group in which he had had mega success as songwriter and lead vocalist (sometimes sharing duties with Eddie Brigati).

When Was told him he had hired Porcaro for tracks on *Dreams in Motion*, Cavaliere said, "What? Are you kidding me? Holy Shit!" "Jeff was a good guy," says Cavaliere. "He and I just really hit it off." Why the instant connection? Felix just laughs and states unequivocally, "We're Italian." It was a mutual admiration; knowing Jeff as I did, I can only assume he was a big fan of Cavaliere's from his iconic work with the Rascals like "Groovin'," "Good Lovin'," "I've Been Lonely Too Long," "How Can I Be Sure," and "People Got to Be Free." And Cavaliere knew exactly who Jeff was. "He was just so good it was ridiculous," Felix says. "When I met him, it was kinda like animals: they admire one another; they admire one another's talent and then there was that nationality bond.

"Don works a little different than other producers," Cavaliere says. "He brings in these monster talents and then he just lets them do their thing. And then he says, 'Yeah, I like that,' or, 'I don't like that,' or, 'Try this,' or, 'Try that.' It's their ideas that are generated." Cavaliere's record-making philosophy is the same. He welcomed the input 100% "A lot of the stuff was actually created in the studio. One of the songs came out like one of the Toto songs (Note: he thinks it was "Youngblood") and Jeff really did the whole thing. I came in with an idea that I played on the piano and the next thing I know, this magnificent drum arrangement took shape. He started playing this groove and I said, 'It sounds pretty good.' Which is how it should be. In the old days, we had fun making records. We had a good time."

Was told me that on this project a few of the tracks were challenging and "Jeff saved the day." Cavaliere concurred. "I know Jeff enjoyed the freedom on this record."

While singing a guide vocal as the musicians cut the track, Cavaliere could really appreciate Jeff's playing. "What a drummer! Ridiculous!" Felix says. "So precise. Tasty. And so easy to work with. Like butter. Just perfect. Sometimes drummers can be a little nutty. And really, a guy with his reputation, you don't know what to expect. But he was such a sweetheart. It was a joy."

Felix says early in the sessions, Jeff invited him over to his house. "He said, 'Why don't you come over and watch the Super Bowl? I just went out and bought a big screen TV so we could watch it.' I went over and we spent a little time together. I was always very thankful that I got a chance to work with him and to get to know him a little bit. He had some of the greatest stories I ever heard, because his dad was around all those famous jazz musicians," says Felix. "He told me a funny story about Miles Davis. Jeff's wife had just had a baby, and Miles came over. She was breastfeeding, and Miles just stood there looking at her. Jeff said, 'I was getting a little nervous because he was spending a lot of time there,' and finally Miles said, 'You know, that kid picked a great place to have lunch.'"

"LUCK OF THE DRAW": 1990

No one could play the song! It wasn't that Ricky Fataar, who had started recording with Bonnie Raitt in 1971, wasn't a great drummer. According to Don Was, the problem was that songwriter Paul Brady had created a drum part that was highly unnatural for a drummer to play.

"Luck of the Draw" was to be the title track for Raitt's eleventh album, the follow-up to *Nick of Time,* which was her commercial breakthrough, winning three Grammy Awards. Explaining what form the song was in when it came to them, Was says: "Paul Brady made a demo of it and played a drum machine by hand, in real time. Nothing was quantized or fixed or anything; he was playing along with a click, and he triggered the pads. He did things that no drummer would do, so it went against the physiology of a drummer, but it was great for the song. It was basically the bass drum not playing a pattern but going with the vocal. No one could get it right. They could come close, but it was like you had to do exactly what Paul did for it to work."

They cut a version that was really good, with a great vocal, but it was missing what Brady had done on the demo. Someone said, "Jeff Porcaro can play that." Was, having never worked with Porcaro at that point, said, "Really? OK. Cool." He called Jeff in to overdub drums onto the track. "We said, 'It's complicated, man. It doesn't make any sense.' He said, 'Just play it for me.' We played it for him once. He wrote it down as it was going by, then went out and played it perfectly in one take. It was unbelievable," Was says, still in astonishment today. "Listen to it. It's not what you would play on the bass drum, but he understood why it worked for Paul and he figured out what it was. He just listened to it one time, made some notes and executed it perfectly. I've never seen anyone do that. And it's not just that he got the mechanics right; he played it so soulfully.

"There are a lot of guys who had technique and there are also a lot of guys who could play with feel but didn't have the technique. Jeff had them both," Was continues. "And he had great ideas. There was truly nobody like him. When he died it was like, 'Wow, there are certain kinds of records no one is going to be able to make again,' because he was the only guy who could play on it. There hasn't been a new Jeff Porcaro. When he passed so did a certain kind of music."

WHO CAN WE GET

by Steve Forman - August 6, 1992

who can we get
on such short notice
in less than half a lifetime
a tour barely begun
the band so tight like brothers
all up inside each other
so exquisitely knocked way back
instantly infinitely locked
in the pocket
like family
they don't even
rehearse they
just play.

who can we call
to count four free
to set up the chorus
with that kind of feel
who can fill
with just one stroke
the turn-around
who could possibly fill so
perfectly the crucial spaces
for the killer mix
the living room
the tiny faces
just by being there
Oh Jesus
who do you call

who could we get
for the big band
for the rest of us
forget it babe
that's all
its a ten
its a wrap
its the moment
till they put out the new calls

and who can I get
to keep my own thing steady
I've gone thru every book
the AFM the RMA
my own best list
today so small
with nobody quite reliable
to walk clear over here
from way across the hall
just
to wrap an arm around my soul
sticks in the other hand
still ready
God who can I get
who plays like that

STEVE FORMAN

Percussionist **STEVE FORMAN** felt Jeffrey could never be replaced. In complete bereavement, he wrote that poem the day after Jeff passed. It was the only way he could get in touch with his grief and express his feelings to the Porcaro family. They asked if they could include it in his Memorial Program. "I can't diminish how important my association with Jeff was to me," says Forman (via Skype from Scotland, where he resides). "Jeff's acknowledgment and support of me—and the same thing with Joe—was so sincere and direct. I really worked with him rarely, but I ran into him a lot."

Coming from Phoenix, Arizona to Los Angeles in the early '70s, Forman really didn't have any connections and wasn't very active socially. "Somehow Jeff really got me," he says. "He supported me and promoted me as well. He made recommendations, got me on sessions once in a while, and he even put me in the running for Toto—but I got out-schmoozed by Lenny (Castro), who is a force of nature and a wonderful player." Forman ended up amassing credits with such artists as Warren Zevon, James Taylor, Sarah Vaughan, Linda Ronstadt, Al Jarreau, Steve Cropper, the Beach Boys and a long list of others.

The few times Steve did play with Porcaro, he says what he heard in his headphones was "generally perfect! The touch, the balance was remarkably clear. He and Paich and the guys he grew up with had an understanding of pop music; they were born with it. By high school they were super in demand."

Forman will never forget one night when he sat in on just tambourine for one tune at the North Hollywood club Donte's. Jeff was in the audience "I don't remember much about the experience, just Jeff's comment—which wasn't to me; it was to somebody else we were standing with—and he described it as 'right in the pocket.' That was enough mileage for me to have confidence in myself for the next year or two. It wasn't because he was well-known and all that. It was because I had worked with him, had heard his playing and knew what it felt like to play with him. It was perfect. It was always perfectly in the pocket; 'coherent' is the word I have used to describe him when I taught rhythm theory to my students. I would tell them there was never clutter. He never played a lot of notes. He had a certain intangible thing. I use the words 'momentum' and 'continuity'; the phrasing. It was always about the song. Jeff had tremendous facility and technique. He had great chops and could play a million notes, I suppose, but I never heard him do it. What I always got was so good. I only played a fraction of what I wanted to with him, but every time I did, it was a delight."

Although Forman cannot recall the track or the artist (and I did my best to research it to no avail—it may not have even been released), but he remembers being in the studio with guitarist Oscar Castro-Neves and Jeffrey, cutting a straight-ahead samba. "The feel was like no other American I had ever played with," Forman declares. "I had recently been back and forth to Brazil a couple of times; in those days I was deeply engrossed in Brazilian music. For one thing, Oscar called Jeff when there were all kinds of Brazilian drummers around town. It was just gorgeous."

Rural Still Life playing at Andy Leeds Bar Mitzvah. L to R: Doug Wintz, Gary Bivona, Frank Szabo, Steve Leeds, Dan Sawyer, Jeff Porcaro, David Paich, Cliff Gordon, Scott Shelly, Gary Sherwood. (Courtesy of Andrew Leeds)

Chapter Two

The Seventies

MILLIKAN JR. HIGH

STEVE LEEDS was in Jeff's inner circle and at the core of his early musical experiences. For Steve, Jeff was a part of Steve's most rewarding musical moments. And because they were so very connected, Steve was able to not only share so many wonderful memories, but in doing so, illuminate pieces of Jeffrey that might not be as well known. In fact, he disclosed many stories that were new to me.

Steve met Jeff in around 1967 or '68 playing in the orchestra at Millikan Jr. High School under the direction of David Winseman. He remembers well Jeff's black horn-rimmed glasses, but Steve had his own group of friends and they really didn't get to know each other for a little while. Once they did, they walked to school together. Leeds would walk to his house at 7:00 in the morning and they would walk together, although sometimes Leeds rode his bicycle with his baritone sax strapped to the rack on the back of the bike.

Recounting one of the fun times, Steve recalls, "We had a home court basketball game in the Millikan gym and Mr. Winseman decided we were going to have a pep band because we didn't have a legitimate pep band. He picked about eight or ten guys—Jeff was one of them. I went with my bari sax and we sat in the bleachers and we jammed Dixieland. I think Jeff was playing snare drum and another kid was playing bass drum."

Steve and Jeff were three weeks apart: Jeffrey born April 1, Steve on April 27 in 1954. In 1969 they were 15 years old and their parents drove them to gigs; one would take, one would pick up. They had already been in a Battle of the Bands as the Merciful Souls, but in 1969, the four-piece Jazz Youth Workshop entered the competition

Jazz Youth Workshop, 1969 Combo Division. L to R: Scott Shelly, Jeff Porcaro, Steve Leeds, Gary Sherwood. (Note: Tom Scott and The Carpenters also competed in prior years of this event.) (Courtesy of Steve Leeds)

at the Hollywood Bowl, and they were one of the three finalists. They played three tunes: "The Holy Land" (a David "Fathead" Newman tune) and to show their versatility, Scott Shelly moved from guitar to vibes to play the Herbie Mann version of "Hold On, I'm Comin'" and a Tom Scott tune in 7/4 called "Blues for Hari."

Steve says Papa Joe's tutelage was invaluable. "We rehearsed at Jeff's house just so Joe could be there. First of all, he straightened Jeff out on how to feel on some of these things," Leeds explains. "We would listen to it all the time. We were struggling with the 7/4 groove and Joe worked with Jeff privately and the next day we played, man,

Jeff just had it. You didn't have to tell Jeff twice. Once he figured out how to subdivide it and keep playing the groove and play the fills, that was it. And he made us keep up with him!"

In the Merciful Souls, they were playing tunes by Smokey Robinson; Blood, Sweat and Tears; and songs like "Get Ready" by the Temptations. Leeds' father outfitted them in iridescent green Nehru jackets and they entered the Teen Center Battle of the Bands competition in the San Fernando Valley. "We worked our way through a couple of rounds, and we got to the last round and came out there with our Nehru jackets and did 'Get Ready, Here I Come' and the horns were doing steps," Leeds recalls. "We had another drummer, who got us through the first two rounds, but when we got to the third round, for some reason the drummer left us, and we didn't have a drummer. I don't remember exactly what happened, but Jeff came in at the last minute."

Jeff, who was still at Millikan Junior High while the rest of the band was in high school, had one rehearsal and a run-through of the show and a couple of days later they went out and played the final competition. "Most of the guys in the other bands were older than us and they played loud," recalls Steve. "The prize was $400 and these guys who had four-piece bands thought they were going to ace it. But we had ten guys on stage to split the $400 ten ways. We were in the second half of the line-up and heard the other bands playing. Joe Porcaro drove us and was there. We were getting ready to go on, and I went up to Joe and said, 'Some of these bands are really good, Joe.' And Joe said to me, 'You can beat 'em.' And with that, we went up there and we kicked it, and they chose us to be the winners. They gave us the money and took our pictures and put us in the *Green Sheet* (newspaper)

May, 1969

Teen Times

for teens, by teens, about teens

MERCIFUL SOULS WINS TEEN CENTER BAND BATTLE

by David Robinson

"Merciful Souls" won the Teen Center Battle of the Bands Friday night, April 11, and captured a $400.00 cash prize which they plan to split among themselves.

The "Souls" won out over 39 other bands who had entered the four-month long battle. The Merciful Souls have been together since February

Members of Merciful Souls from lett are Harvey Licht, trumpet; Frank Szabo, trumpet; Doug Wintr, trombone; Jay Sacks, saxophone, Steve Leeds, saxophone; Gordon Strother, singer; Jeff Porcaro, drums; Elias Alcantar, singer; Gary Sherwood, bass; Scott Shelly, guitar; and Rich Aronson, organ.

Harvey, Doug, Jay, Steve, Scott, Gary and Gordon all attend Grant High School. Frank, Richard and Elias attend Van Nuys High School and Jeff attends Millikan Junior High.

The group plans to do some recording for the Harmony Recording Studios and is tentatively scheduled to play the music for the sound track of a new movie, "The Activist."

Asked what he thought the group owed its success to, Harvey Licht replied, "Our great talent."

Teen Times Battle of the Bands story, 1969.
(Courtesy of Andrew Leeds)

and the *Daily News* (Valley newspaper)."

Steve says after school he would ride his bike over to Jeff's house and they'd sit in his room and listen to music. Of course, at the top of Jeff's list was Hendrix, and Steve recalls Eileen picking them up from the Hollywood Bowl after they saw Hendrix. He says he appreciated Hendrix, but being a jazz sax player it was "a little over the top for me, but Jeff loved him. He didn't have the kind of restrictions I did; Jeff heard things and sensed things musically that I did, but didn't appreciate or didn't want to go in that direction."

Leeds says there was only one time that Jeffrey and he got into a fight and it actually turned physical. He doesn't remember the details of why it happened, but he says he is pretty sure it was because Jeff was bullying his brother Steve. "If I remember correctly, he was breaking Steve's balls, making him cry and I got in between them, 'Don't do this, leave him alone,' and Jeff didn't want to hear it. We ended up on Jeff's front lawn of the Milbank house slugging it out. And we actually head-butted each other. Joe finally broke it up. I don't remember what happened after that, but we were both out of breath. That was the one time we were completely at odds. We were both firstborns and both had little brothers and it was a pecking order, but I thought Jeff had gone over the line." They didn't hold onto the anger for any period of time. Just like brothers, Steve says. They got right over it.

Joe was a mentor for Leeds—just being around him and seeing how he functioned in the music world. His own father was in what was commonly known as the "schmatta (or clothing) business," so his father told him honestly there were some things he couldn't help him with. "Sometimes Joe would pick Jeff up early from rehearsal and listen to a few tunes. He'd hear us and tell us the horns were playing out of tune or easy stuff, not critique on a rubric like being a judge at the Hollywood Bowl or anything, but little stuff like, 'You guys should get in tune.' It made a difference because earning his respect was a valuable achievement goal for anybody who wanted to be in the music business. And in all the groups we were in, Jeff just made everyone who was in the band want to be a better musician; want to go home and practice and get the damn part right."

Steve also got his love of Italian grinders from Joe. Joe turned him onto the Italian grinders from Salerno's in Toluca Lake and Steve would pick them up and bring them home for him and his brother. Steve also remembers Eileen's spaghetti; how he'd ride his bike over to the Porcaro house after school and he'd smell dinner cooking. "I'll never forget one day Eileen was cooking, and I was smelling that sauce coming out of that kitchen. Somehow, I got invited to stay for dinner. When I ate that spaghetti with that sauce I was going, 'Man, this is the best sauce and spaghetti I've ever had and this salad with the Italian dressing! My mom doesn't cook like this. Would you please give the recipe to my mother.' I begged her. And then I went home and begged my mother to call her until she did and she made it."

When it came time for high school, Steve was in the North Hollywood High district (as was Jeff), but most of Leeds' friends were going to Grant. His parents permitted him into Grant, but Porcaro went to North Hollywood High, and (as the story has been told) when Jeff was bullied his mom had him transferred to Grant High. (Once Leeds and Jeff were permitted into Grant, their siblings were automatically allowed to go to Grant.) "When Jeff came to Grant, things gelled in our musical circle," Leeds says.

Soon after their Teen Battle of the Bands win, Merciful Souls' keyboard player left and that's when Joe said, "I know a guy…" and David Paich entered the picture. Steve remembers that first meeting with Paich in Leeds' bedroom. His recollection was they were playing with a different drummer first and then he left and Jeff arrived. For thirty minutes Jeff and David played Joe Cocker's "Feelin' Alright." "And the rest, as they say, is history," Steve says.

For a little while, Merciful Souls and Jazz Youth Workshop were both active. Jazz Youth Workshop was Scott Shelly, Jeff, Gary Sherwood and Steve, and they would jam John Coltrane's "Equinox," funk tunes, blues, and make up their own songs. Sherwood's older brother Jeff had heard the band playing and he attended UCLA and was enrolled in an Intro to Jazz class taught by trombonist Paul Tanner (who helped invent the theremin and played it on the Beach Boys "Good Vibrations"). He told Tanner about his brother's "little jazz band" and Tanner invited them to play at UCLA. Porcaro, Shelly, Gary, Steve and David Paich all got permission to take the day off from school to play at the university at 11:00. "We played for the class in a hall with a stage; it was a really cool gig. We played jazz for an hour—like 'Goin' Home,' Ernie Watts. They loved us."

They weren't Merciful Souls for much longer due to personnel changes around 1969. The lead singer, Gordon Strother, graduated and they decided to change the name to Rural Still Life after the Mike Lang composition "Rural Still Life #26" (performed by Tom Scott). In that band Scotty Page, Frank Sazbo, Doug Wintz and Leeds comprised the horn section alongside Paich, Shelly and Jeff, and there was a singer named Cliff Gordon. They were listening to artists like Delaney & Bonnie, and they played the Grant High School dances, proms and homecoming events organized by Mr. Arthur, who paid them $100.

Leeds says it was Paich who turned Steve on to Delaney & Bonnie (*Accept No Substitute)* and he began to listen to sax player Bobby Keys. "Jeff didn't like it at first, but David kept his thumb on it. 'Check this out, check this tune out, 'Ghetto,'" Leeds recalls. "That's how Jeff learned about Jim Keltner. It was through David putting his thumb on Delaney & Bonnie."

Steve got a car at 16 and he could drive around the corner, and the first guy he would pick up was Jeff (and his drum set) to go to a rehearsal. "When we couldn't rehearse because too many members couldn't make it, we would just jam together in Jeff's music room, where Joe would have his marimba and his congas and Jeff would have his drums set up, and there was a piano and a couch."

Also during high school, Leeds' neighbor William Blinn, who wrote "Brian's Song" and many other film and TV projects, would often hear the band rehearsing. One day, around 1970 while on the Warner Brothers lot someone said some high school musicians were needed for an Andy Griffith show called "Headmaster," and Blinn immediately thought of them. He recommended that they call Steve, who put together some musicians for what is called a "sidelining gig" or miming to a pre-recorded track. He got Jeff, Doug Wintz on trombone, Gary Sherwood on bass, and he can't recall if there was anyone on keyboards and perhaps a couple of others. Again, they had to get permission to take time off from school and they also had to be what is called Taft-Hartleyed—when someone is not a member of Screen Actor's Guild and they had to have an onset teacher. "They dressed us up, and sent us to make-up where we sat in the make-up chair."

They desperately wanted Rural Still Life to play a cool club called the Brass Ring and Steve relentlessly begged the owner, but they were underage. Finally around 1970, the owner agreed with the condition that they wouldn't drink. Percussionist Bobby Torres was in the band at the time and Leeds says they pulled in a good crowd which brought good "door money," but when they went to get paid at the end of the night, the owner ended up taking a big cut. It didn't matter, though. "It was the Brass Ring and Delaney & Bonnie would play there," Leeds says.

They worked the same deal at Donte's, where they would go

all the time to see acts like Victor Feldman, Louie Bellson and Tom Scott. Leeds got to know the doorman and he kept talking about the band until he finally gave in when Leeds suggested they could play a Sunday afternoon. It was 1970. "We played there and did really well and a couple of months later we got a call from the owner because one of their acts cancelled at the last minute and they wanted us to fill in, so they called us back for an encore at Donte's."

Leeds says some of the other music Jeff loved was Sly and the Family Stone. "He'd put on 'Everyday People,' and he'd say, 'Dig the way the drummer plays. He's so simple. Dig the horns, they're so funky.' Who else did we listen to? Buddy Miles. Big Buddy Miles fan. He loved Buddy Miles. If you listen to everything Jeff played, including all the Toto stuff, there was a Buddy Miles undercurrent to all of it, especially the fills, even more pronounced to anything Bernard Purdie played or Jim Keltner played. We did 'Them Changes' I don't know how many times and we had a full horn chart on it."

He says they would listen to Seals & Crofts and Lee Michaels up at their keyboard player friend Mark Lewis' house. Of course, Jeff loved Led Zeppelin, which Leeds admits he didn't care for. "Another band Jeff dug a lot was Three Dog Night—Floyd Sneed," Leeds recalls. "We did a few Three Dog Night tunes in Rural Still Life including a tune called 'The Loner.' You shoulda heard Jeff play on that. There was a theater called the Valley Circle Theater on Ventura Blvd., and Three Dog Night was playing there. Jeff asked me to go, but I didn't. He went with someone else. He was really into Floyd Sneed."

Then something cool happened when Steve and Jeff went to rent their usual PA for a dance they were playing. Joe's cartage service in Hollywood gave them a break, so they would go into Hollywood to rent what was then the state-of-the-art PA system for all their gigs: a Shure Vocal Master PA. On one of those trips to the cartage company, the owner whispered to Jeff that Floyd Sneed was in one of the rehearsal rooms. They put the gear in the car and went back in and cracked open the door to the rehearsal room and watched Sneed and some other musicians (not Three Dog Night) rehearsing. They hung out for about ten minutes and Jeff was stoked.

We all know that Jeff loved Bernard Purdie and couldn't get enough of *Aretha Live at Fillmore West,* but Leeds says another one of Jeff's favorite Aretha tracks was her single "The House That Jack Built," with Roger Hawkins. "Jeff said, 'This is the way our band should sound.' The other one Jeff used to talk about all the time was 'Ooh Child' by the Five Stairsteps," Leeds notes. "He loved that drummer (Jerome "Bigfoot" Brailey)." Leeds mentions another tune Porcaro really dug: "Time Has Come Today" by the Chamber Brothers (a drummer by the name of Brian Keenan was on the track). "Once, Joe Chambers sang with Rural Still Life at some gig in the Valley. I don't remember the circumstances, but I remember he showed up and sang with us."

In the summer of 1970 Leeds, Paich and Jeff (as well as Mike Porcaro) attended a weeklong Stan Kenton clinic at the University of Redlands in Redlands, California, along with a couple hundred other 16-year-old kids. Kenton and his band members were the teachers and Leeds recalls that he, Paich and Jeff roomed together with a fourth musician, who he does not believe was Mike. "We woke up in the morning, went down to the cafeteria, ate some breakfast and then went to one of the ensembles or rhythm section detail or some theory class or jazz lesson. In the afternoon there would be band and around

5:00 we would stop and eat dinner and after dinner Kenton would play for an hour. It was an amazing experience." Leeds says when they first got there they auditioned. It was one of the first times Steve ever auditioned. "When they heard Jeff and David play, they went into the 'A' band. They read better than I did and they definitely played better than I did," Leeds admits.

Steve, David and Jeff were in a band together led by a teacher/ arranger at North Texas State by the name of Dan Haerle. "He had an extra-curricular activity you could try out for called the Improvisational Experimental Band where he got about five saxophones, five trombones, five trumpets, rhythm, congas; all the best guys from the best bands, and we didn't have charts. So here's twenty some-odd guys with a director, and he would dictate to us what to play. He'd go to the rhythm section and say, 'We're in D minor and we're going to do eight bars of this and then we're going to go up a half of a step to E flat minor and do eight bars of that and come back to D minor and then we'll stop and there's a rhythm break. After the rhythm break, there's a trumpet solo and we go back to the D minor.' He just basically spoke the chart to us and we knew the chart. None of us had really played in a big band."

Funny story at the band camp—in typical Jeff manner—they were in a second story dormitory room and at the same time there was a cheerleader's camp going on. Their room overlooked the field on which the cheerleaders practiced. "Jeff would wake up in the morning and look out the window and say, 'Wow, look at that, man!' And there were all those girls with their pom-poms kicking their legs and swinging their arms," says Steve. "One morning David and I woke up and looked at each other and said, 'Where's Jeff?' And you know where Jeff was? Jeff woke up early and he was down on the field where the cheerleaders were doing their drills."

As a senior, Leeds decided to take choir instead of band. Shelly was also in choir and the choir director knew about Rural Still Life because they played the school dances. She got the idea that she wanted to do a year-end concert for choir and incorporate jazz. "She had the chutzpah to call (composer/arranger) Lalo Shifrin to perform the *Jazz Suite on the Mass Texts,*" he recalls. She asked for clearance to perform and get the music and Shifrin said yes. He said he could give her the score, but not the parts. Leeds copied the parts, and they performed about four of the nine pieces of the suite with about an 80-voice choir and a jazz group with trumpet, sax and flute. "We had Jeff on drums, Mike on bass, Paich played piano, Scott Shelly played guitar and we had three or four horns, and it went back and forth between big ensembles with improvisation sections and then it would break out into a jazz swing thing like for alto flute. There were so many people involved it had to be in the gym, instead of the auditorium."

Leeds says Jeff was very adept at odd times. "Jeff had a very refined and mature sense of music, rhythm and harmonic progression. Everything made sense musically to him and it came through him. Stuff like Emerson, Lake and Palmer and Yes. Some of that stuff seemed contrived to me and a little too much toward the classical side, but Jeff got it and could play it. Another guy Jeff said he dug and used to listen to was Billy Cobham and guys like Elvin Jones, really hard-driving jazz drummers. That was part of Jeff that not everyone realizes. John Guerin was always at Donte's with Tom Scott. He played odd times and he was fabulous."

Then there was the gig on Catalina Island that George Bell—

one of the singer/guitarists they hung with—asked them to do. The gig included Leeds, Jeff, Bell and Mark Lewis on keyboards. "The four of us went down to Long Beach Harbor and got on a charter boat with a fuckin' Hammond M3 organ and a Leslie and a drumkit and we set sail for Catalina Island," says Leeds. "I have an inner ear problem and get vertigo from watching virtual reality games. This was one of the worst experiences I ever had with seasickness. We ended up playing a gig at some place like a Moose Lodge, some shithole. We jammed Hendrix tunes and whatever we could think of and they put all four of us in one room in a fleabag hotel overnight in Catalina. Mark and I weren't into it, but Jeff was into it and he was hanging right with George Bell, and they were carousing and having a good ol' time. After the gig they stayed out late and partied, and the next day going home was almost as bad as going there. I think they paid us $100 for the four of us."

On Jeff's seventeenth birthday, Leeds recalls Jeff's girlfriend at the time planning the fashionable "snatch breakfast," where the birthday person would be "kidnapped" in their pajamas early in the morning and everyone invited would also come to the restaurant in pajamas. "We must have had 15 or 20 people," Steve remembers. "We were all in the large booth waiting in the back of the restaurant for him when she got him there."

As Steve's graduation gift to himself (he graduated a year earlier than Jeff), they planned a getaway with Mark Lewis (who was a couple of years older). Mark had a van in which to cart his organ around, so they threw their clothes in the back and took a trip to San Francisco. "We booked a hotel in the Tenderloin, which is really bad now, but wasn't so bad then. It was a cheap motel and we had a room. We had dinner in a Moroccan restaurant where you sit on cushions on the

An overload of taste and finesse: Jeff with Larry Carlton, Abe Laboriel and Greg Mathieson at a surprise concert at the Musicians Institute in Hollywood, 1985. (Photo by Peter van Ham)

A well-deserved ovation: Jeff with Larry Carlton, Abe Laboriel and Greg Mathieson at the end of their surprise concert at the Musicians Institute in Hollywood, CA, 1985. (Photo by Peter van Ham)

All his life Jeff remained connected to the Musicians Institute in Hollywood, CA, where his father Joe headed the Percussion Institute of Technology (P.I.T.) faculty together with Ralph Humphrey. (Photo: Peter van Ham)

floor at a low table. They do the Tajine with the rice and the chicken all on top and you eat with your fingers." The next night they went to see Frank Zappa at the Amphitheatre in Berkley, even though they had just seen him a couple of weeks prior in Los Angeles, they enjoyed the sights of San Francisco, like the Golden Gate Bridge and Haight-Ashbury.

Soon after Jeffrey got the Sonny & Cher gig, he moved out of the Porcaro house. Steve remembers Jeff's first apartment near Donte's in North Hollywood, near the Shanahans. He would go over to the apartment, and they would listen to music, and he remembers how everyone smoked Marlboro cigarettes. "We're sitting in the apartment one day—and he had only been in it for a couple of weeks, but he was going back out on tour again," Steve remembers. "I asked him if I could stay there, and he said yes. He gave me the key and said, 'Don't do anything I wouldn't do,' and he asked me to clean up after myself and not leave the door unlocked. It was just a bed and a sofa and some pots and pans, but it got me out of my parents' house, and for me it was like a sanctuary. Jeff was big-hearted enough to do that, so generous, so good-hearted to say yes to me."

One day, after both Jeff and David were with Sonny & Cher, Steve recalls that David's father Marty was scoring the TV show "Ironsides" at Universal. "I used to go and hang out there with David and sit next to Bud Shank, the sax player, and watch him play the cues down. One day Marty said, 'We're going to do some stuff in the show and I want Jeff to play the drums.' And Jeff was the drummer on 'Ironsides.' I went and Jeff said it was the only time the fear of God came over him. He said, 'I am sitting in a room with Bud Shank and Ray Brown and a string section on a sound stage with (music contractor) Sandy DeCrescent with a clock running at Universal and they want me to sight read parts.' That was the one time that he actually confessed he was a little bit nervous. He killed it, but he did admit it was the most pressure he had ever been under. It was like being in the trenches, under fire. Sandy DeCrescent is looking at the clock going, 'Marty, we've got ten minutes to do three more cues, can you do it?' And there are 20, 30 guys and they're sitting back in their chairs, like it's no big deal because they do this every day. But if you mess up, you mess up 30 people."

As Joe reported in *It's About Time*, he played on a TV show with Jeff—it may have even been the "Ironsides" session—during which Jeff mouthed to him "I can't do this," which Joe took to mean he just didn't dig it.

Leeds recalls that after the "Ironsides" job he had to get David and Jeff to LAX airport to catch a plane to Las Vegas for a Sonny & Cher show in rush hour traffic. "They barely made their plane by ten minutes."

In 1973, Jeff, David and he recorded for a producer named Shannon O'Neill at a little recording studio called Independent Recorders on the corner of Colfax and Ventura Blvd. in the San Fernando Valley. He doesn't recall how he found them, but they would go in at night and cut tracks including one for Christopher Paul (Engemann) called "The History of Rock and Roll." He was the nephew of the executive producer Bob Engemann (an original member of The Lettermen) and it was for a label called MGM South. His father was Karl Engemann, a record company executive.

As time went on, Jeff recommended Leeds for various gigs including a Wolfman Jack album and a Boz Scaggs tour in1976. "When we were getting ready to leave for the tour with Boz, Jeff was living in Laurel Canyon," Leeds remembers. "There was a limo coming to Jeff's house to pick him up. I got all the info from the management company and I would have to meet everyone at LAX and Jeff said, 'Come on up to my house and ride in the limo with me.' And that's what I did. Jeff also gave me a very, very good piece of advice while we were rehearsing a couple of weeks before, when I asked, 'What should I bring? What should I bring?' And he said, 'Bring condoms.'"

THE YOUNGER LEEDS

Younger brother **ANDREW "ANDY" LEEDS'** memories of the Porcaro family begin as a fifth grader at Riverside Dr. Elementary School. Steve Porcaro was in the fourth grade, Mike Porcaro was in the sixth grade and as we know, Jeff and Andy's older brother Steve met at Millikan Jr. High in Sherman Oaks.

The Leeds family lived in Studio City near Beeman Park and the Porcaro family was around the corner from them. "At some point in time, although I can't tell you exactly when, my brother was hanging out with Jeff, and I remember going over to their house on Milbank all the time after school. But my parents both worked, so eventually the hang became at my house because there were no parents at home," Andy says with a laugh. "Later, Steve Porcaro and I would roadie for the band. Once in while they'd let us get up behind Jeff and play cowbell or something. We had a blast."

Jeff's early band Rural Still Life played at Leeds' 1971 bar mitzvah; the venue was the Ventura Catering Hall (now a Poquito Más restaurant) on Ventura Boulevard in Sherman Oaks. At the time, the band consisted of Scott Shelly on guitar, Jeff on drums and Andy's brother Steve on sax. They played a lot of soul music. Everyone was taking music lessons, but obviously some of them exceeded the others in talent. Andy recalls how Jeff, while in high school, would go over to Valley College and sit in with the big band. ("My brother was in the big band over there," Leeds recalls.)

Andy remembers how Jeff started at North Hollywood High School but was transferred to Grant High when a certain portion of the North Hollywood High School students, who did not care for the hippie population, began to bully him. Jeff's mom was able to change his school.

Andy also remembers going with Steve Porcaro to the Sahara Hotel to see seventeen-year-old Jeff play with Sonny & Cher: "We were sixteen, and our parents let us go by ourselves with our older brothers. They were performing every night, and we were hanging out. It was David Hungate, David Paich and Jeff. It was a lot of fun, and they were having a blast. Jeff was right out of high school, flying around on a Playboy Bunny jet."

STEVE PORCARO confirms that he and the two Leeds brothers did, in fact, go without parental chaperone to Vegas to see Jeffrey with Sonny & Cher. Steve reminds me that at seventeen, he went on the road with Gary Wright. "Steve Leeds (Andy's brother) was driving," Steve recalls. "And at that age, what trouble were we going to get into? We went to see Jeff and we were so proud of him. Paich was on the gig, along with Dan Ferguson, and it was really fun."

Leeds has vivid memories of attending Steely Dan rehearsals with his brother, at Jeff's invitation. "Jeff would say, 'Come down to rehearsal,' and I'd go, 'You're kidding me!' Steve and I would jump in the car and go down to Modern Music, which is now the CNN building at Sunset and Cahuenga. It was the original band with Skunk (Jeff Baxter), double drums (with Jim Hodder) and Michael McDonald on background vocals. To this day I still work with Donald (Fagen) very closely as his travel agent."

Rural Still Life went through several incarnations, a couple while Jeff was in the band (discussed in *It's About Time*), but once he left with Sonny & Cher, the group took on a new form. They dropped the "Rural" from the name and at first, played soul music. Andy recalls: "After it was my brother's, Jeff's and Paich's band, it became Steve Porcaro, Dean Cortez, Carlos Vega and me."

Andy met Carlos Vega while the two were ushers at the Hollywood Bowl. "As soon as they turned out the lights, the two of us would sit down on the staircase and start smoking pot," Leeds recalls with a laugh. "We wore these little blue blazers and bow ties, but we saw some great symphony concerts, and Elton John where he had the doves fly out of the piano. There were some major shows in the two years we were there."

Eventually, when Jeff got the gig with Steely Dan, Still Life became a two-guitar band with Steve Lukather and Mike Landau. Leeds recalls one epic night that this revamped, guitar-centered Still Life was playing at Grant High School and Jeff showed up with Donald Fagen. "We were doing all the tunes off the *Katy Lied* album, which hadn't come out yet—Jeff had gotten us the demos," Andy remembers. "They were standing way in the back. There were also times Paich would come and sit in with us, like at the Beverly Hills High School prom at the Beverly Hills Hotel. He would just show up."

Andy and Mike Porcaro became roommates, and with some financial help from his father, in 1978 Andy founded Leeds Musical Instrument Rentals. Jeffrey was "100% instrumental in the success of my company," according to Leeds. Jeff lived on Kirkwood Drive with a friend named Chris Cotton from New Hampshire. In L.A. Chris worked at S.I.R. (Studio Instrument Rentals) and Jeff knew Andy was looking to open a business—perhaps buy a music store or something like that—so Jeff told Andy there were no good instrument rental businesses and he should start one with Chris. Andy took his advice and "Jeff promoted it like crazy."

"Every time something broke down on a session, Jeff would say, 'Call this guy right now and he will take care of you,'" says Leeds. "I would jump in the van and drive the instrument down, whatever time of day it was. He used to call me from Sound City with Keith Olsen at 2:00 or 3:00 in the morning: 'We need a synthesizer down here.' I'd go open up the store and drive it over there, hang out for a little while, listen to the session, then go home, go to bed and go back to work in the morning. He would be on a session and they would order in a Fender Rhodes or an amp or something, and the only place back then to get anything from was S.I.R. and Jeff was the guy! If he said 'boo,' every producer listened."

Leeds says he went to many sessions and delivered everything himself, and then he would hang out. A couple of years after they

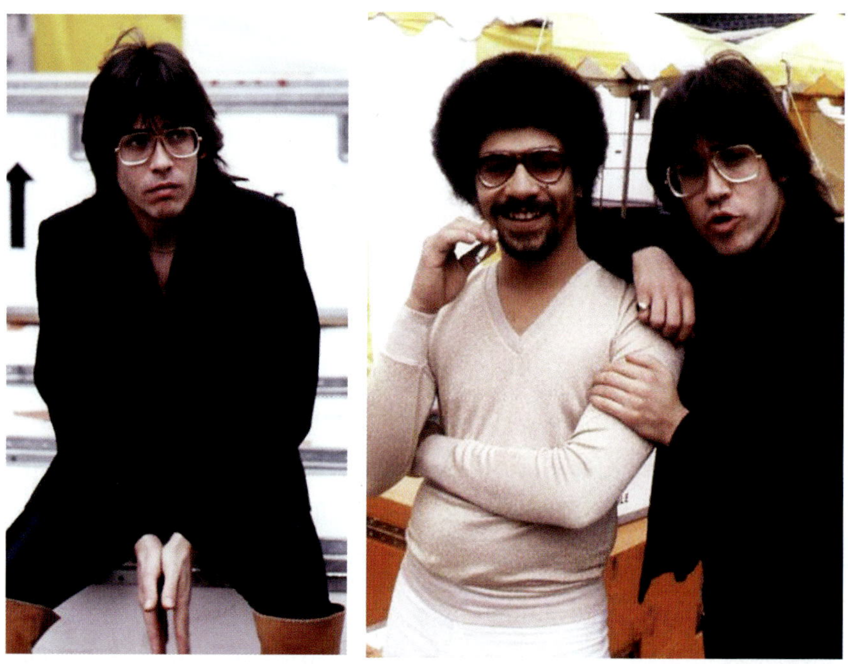

Left: Jeff backstage at the Los Angeles Memorial Coliseum during Toto's 1979 U.S. tour. (Courtesy of Barney Hurley). Right: Lenny Castro and Jeff backstage at the Los Angeles Memorial Coliseum during Toto's 1979 U.S. tour. (Courtesy of Barney Hurley)

Jeff, Paul Jamieson, manager Larry Fitzgerald, and Steve Lukather, Japan, 1980. (Courtesy of Andrew Leeds)

Toto, Japanese garden, May, 1982. (Courtesy of Andrew Leeds)

Jeff, with fans, waiting for the Bullet Train, Japan, 1980. (Courtesy of Andrew Leeds)

Jeff jumps in the bus driver's seat, Japan, 1980. (Courtesy of Andrew Leeds)

Jeff, lighting director Leo Bonomy, and two Udo artist reps, May, 1982. (Courtesy of Andrew Leeds)

Jeff after a show in Japan, 1980. (Courtesy of Andrew Leeds)

started the business, they moved down the street and bought two side-by-side buildings, with the rental business in one and a rehearsal studio in another—and it took off. "In the early days, I traded rehearsal time with Toto to go to Japan with them," says Andy. "'I let you rehearse for free, and you buy me a ticket to Japan.' We did that twice."

The first trip to Japan was soon after the 1980 Paul McCartney Japan marijuana bust, and Andy recalls the partying climate was tough for the band. "They were like gods over there at the time," Leeds says. "There were fans chasing us down the street as we were driving away from the hotel to the venue."

During the second trip, Leeds was helping Yamaha to sponsor their equipment. Paich and Steve Porcaro were already involved, but Leeds was assisting with the coordination. "We went to the Yamaha factory to see the prototypes of some synthesizers. It was Steve (Porcaro), Paich, James (Newton) Howard and me," Andy says.

SCOTT SHELLY

When 13-year-old guitarist **SCOTT SHELLY**'s family moved to Sherman Oaks, he began going to Millikan Jr. High and he quickly put a four-piece band together for a battle of the bands. They went up against a "power trio" called Haze of Saturn with Ron Ravenscroft on guitar, Kerry Morris on bass, and Jeff on drums. "They did a Hendrix tune, and we did an original song. They won, of course," says Shelly (via Skype from his home in Australia, where he has resided for 22 years). "I went up to Jeff and said, 'Man, that was great! Incredible drumming. We should stay in touch.' So we exchanged numbers; we were little kids, you know. That was the start of it. He lived over near

Studio City Park; Steve Leeds lived over near there too. I met Steve over at Millikan Jr. High about the last part of grade eight. Steve was responsible for a lot of this. He had a band called the Dead Beats with Jay Sachs and Dan Sawyer, and Steve did all the charts. Somewhere in there, around the age of fourteen, we all marched down to Local 47 to join the union!"

When the kids all hung out, they would "soak up a lot of music" by listening to records. They got together a lot at Kerry Morris' home in Burbank, where Kerry turned them on to tons of great music including Pink Floyd, Weather Report, and Chick Corea—and they would learn music off the records. Their band the Merciful Souls began as a soul band and expanded with Blood, Sweat & Tears and Chicago tunes. When their keyboard player left, David Paich entered the picture. (Note: Refer to this story in *It's About Time*.) That band became the first version of Rural Still Life. "That was a fun band," Shelly recalls. "We played a lot of high school dances, proms and that kind of thing."

For one semester of the eleventh grade, Jeff attended Grant High—the same school as Shelly. They often went to the Pilgrimage Theater for the free jazz concerts on Sunday afternoons, where they heard great artists like Stan Kenton and Tom Scott. "Besides being one of the best drummers on the planet, Jeff was one of the best people," Scott asserts. "Often when people that you know become famous and then more famous, it can become an awkward thing, but in my experience, Jeff never was like that. He was extremely humble about it, extremely generous with his time and his talent, and he would always go the extra mile to do things."

A little Burbank coffee shop called Patty's, near NBC Studios, was another favorite hangout. "They made a thing called 'scrabble,' which was basically scrambled eggs with hamburger and spinach added. We probably went there a half dozen times for breakfast," Shelly recalls. "We wouldn't talk about music necessarily, but about what it was like to be the eldest son in your family and stuff like that. Life stuff." Scott remembers going over to Jeff's apartment one day and listening to Steely Dan's *Can't Buy a Thrill.* When the music ended, Porcaro said, "I'm going to play with these guys someday." "It wasn't, 'I *want* to play with them,'" Shelly points out. "It was like he was putting the word out to the universe: 'I'm *gonna* play with these guys someday.' Then in '74, I remember going to see him at the Sopwith Camel (club) for one of the early Dan shows where he played double drums with Jim Hodder." Later that year, Shelly was on tour with Spirit and had a night off in Detroit, and he saw Jeff play with Steely Dan again, in Windsor, Michigan.

After their time in Rural Still Life, Shelly recalls Jeff calling him to come over to the Valleyheart Drive house garage to check something out. When he arrived, the second edition of Rural Still Life was rehearsing. It was Carlos Vega on drums, John Pierce on bass, Mike Landau on guitar and Steve Porcaro on keys. "That was my first exposure to those guys. It was mind boggling," Shelly says. "Jeff was laughing the whole time."

Scott hadn't seen Jeff in about six months when he got a call from him one Monday morning. "He said, 'What are you doing? Come on over. Steve (Porcaro) is here. I'm gonna make him breakfast, we're having greasy eggs and bacon.' This was after I had done a twelve-week summer tour with Dan Fogelberg, one of my favorite tours. I go over and Jeff says, 'You should go out on the road with Boz,' and I said, 'but Mike Landau is playing guitar,' and Steve goes, 'No, man, you're going to play synthesizers. I'll show you everything you need to know.' A week later, after five rehearsals (at which Steve gave me the Oberheim manual and Minimoog manuals), I got the gig. Honestly, there were half a dozen guys with reputations who could play circles around me, but it was because Jeff and Steve marched me in there (that I got the job). I learned a lot, and Boz was great."

The last call Shelly got from Jeff was just a few months before he left us. "I don't know if I should say this…" Scott paused. "But he did tell me a couple of times that he had the feeling he was not going to be with us for a long time."

THE SHANAHAN CONNECTION

While in high school, Scott Shelly recalls, Jeff would take him over to his friend **KELLY SHANAHAN**'s house, and they'd listen to records. "(Jeff and Kelly) were friends forever," says Shelly. Kelly met Jeff in the marching band at North Hollywood High School. Shanahan was in his senior year there and was the section leader of the drum squad. It was his job to assign the drummers to their different instruments, which were snare drum, tenor drum, bass drum and crash cymbals. Kelly didn't like the position because whoever got put on crash cymbals or bass drum was always disappointed. The best drummers would be assigned to snare drum or tenor drum.

Jeff and Shanahan's younger brother Danny were freshmen. Kelly knew his brother was good, so he put him on snare drum. There was one opening left for snare. "I had Jeff play me some rudiments. He was very good, but Charlie Yacoubian was a senior and next in line for snare, so I put Jeff on crash cymbals," Kelly recalls. "That day, after school, my brother Dan said to me, 'You know that guy Jeff who you assigned to crash cymbals? I have him in another class, and we got to talking. His dad is Joe Porcaro! Jeff is an incredible drummer.' Joe and our dad, Dick Shanahan, knew each other from working in the studios together on movie dates where my dad was on drums and Joe was on percussion."

The next day Kelly broke the bad news to Charlie Yacoubian that he was now on tenor drum and Jeff was on snare. "That day I invited Jeff over to my house after school. We had a semi-soundproofed studio in the back with drums set up. Jeff and I exchanged drum ideas back and forth. We hit it off and became best friends," Shanahan remembers. "Halfway through football season, Jeff and I got bored with the typical drum cadences, so I let Jeff write a new one. It was a rock beat from a Vanilla Fudge song with a real tricky bass drum part, so Jeff and I played bass drums and the other guys just played 2 and 4 on snares."

Shanahan remembers going to watch Jeff play in his band Rural Still Life: "I was always amazed at what Jeff could do with his bass drum. I would usually sit in on a tune when Jeff got cramps. It seemed like every gig his hands would cramp up at least once. Jeff always wanted me to sit in on a song and play a drum solo. I was pretty good at drum solos; I played a solo every night at Disneyland when I was sixteen years old while filling in for my dad the whole summer with The Elliott Brothers Orchestra."

North Hollywood High School marching band. Jeff in bottom row, second from left. (Courtesy of Kelly Shanahan)

As soon as he got his driver's license, Kelly bought a red Volkswagen bug with the savings from his gig at Disneyland. "Because I was the only one of our friends who already had a car, I was always the designated driver when we went to concerts," Shanahan recalls. "One memorable concert I went to with Jeff and my brother Dan was Jimi Hendrix at the Forum in Inglewood. Opening the show was a funk band with horns called Ballin' Jack that was really good, and the Buddy Miles Express. The next day at school I realized that Jeff was also an artist. He had drawn a cartoon of us trying to find our car in the parking lot, which was hilarious. I wish I still had it. Jeff was an amazing friend. At one point he lived next door to me. He would always come over to hang out and play me the newest tracks he played on, like Seals and Crofts and so on."

Kelly and Jeff became immediate fans of Steely Dan after their first album was released. One time, after Kelly had just returned from a tour with John Sebastian, Jeff brought over a track he did with Fagen and Becker for a Schlitz Beer commercial. (It never aired.) "I remember thinking, 'Oh my God, this is the best Steely Dan has ever sounded, and it's just a beer commercial,'" says Kelly. "Later on, I wasn't surprised when Jeff told me Fagen had asked him to go on tour with them. The Sonny & Cher TV show had been a cool gig for him, but I knew this was Jeff's big break. He was so excited when he came back from the first rehearsal and said it went really well."

Shanahan was part of the one project Jeffrey produced (outside of co-producing Toto): The Strand. "It all came about after we replaced the soon-to-be Toto guys as Boz Scaggs' road band," says Kelly. "When Jeff and Paich got the Toto record deal, they had to recommend replacements for Boz's road band for the Japan, Australia, and New Zealand tour. That was us—Scott Shelly, Dean Cortez, Peter Reilich and me. While we were touring, Boz had promised us we would play on his next album, but understandably he used the Toto guys again. Boz's manager Irving Azoff felt kind of bad for us, so he paid us to go in the studio and make some demos, so we could try and get our own record deal. We eventually got our own deal on Island Records. They told us we could choose our own producer, but that Chris Blackwell wanted to produce us. Chris was the head of Island at the time and had just produced Stevie Winwood and the B-52's, but we didn't want to use him because we were afraid he was going to try to make us sound like the B-52's. So we talked Jeff into producing us—which is probably why Island didn't put any money into promoting us. They were insulted we didn't use Chris Blackwell.

"Jeff was a great producer. We were all pretty much rookies in the studio, so Jeff made us feel comfortable and built up our egos. The only problem was the singer we chose: Moon Calhoun (who was a great singer and also a very good drummer). On the demos I played drums on two tracks and Moon played on two. Island Records wanted the sound we got on the tracks I played on, so they wanted me to be the drummer. Moon resented me for it. He would get drunk and call Chris Blackwell at his home in the middle of the night and tell him that he should be the Strand drummer instead of me. Moon also gave Jeff a hard time doing his vocal tracks, to the point where Jeff said he never wanted to produce again. Then, when it came to the final mix, they didn't even have Jeff there. Chris Blackwell mixed it. Jeff's mixes were way better, by the way. And then they didn't pay Jeff on time, to the point where he almost had to sue them. Although Moon pretty much ruined the experience for me, working in the studio with Jeff made it all worthwhile. While we recorded our tracks in studio B at Sunset Sound, the Toto guys were doing overdubs for *Hydra* in Studio A—so there was a lot of partying going on back and forth."

"Towards the end, I said, 'We need a shuffle, let's do a shuffle.' I started playing something on the piano, and Jeff started singing this little melody over the top of it," recalls Scott Shelly. "He said, 'That's gonna work great.' I said, 'Well you just sent me the melodic hook, so you're going to get part writer's credit,' and he responded, 'I didn't do anything; I didn't write anything.' I said, 'Actually, you did, so now you're a songwriter as well as a producer. Go down to ASCAP, pick a name for your publishing company—Cowbella Music—and now you can go back to Toto and say, 'I'm a producer and a writer, start including me into the process.'"

Looking back, Shelly feels that although the playing was great, the writing was weak—but he feels fantastic about the fact that they approached Jeff to produce the project. He says Porcaro was a wonderful producer. "Jeff had the chops and ears to produce," says Shelly. "He absolutely knew how long we should spend on a track, and he knew if a track was making it or not. Because he knew us—especially Kelly and me—we'd do a take and he'd know what was our best or not. He'd say, 'Okay, let's do one for real now,' to piss us off, just so we'd do better. He'd kick us in the ass, and it was a good experience for that. There were a lot of laughs and a lot of good hangs. It was just so much fun to hang with Jeff—he was just a sweetie and funny and really, really smart. He was something."

Shanahan says Jeff was a great friend who was always there for him when the chips were down. "One time when my drums were

The Strand album inside sleeve pic. L to R: unknown model, Scott Shelly, Peter Reilich, Moon Calhoun, Kelly Shanahan, Dean Cortez, David Batteau, Jeff Porcaro. (Photo by Jim Hagopian, courtesy of Scott Shelly)

stolen, he let me borrow one of his best Gretsch sets," says Kelly. "He recommended me for that Boz Scaggs tour when he couldn't leave town because Toto was recording their first album. That was probably the highlight of my career. He also recommended me for a Seals and Crofts tour, which didn't turn out so well. Jimmy Seals hated me. I played with them for a while, but Jimmy was never happy with me. They finally let me go and hired Jeff back when he was available. Jeff said to me, 'Don't feel bad Kel, I just got let go by Steely Dan and replaced with Bernard Purdie.' Jeff was like a brother to me, and I was devastated when he died. I still am."

Kelly's younger brother **DANNY SHANAHAN** was Jeff's age. His brother Kelly, his father and Jeff were the three greatest influences in his life. While at Walter Reed Junior High, some of his drummer friends at Milliken Junior High mentioned Jeff to him. By the time they both ended up at North Hollywood High, Danny was very familiar with the name Jeff Porcaro.

Danny describes Kelly as a child prodigy who, at fifteen, was already subbing for his father in big bands. As stated before, Kelly was the section leader in marching band, and that first day in the class, Danny says he didn't know who was who—including Jeff—because the roll was not taken. Danny confirms the story that Kelly put him on snare and Jeff on cymbals, and when they went on to their next class (which was English), Jeff sat next to him. The teacher called the roll, and when he said "Jeff Porcaro," Danny made the connection. As the class progressed, Porcaro became the class clown with his huge personality.

Riding home with brother Kelly after that first day of school,

Danny said, "There's a guy in band named Jeff Porcaro and I know you put him on cymbals, but I think you need to change him over to snare drum, because he has quite a reputation." At school the next day, the drumline positions were revisited. "Kelly says to Jeff, 'Let me see you do some paradiddles,'" says Danny. "So Jeff goes to the snare drum and does them—and we all know how good he was. Then he does some double paradiddles. Kelly was impressed, so he starts playing along with him on the paradiddles. They were going back and forth in front of the whole class, and everyone loved it, because they were going faster and faster, probably for about ten minutes. Finally, Jeff threw his sticks down and went, 'Ok, man, you won.' Kelly goes, 'You're on snare drum.' And that was the start of our friendship."

Danny also remembers the previously mentioned Vanilla Fudge cadence. "Jeff came into class one day and said, 'Dig this, I have an idea for a new cadence. I'm going to play bass drum and I have this great Carmine Appice feel I want to do for a cadence.' He and Kelly wrote out the bass drum part for the drummers marching out on the field. We were doing eighth notes and accenting 2 and 4, and it was so cool. After the game our music teacher looked at us and said, 'That was kinda neat, but don't ever do it again.'"

Jeff was soon asked to join the school jazz band. One night, after an evening rehearsal ended early, Danny waited with Jeff for Mrs. Porcaro to pick them up. Jeff had his dad's vintage Camco drums with him. Turning to Danny, he said mischievously: "I have an idea." "I thought, 'Oh boy! He's got an idea!'" Danny recalls. "We took the drums out and set them up on the 50-yard line of the football field and just started playing, with them echoing all over the place. I never would have done that without him," Danny says, laughing. "We had so much fun together."

GRANT HIGH MARCHING BAND

When Jeff left North Hollywood High School, he enrolled at Grant High School and joined their marching band. That's where he met **MERCY** (real name Marla) **BARON,** who had joined the Grant High School marching band in her freshman year of high school in 1970. Baron says, to her best recollection, Jeff joined in his senior year. Marching band was a daily class at school, where they learned the music and field drill, and the students were required to attend all the football games. "I had paid my dues in the drum section and (of course) I was the only girl in the drum section back in those days," Mercy recalls.

Paying dues meant starting out on the bass drum and proving you could read well to finally reach the goal of playing snare drum. "I was really looking forward to being section leader," Baron confides. "As soon as Jeff joined, Mr. (Miles) Neill, who was the band director, and everyone, was blown away. Here comes this sixteen- or seventeen-year-old kid who could just literally drum circles around us. He stood out whether he wanted to or not. The humbleness of Jeff was always there, but so was the hipness; he was so hip for his age, and he was so humble on top of it and sweet and kind and all those things. But I was pissed. Immediately Mr. Neill wanted to make him section leader, and I was like, 'What? I've been in here three years already!' I think there had been some promise of section leader coming the next year because I had stuck with it all that time, so it was a little devastating for me when he made Jeff (who I didn't really know yet) section leader. I thought his playing was phenomenal, but, I mean, in marching band, how phenomenal can you be? I think at this point the band Rural Still

Life was together and playing."

When Jeff was made section leader, he took Mercy aside. "He said something like, 'Look, I'll tell you what. I know he made me section leader, but you've got seniority, and you've been here for a long time,'" she recalls. "'So how about if you kind of really are the section leader and do all the things the section leader does, and I'll write the cadences and work with the guys on stuff.' It was so magnanimous of him and so generous and kind, how could I not fall in love with him on the spot? Which is pretty much what I did. I ended up having such a crush on Jeff even though technically he was miles beyond me. He taught me everything he knew; I still have this cadence he wrote—it was so funky that we could not march straight to it." Years later, when she saw Jeff at a Valley Arts Guitar special in-store show, she had him sign the cadence.

Jeff and Mercy Baron at a Valley Arts Guitar store appearance, 1982. (Photo courtesy of Mercy Baron)

When the drum line wasn't on the field, they would sit in the stands together, and Jeff would teach them. "Jeff would show us cadences he made up," Baron recalls. "There might have been maybe six, seven or eight drummers and to keep us from being bored, he would have each one of us play a different time signature. We would have to be kind of quiet about it—we couldn't play our drums; we would play on the rims, and it was mind-blowingly phenomenal because I would have never done this otherwise. Then Jeff would have us play these different time signatures that would blend together. I will never forget the sound of that. We would do it for a few bars and then literally fall apart, going, 'Holy shit! Are you kidding me?' To say that I learned from him is an understatement. We were so lucky!"

When the marching band had games at other schools, they travelled on buses, and once again Baron describes the scene as the drummers sat together, playing cadences led by Porcaro. Every member of the line had their sticks constantly in hand, trying to emulate Jeff, and trying to absorb every shred of knowledge he would impart, "which he loved doing," Mercy says. "And there was never any ego involved. He was just happy to see us eager to learn."

Mercy was part of a group that also hung out socially with Jeff, and she recalls seeing Rural Still Life at school functions. Sometime during high school Mercy's father—a fledgling songwriter—took the band into the studio to cut some of his songs. Mercy says watching Jeff in the studio was phenomenal. "He knew how to get the right drum sound already," Baron says. "I don't remember who the engineer was or even where it was recorded, but I'm sure it was somewhere in the Valley. We were all in awe of the rest of the guys in the band, too. It

Senior high marching band drum cadence written by Jeff. (Courtesy of Mercy Baron)

wasn't just Jeff. They were all mind blowing at their ages. All of them were sixteen or seventeen years old, and I remember thinking, 'Where did all these guys come from? Who could play like this?'"

Jeff dropped by to say goodbye to Mercy the night before he left for the Sonny & Cher gig. Mercy had "awesome" parents who let her have her own apartment in North Hollywood at seventeen. Jeff was impressed that she had a kit of practice pads set up. When Jeff inquired about the noise that practicing must create, she told him "I live right above the manager, and every time I sit down to practice, she takes her broom and hits the ceiling like, 'Shut up!'" Jeff loved it. "He just cracked up over that," Mercy recalls. "He thought that was so funny. I was so excited to see him and really, it was the last time we hung out together because, as you know, his career just took off into the stratosphere after that. We kind of lost touch because back then there were no cell phones."

They graduated in '72 and Mercy remembers going with a group from high school to see Jeff play with Steely Dan at the Sopwith Camel in Glendale in 1974. "Steely Dan was already pretty well known," says Mercy. "The night was very memorable because of something sad that happened to Jeff that night. We're all watching the gig and Jeff is playing like a motherfucker—as always, so good—but in the middle of the set, Jeff's hands completely freeze and seize up, and he falls backwards off the drum throne." Baron is still unclear as to what exactly happened. I know at times Jeff's fingers froze around the sticks so tightly that they actually had to be physically uncurled and removed, so it's possible that's what Mercy and her friends witnessed. Baron is just sure everything stopped, but from what she recalls, he recovered and finished the set. She doesn't remember talking to him about it later.

Scott Shelly, who was there that night, doesn't recall this episode, but he did tell me he knew that Jeff had a severe issue with his hands cramping up, even at fourteen years old. "He didn't tell a lot of people about it, but I remember a couple of times at somebody's school dance, his hands would cramp, and we would have to massage his hand to get the stick out of it—it was that much of a deal," he says. "It happened enough that we wondered what the hell was going on, but he didn't really want to talk about it."

JODY CORTEZ

Ten-year-old **JODY CORTEZ** moved with his family from Miami to L.A. when he was in the sixth grade. Entering Milliken Junior High in seventh grade, he met Joleen Porcaro, the youngest of the Porcaro kids. Jody's older brother Dean was in a band with Steve Porcaro. When the drummer got sick, Jody replaced him—and found himself playing Jeffrey's Camco set in the Porcaro garage. "Jeff would come to our gigs and play cowbell and tambourine behind me. He would often find a riser and have me play on it. His influence soon enveloped me, and I became a Jeff worshipper. Joe (Porcaro) would tease the boys and tell them I had better time (laughs). I loved Papa Joe like a father," says Jody, who also took lessons from Joe for about a year.

In 1971 Jeff recorded that first Jack Daugherty session with Jim Keltner (for the album *Jack Daugherty and the Class of Nineteen Hundred and Seventy One*) and Jody recalls attending a concert at Valley College where Jeff and Jim Gordon played double drums for that project. "I was eleven years old with my mouth on the ground," Cortez says. "Jeff used to call me 'little Buddy Miles,' and I would play with marching sticks, and I hit those drums! Jeff was literally levitating off his drums that night, jumping up catching cymbals, jumping off the drumkit, reminding me of a gymnast. I'm thinking, 'This guy is from another planet, truly ahead of his time, totally like a Gandalf.' I've always considered him a Gandalf, period. He was my Gandalf. At this concert there was an intermission, so I ran to the restroom. I'm standing at the urinal and in walk Jeff and Jim Gordon, and they stand next to me. Jeffrey is to my right and Jim Gordon is to his right. I turn to Jeff and go, 'Jeff, you're like the best drummer in the whole world, man,' and he goes, 'No, *he's* the best drummer in the whole world,' so our heads all turn to the right and our heads all look up at Jim Gordon," Cortez recalls, laughing.

Jody moved to Germany from 1974 to 1978. When he returned, Jeff had plans for him. Cortez recalls that Jeff told him he wanted him to play with Larry Carlton, but Jody told him he had enrolled in junior college and wanted a few years to figure out his life. Before the third year had ended, he got a call from Jeff. "At that point, I was planning to become an optometrist. Jeff grabbed me and said, 'Yo, dig! You're going to play drums!'" Cortez recalls. "He called me up and said, 'Come on down to Leeds, I'm in the big room.' I show up and he's smoking a joint. Jeff introduces me to Jimmy Scaggs (Boz's brother). Carlos Vega had gone with Olivia Newton John for more money, and Jeff says, 'So dig. You're Boz's drummer. Who do you want in the band?' So I was playing Jeffrey's shit at a super early age in his garage, on his drums, shitting myself because Joe's in the next room and the family is in and out and I'm going, 'How did this happen?'

"Later on, there was another call from Jeff, 'Hey, do me a favor.' 'What's that?' 'Could you drive to Santa Barbara for me?' 'Sure. What's going on?' 'My buddy Christopher Cross is there. He needs you to play some drums for him.' 'For sure. I'm there!' That started my twelve-year touring and recording career with Chris," Jody states. "We did some Japanese imports with Jeff, Vinnie, Carlos and me. The first record I did was called *Rendezvous*, which was a Japanese import. Jeff did the title track and a ballad called 'Is There Something.' Both tracks are killer."

SHAZAM!

In about 1974, two burgeoning stars collided: Jeff Porcaro and a young film and TV composer and producer named **RANDY EDELMAN**. Edelman had been called to write an arrangement to conduct the orchestra on *The Sonny & Cher Comedy Hour* for their guest Jim Nabors (a.k.a. Gomer Pyle). Edelman describes himself back then as a "20-year-old punk kid" elated to be doing odd music-directing jobs. He has gone on to score films such as *Twins, Ghostbusters II, Kindergarten Cop, Beethoven, The Mask, Dragonheart* and has contributed to many others.

Nabors was a big star at the time from his five seasons on *The*

Andy Griffith Show. "Jim had an extraordinary operatic voice, totally unlike his comedy Southern routine," says Edelman. "At the time there was a hit song called 'Good Time Charlie's Got the Blues.' It had a country-ish feel that Jim liked, and he thought I could do a cool arrangement that would 'hip' him up (which was impossible). I did the arrangement with a very cool drum fill before the chorus—with big toms, etc., which was all the rage then. With a TV studio orchestra, I figured at the run-through I would have to explain the tempo change, the number of hits in the fill, and the sound of the toms. I anticipated a fucking nightmare. We started the run-through and it was all ok. Then we got to that spot before the chorus and I almost fainted. Suddenly, right on cue, in the exact tempo and the most explosive sound you've ever heard coming out of the deep toms came precisely what I had concocted and imagined. I was in shock, with the biggest smile on my face—and on good ole' Jim's. After two run-throughs, which were all the same—perfect—I strolled back to see who had delivered this joyful moment and performance. Lo and behold, it was a skinny little kid, maybe sixteen or seventeen years old. I did not shake his hand; I hugged him, and he told me his name: Jeff Porcaro."

It obviously was not a name Edelman forgot, because when it came time to record his solo album, *If Love is Real,* a couple of years later, he had Jeffrey on all the tracks. "Jeff was a virtuoso sitting back playing his drum kit," Edelman says. "Especially for me recalling my album *If Love is Real* with both him and the great Steve Cropper playing electric guitar over at Producer's Workshop in Hollywood with Bill Schnee at the console. I've had quite an association with Jeff's family; Joe played percussion on many of my movie scores, Steve is a close friend who has worked on a million things with me, and even Mike played bass on 'Don't Let Go of Me' from my *You're the One* album."

JEFF BAXTER

JEFF BAXTER, also known as "Skunk," says he probably met Porcaro on a record date but doesn't recall which one. In those situations, Baxter explains, it's usually pretty much business as usual, so there's not much time for small talk, thus the meeting was not memorable. He *does* recall one session where he was "egging Jeff on" because the track lacked energy and needed an injection of Porcaro's personality and energy. "Jeff was one of those guys who not only could inject energy, but because he was a groove master, he had a pocket that was unique," Baxter notes. "He had more than one pocket, actually, and he was able to adapt to the artist. The pocket for this song was forward-leaning. He really needed to drive this song, and he nailed it in one take.

"Every drummer has a different pocket. They're all expected to keep time, just like every guitar player is expected to play in tune and be able to perform, but the way Jeff Porcaro would interpret the rhythm—he had a way of leaning forward but playing the snare just a nanosecond behind. He understood the subtleties of where to put things. The way that he laid the snare back in the music was a presence behind the whole band. It was like he was wrapping his arms around the whole band and helping everyone to walk. I always felt like he was right behind me with support. Not that he wasn't leading, but he was always supporting, so I knew I could try things and step out rhythmically and always know that Jeff was there. It doesn't happen with a lot of drummers, because they get confused when people start slightly varying from the road."

Baxter cites Jeff's confidence as one of the traits he admired.

"You have to have a lot of confidence as a studio musician," he asserts. "You have to feel invincible, like there's nothing you can't do. Some people have arrogance to them where that confidence manifests itself. Jeff had a benevolent confidence. There was always humor. Certainly, you wouldn't mistake his body language and his personality as a shrinking violet, but it was never arrogant. I loved playing with him."

Playing with Jeff was joyful, according to Skunk, and in live situations there was a different energy and a performance element. "In Steely Dan, because the music wasn't, of itself, driving rock, having Jeff and Jimmy Hodder (who was an excellent drummer) playing together, they both understood the need to lean forward live," says Skunk. "Jeff was really good at that. He loved to play live, and of course Toto really defined that."

Baxter recalls having a lot of fun on stage with Jeff, sharing private musical moments between them: humorous and whimsical musical "inside jokes" that the audience might not notice, but would provide a laugh and a wink. Speaking of sharing laughs, Skunk says they both loved dumb jokes. "Like when I was playing in Linda Ronstadt's band with Andrew Gold, we were both big fans of Rodney Dangerfield and Henny Youngman; that kind of humor," he explains. "It was like Hal Blaine and his humor. You couldn't shut him down. Jeff and I shared the love of offbeat humor: not salacious, but dumb."

TEASER

Jeff mentioned Tommy Bolin's *Teaser* album a couple of times in conversations we had through the years, kind of like the yin to a Barbra Streisand yang. He'd mention both Bolin and Streisand in the same sentence, as if it were a yardstick measuring the broad stroke of his abilities, a proud proclamation of the diversity of his studio capabilities. In fact, he implied that he once went from a Streisand session directly to work with Bolin. I don't know if that's entirely true, but it seemed as if that was what he was getting at. He said in those kinds of situations he would change his attire to match the music, sort of like getting into character. I always felt he was very tickled that he was called to play on *Teaser* because it was a little bit out of the ordinary.

Bassist **STANLEY SHELDON** (Peter Frampton, Lou Gramm, Warren Zevon, Delbert McClinton) met Jeff at the Record Plant in 1975 on what he recalls as two days of sessions wherein Jeff cut four tracks for *Teaser*. He says they clicked instantly, and he felt Jeff's excitement and enthusiasm. Actually, he felt a bond almost as though they were brothers—even before they met. People had told him he even looked a little like Jeff. "He was such a great guy. We even had the same pants on one of the days," Sheldon says with a laugh. "They were these crazy looking almost quilted looking white pants that when you put them in the dryer they puffed up like popcorn. I think I got them at Fred Segal's."

Stanley agreed with me that the session wasn't Porcaro's usual call. "He played so great on the tracks we did together," says Sheldon. "Those are some of my favorite tracks." They cut live in the room; just he, Jeff and Bolin. "David Foster came in later and did some keyboard overdubs, and Tommy did a lot of his own overdubs. But when we cut the basic track, it was just the three of us. I remember Carmine Appice was there, just hanging out. Carmine is a character. He came in and there was a hit song that had just come out called 'Standing on Shaky Ground' by the Temptations. We all loved it, and Jeff and I were talking about it. Carmine tried to show me how to play the bass part. I said, 'No Carmine, that's not it.' After Carmine left, Jeff and I were joking about it: 'What the hell is Carmine doing trying to show me how to play the bass part?'" Stanley recalls, laughing. "I can remember it like it was yesterday."

According to Sheldon, Bolin was a Steely Dan nut (hence the hiring of Porcaro) and they got all the songs on the first or second takes. Jeff's hi-hat work on the title track is something that Sheldon specifically mentions as memorable. "It's classic Jeff hi-hat," Stanley remarks. "I love the feel on that. I wasn't crazy about that song, quite frankly. It was too poppy. But when Jeff put that groove to it, I was a fan. 'Dreamer,' which he played on, was the only ballad on the record."

Bolin was not a schooled musician and didn't write charts. He'd play the song and give a description like, "Here's the groove, we're going to do eight bars of this, two bars of this, and let's do it." Then he would let the musicians do their thing. According to Sheldon, the "Teaser" hi-hat part was Jeff's idea. Also, Sheldon recalls, "At the end of 'Teaser' Jeff dropped his sticks and said, 'Let's go dig it, man,' and got up to go listen to it in the control room. Tommy kept it on the record; you can hear it plain as day. I always thought that was so cool; Jeff always knew when we had it."

They recorded the first part of the album, and then Bolin went on the road with Deep Purple. At the same time Peter Frampton was releasing his groundbreaking *Frampton Comes Alive!* with Sheldon. It complicated matters in the recording schedule of *Teaser* as well as creating promotional consequences when *Teaser* was finally completed. The first four tracks of Bolin's record were done in Los Angeles with

Jeffrey and then the second half of it was recorded in New York with Narada Michael Walden.

A HERO'S PERSPECTIVE

(Note: I had never heard a lot of the information Bernard Purdie shared with me, and he could not place some of the details or timeline. Although I tried to research to the best of my ability, I could not independently verify anything that follows.)

Anyone who knows about Jeff Porcaro knows one of his major heroes was **BERNARD PURDIE**. According to Purdie, he met a teenage Jeff while working with Joe Porcaro on a project after Joe asked if he could bring Jeff to the studio. I had never heard this story, and of course Joe is not here to confirm this. While I did try to find a project on which Purdie and the senior Porcaro worked together, I could not, but that does not mean the story is not true. (Many sessions never get released.) "Joe told me about Jeff and asked if he could watch," says Bernard, adding that Joe had told him what a fan of Purdie's Jeff was. Bernard told Joe he could come anytime. "I love it when he comes. I said, 'He can always come. He can sit on the floor.'" Purdie recounts. "Joe said, 'I don't want him to be in your way.' I said, 'He's not in my way. I love it when he's there. He might suggest something. I like the idea if I'm helping him, I love it and it makes it work for me.'" Once in a while, they would go to eat "because I always love to eat," Purdie says with a laugh. "He would ask me questions. He asked me about my shuffle, about my playing, the kind of things that I did and what put me in the position of what I was doing. It was easy to talk with him and I enjoyed him because he loved what he was doing."

Bernard can't recall at what stage Jeffrey was at in his work during this time. Of course, the song "Rosanna" was not released until 1982 and Jeff would have already been 28, but Purdie and I spoke about how Porcaro always gave Purdie credit for the shuffle feel on "Rosanna." "He was learning the Purdie shuffle, but he learned it on his own, the way he felt it," Bernard says. "What he did was he put the backbeat on 1 instead of 3. I thought that was wonderful. He took my shuffle and made it his—and that was the kind of thing we always talked about: No matter who you want to emulate, if you do it your way, it's always going to work. Whether you're placing the beat in front or behind, it's all about what you do with it. If you're going to make it sound like my beat, wonderful, as long as it works for you. That's what counts."

Bernard acknowledges that Jeff was called for his version of that shuffle and says, "He wrote things around it. He never switched and went back to 3. He put the backbeat on 1 and it worked. It now became his little thing," Purdie says, as we agree it became the Porcaro-Purdie shuffle. Purdie was very flattered that drummers found it something to adopt in their playing, and says that he and Jeffrey became friends. At the time, Purdie was traveling back and forth between L.A. and New York every two weeks or so, and he always knew where Jeff was playing and would make it his business to see him. It was a mutual admiration; they always made it a point to see each other when they could. "People thought drummers were in competition with one another," Purdie says. "They've never been in competition with each other."

In fact, Purdie told me something I never knew: Jeff was the one who connected him with Steely Dan and was responsible for Bernard playing on "Kid Charlemagne," "Babylon Sisters" and "Home at Last."

"The first time they called we talked about Jeff, and I said, 'Yeah, I know Jeff quite well,'" he says with a laugh. "People should stop trying to pit one against another and you find out that they love one another."

Bernard is grateful for all the time he spent with Jeff. "It sure hurt when he left," he says.

LES DUDEK

Guitarist **LES DUDEK** laughs as he recalls the long and winding road that led him to Porcaro. He had just finished a tour with Boz Scaggs and had been invited to play with a new group called Journey. While rehearsing with Neal Schon, Ross Valory, Aynsley Dunbar, and Gregg Rollie at Studio Instrumental Rentals in San Francisco, he received a call from Columbia Records requesting a meeting at their nearby office. Dudek excused himself, saying he had to go across the street and would be right back. At the meeting, the president and vice president of the label offered him a solo record deal on the spot. Later the same day, Capitol Records called, also offering a deal.

"I went from not knowing how I was going to pay my rent that month to having three things I could do in one day," says Dudek. A decision had to be made as to whether he should continue with Journey; sign with Columbia, with Boz Scaggs as producer; or go with Capitol, with Steve Miller producing (who had helped bring him out to California). Feeling loyalty to Scaggs, with whom he had worked for about five years, he chose Columbia, thereby ending his being "a founding member of Journey for about two hours," he jokes.

Dudek had some players in mind, but he hadn't thought of

a drummer. "Boz and I flew to L.A. and had an audition with this drummer named Jeff Porcaro at Studio Instrumental Rentals on Sunset," he recalls. "Boz and I had just had lunch at La Scala Boutique in Beverly Hills. We walk into S.I.R. and Porcaro is sitting there on his drum throne. We say our greetings—'Hi, I'm Les, I'm Boz, I'm Jeff,' —and I said, 'Let me hear you play something; play me some grooves,' so Jeff started playing. Boz and I looked at each other, Jeff looked at us while he was playing, and then he stopped and said, 'You guys wanna plug in and play something with me?' I said, 'No, you're hired, man, let's go make a fuckin' record.' Jeff was the first and last drummer we auditioned. I picked him on the spot and told Boz we found our guy."

Dudek, feeling that he has an innate ability to spot great musicians, knew instantly that Jeff had it. "I just had the knack, playing with really great players over the years; making records with the Allman Brothers, Boz, and doing sessions," he says. "I turned down a lot of stuff, like the Marshall Tucker Band."

The first self-titled Les Dudek solo record was cut in 1976 at Davlen Sound Studios, and he says it was an incredible experience. Playing a track back in the control room, Dudek remarked to Scaggs that it would sound great with some B3 organ. "Jeff goes, 'I know this guy. David Paich could play the shit out of this,'" Les recalls. "'How do we get hold of him?' I asked. Jeff says, 'He's out in the hallway.'" Paich returned the favor for Dudek while working on *Silk Degrees.* Dudek will never forget Porcaro telling him: "They were recording 'Jump Street,' and Boz and Joe Wissert said, 'We should put a slide guitar on this song. Who can we get that plays slide guitar?' Jeff said it was David Paich that spoke up and told Boz, 'You've only had one of the best slide players around playing in your band for over five years; that's a no-brainer: Call Dudek,'" Les recounts. "After all the years I played with Boz, Jeff couldn't believe my name wasn't first in the hat. Go figure."

After the album was released, Dudek was booked to play at Spartan Stadium in San Jose with the Doobie Brothers, War and Pablo Cruise. He didn't have a drummer. "I had to call the promoter and tell him I couldn't do the gig," says Les. "He said, 'What do you mean that you can't do the gig? You're already on the poster.' I said, 'I don't have a drummer.' He said, 'You better find one.' I thought, 'Well, let me call Porcaro and see what he's doing, for shits and giggles.' I called him up and said, 'Jeff, what are you doing next week?' And he said, 'I don't know, what are we doing?' I said, 'I'm playing a gig next week with the Doobie Brothers at Spartan Stadium and I don't have a drummer.' And he said, 'So where's my fuckin' ticket?' That's the way it always was with Porcaro. He would drop shit for me."

On 1978's *Ghost Town Parade,* Porcaro and Keltner played double drums on two tracks: "Bound to Be a Change" and "Friend of Mine," cut at the Record Plant in L.A. According to Dudek, on "Friend of Mine" Jeff and Keltner were jamming so intensely that it got to the point where Jeff was kicking all the drums over. "At the end of the song you can just hear Porcaro on the hi-hat, but what people don't realize is that's all he had left to play. I'm looking up and there are no drums there. He just had a hi-hat," Dudek recalls with a big laugh.

"On the song 'Central Park,' we wanted to add some more drums, so we set Jeff up in the parking lot and put mic's all around—because the whole theme of the song was when I was in New York City at some CBS event, I had my windows open, and I heard some drum thing going on, echoing through the buildings in Central Park. There had been about forty drummers in the park just grooving together, and that's how I got the idea for the song," Dudek explains. "To recreate the way it was reverberating through the buildings, Bruce (Botnick) and I got the idea to set Porcaro up in the parking lot."

Dudek never toured with Porcaro, but living in the Bay Area at the time, Les played Boz Scaggs' dates at Oakland's Paramount Theatre with Jeff in the band. He recalls a whole crew of the musicians going back to his apartment in Mill Valley after the gig and "getting blitzed": Steve Miller, David Paich, Willie Weeks and Boz. Dudek played the Oakland shows for several years in a row, when Boz would roll through town.

What did Jeff bring to his music? "Everything," says Dudek. "He brought everything. The thing that I noticed right away about Porcaro is he didn't just play a groove; he played the song. He interpreted his drum playing to fit the song. It wasn't just 'wham, bam, thank you ma'am.' He was telling a story. He would lift when it required a lift or he would suck it back and pull it into a pocket when it needed that. He just had a really great overall feel of how to approach a song and turn it into a story." According to Dudek, Jeff liked to hear a demo, he'd write a chart of the arrangement and they'd run the tune down softly, but when the engineer hit the record button, "Jeff transformed into a monster." He mentions the reversed hi-hat on "City Magic" from his first album, and also Jeff's love of water cymbals and how he would hit the crown and wave his hand over it to get an interesting sound.

When Dudek was in Denmark recording *Deeper Shades of Blues* (released in '94, after Jeff's death), he says neither the drummer nor the studio was cutting it. "The sound was bleeding through the walls,"

Dudek recalls. "I said, 'This isn't happening. I would like to do this with Jeff Porcaro,' and the engineer goes, 'You can get Jeff Porcaro?' I said, 'Give me the phone. You got the money? I can get Porcaro.' He said, 'Yeah, whatever.'" On the phone from Los Angeles, Jeff started to try to figure out the logistics of getting his drums to Denmark when he looked at his calendar. "Shit, I'm doing Bon Jovi and Bruce Springsteen this week. But I have two days open. Can you come to L.A.?" Dudek asked him to book a studio for the two free days. They convened at Schnee Studios for the last time they would record together. "He sandwiched me in between Springsteen and Bon Jovi," Les says with a laugh. Standing at the piano, they reminisced about the recording of Dudek's first record right next door at Davlen Studios, and about how many years had passed since then. In all, Jeff appears on five of Dudek's albums. There are even two songs on 2003's *Freestyle* featuring Jeff—"Wild Hearted Weekend" and "Hot Fun in Dixieland"—that had been recorded before Jeff passed away.

DRUMMER TO DRUMMER

TRIS IMBODEN's band Honk was scheduled to open for Steely Dan, but the headliner decided to do the show without an opener. The night was not particularly memorable for that reason, but it was unforgettable because it was the first time he saw Jeff Porcaro play. When Honk was canceled, the band received tickets and backstage passes to the concert as consolation prizes. Jim Hodder and Porcaro played double drums that night, switching off from song to song. Tris recalls it as being late '73 or early '74, because Jeff "Skunk" Baxter and Michael McDonald were still in the band.

Imboden didn't meet Jeff that night. That opportunity finally came around 1975, when Honk was playing at the Troubadour, one of Los Angeles' premier clubs at the time, and Jeff was playing in the opening band (Tris cannot recall the group's name). "We became fast friends," says Tris. "I was so taken with the guy he was—how humble and how cool. I was really knocked out by him—not to mention how I adored his playing."

Fast forward to 1977; Tris was with Kenny Loggins. Jeff was on the road with Boz Scaggs, and Tris recalls some shows with Loggins, Fleetwood Mac and Scaggs. "I remember a show in Toronto where Jeff and I got to hang and he had those beautiful Camcos that I just loved," Tris recalls. "They had that black piano finish on them with gold hardware." Imboden also remembers that Jeff had a set of Syndrums—the first electronic drums—that were completely unknown at the time. "I was checking out his set, and Jeff said, 'Have you heard these? See those pads up there?' I said, 'No, I haven't heard them.' He said, 'Stick around, buddy.' That was a given. I wanted to hear him and the band. I loved Boz, and I loved the album. When I heard (the Syndrums), I thought they were the coolest things ever. On the first album I did with Kenny (*Nightwatch, 1978*), I ended up buying a cheaper version called Synare, and I used them on two songs in an attempt to make them sound like Jeff."

Which brings us to the moment Jeff blew Tris away. After *Nightwatch* was released, and Loggins had the hit "Whenever I Call You Friend" with Stevie Nicks, Loggins was returning from a tour in Japan. As is often the case with bands traveling to Japan, they stop off in Hawaii for a show. "We did a show in O'ahu, and because I love the island of Kauai so much, I flew there with my then-wife Celia, who I had taken with me to Japan," Tris recounts. "Driving to the north shore in a rental car from the airport, we passed a hotel on the east side of the island. At the time, it was called the Kauai Resort Hotel, and I saw this giant sign that said 'TONIGHT: TOTO.' I said, 'No! How can that be?' So we got to our hotel on the north shore, all the way in Hanalei, and I called the hotel and asked if Jeff Porcaro was registered, and they put me through! He said these were Toto's very first shows. Long story short, he said, 'Why don't you come hang this afternoon.' So I drove back to the hotel to hang with Jeff. He met me in the lobby, and started complimenting me on the Loggins' album. I was going, 'Ah Jeff, I can't even listen to it.' We all are so critical of ourselves—I guess we have to be—but I honestly thought I sucked on the record. He said, 'No man, when you come to your senses, you'll see what I'm talking about.' He had his Billy Gladstone practice pad, and he showed some things to me, and then he picked up the *Nightwatch* cassette and said, 'It's because of this I'm doing this.' I said, 'Get out of here.' That's when I was absolutely floored that I could play something that would catch Jeff's ear. It was so sweet, it was so encouraging, and my heart just soared."

That night Tris and his wife saw Toto perform. These were preliminary shows where Toto was working out the performance bugs, and there was hardly an audience—mainly just some record company execs, since the venue was intentionally under the radar. Toto's official first concert date occurred after the Kauai gigs, on January 15, 1979, at Honolulu's Blaisdell Arena, opening for Peter Frampton.

Toto opened a few shows for Loggins later, in the Pacific Northwest, where Jeff and Tris enjoyed time together. Over the years the two drummers ran into each other at rehearsal studios when Loggins and Toto prepared for tours at the same time, or at recording studios when the two would collide in the hallways between sessions. The crowning glory for Tris came one night in 1982 while he was on the road with Al Jarreau and had a night off while playing a festival in Ludwigshafen, Germany. "Both bands happened to be in the same hotel at the same time—very dangerous," Tris says with a mischievous laugh. "We played the first night and Toto had the night off, so they came to see Jarreau. David Sanborn was opening for Jarreau on that tour, and Dennis Chambers was playing with Sanborn. Jeff had heard of Dennis, but had never seen him play, so I said, 'Oh Jeff, I can't wait until you see this guy,' so we both stood on the side of the stage. Jeff was going, 'I can't believe this guy. He's a motherfucker!' It was so much fun turning him on to that. We played, and as I recall we had a pretty good night. Jeff said, 'You're coming (to the Toto show) tomorrow night, right?' I said, 'Of course.' He said, 'Bring your sticks, buddy.' I said, 'What?' He said, 'Yeah, you're going to play.' I said, 'Are you kidding me?' He said, 'No, you're going to play.'"

The next night, Porcaro informed Imboden that he was to come onstage during Toto's first encore for "Hold The Line." They choreographed a drummer switch backstage. While continuing to play the hi-hat, Jeff would get up, and Tris would take over playing the hats. "As he was getting up, I would slide underneath and get the one on the bass drum, and of course the backbeat," Imboden explains. "We did it seamlessly without getting to rehearse; we talked it out and it worked. Nobody in the band looked up. But Luke saw me and yelled, 'Buddy!' I still can't believe I got to do that. It was like 'Pinch me now.' That was the kind of person Jeff was. He was so generous of spirit, as well as being so funny and so much fun to hang with."

Although cameras were not allowed at the concert, a stealthy

Tris and Jeff. (Courtesy of Tris Imboden)

fan snuck a shot of Jeff playing tambourine while kneeling down beside Tris. "This is the guy that Jeff is," Tris says. "Neither of us knew there was a photo, but the guy contacted Jeff and sent it to him. Jeff had it blown up and gave it to Harry McCarthy from Drum Paradise (my cartage company back then) to give to me. I just loved the guy. He was the kind of guy you would just jump on a grenade for."

THE NIGHTMARE ALBUM WITH A GREAT DRUMMER

In 1977 Hall & Oates, coming off the success of such hits as "Sara Smile," "Rich Girl" and "She's Gone," recorded *Beauty on a Back Street*. Although both Daryl Hall and John Oates were New York guys, they had made their last three (and a half) albums in L.A., and they hired Porcaro to play on the entire new one. "In the process of being in L.A., of course we started meeting people and hanging," **JOHN OATES** says. "We started hanging at the bar at the Troubadour, meeting various people. We knew Toto; the music business was so much smaller then. There was a lot of mutual respect between the Toto guys and David Foster and all those people. We were all kind of hanging around. Through the years Daryl and I have been very fortunate to be surrounded and play with some of the greatest musicians ever. One thing I've always noticed about great musicians is that they love to play great songs, so we've attracted the cream of the crop from the earliest days at Atlantic, with drummers like Jim Gordon and Bernard Purdie and so on. As any musician will tell you, it all starts with the groove; it all starts with the drummer. Having a great drummer is the first building block to having a great session. I always wanted to work with Jeff, but whether it was his touring schedule or our touring schedule, we didn't come together earlier. But it came together then."

Oates offered a disclaimer upfront: "The album we are talking about is my least favorite album we ever made," he admits, explaining the album was made under duress. Their producer and former guitarist, Christopher Bond, who had helmed the previous two hit records, had let success go to his head. "He had a lot of personality problems and a lot of substance problems. The album was very difficult to make," Oates says, presenting an illustration: "There was a point during the making of the record, literally during a session, when he collapsed onto the console. His face smashed into the thing, the EMTs had to be called and he was rushed to the hospital. That was the feel of the record. Obviously, the bright spot was having someone like Jeff Porcaro, because, quite frankly, maybe the album wouldn't have gotten made if it hadn't had amazing musicians. I thought the songs were mediocre and dark—it was a dark period of time. The saving grace is that we had great musicians playing some fricken weird songs."

John and Daryl always directed the musicians on their projects, but, "my personal philosophy on making great records—and what I learned from working with great producers like Arif Mardin—is you surround yourself with the best possible players who you think are appropriate for the music you want to make, and then you let them do exactly what they do. You direct, but you don't dictate," Oates says, explaining that, particularly with vocals, they might have to give direction when it comes to phrasing, and stop to pick up the tempo or slow it down. "You didn't have to dictate anything to Jeff Porcaro. You just told him what you were going for. He heard the song; he listened to it with his musical sensibility and then he just played, and everything he played was just amazing. That's how you get the best out of the people you surround yourself with."

Oates can't recall the first time he met Porcaro, but says it was probably socially, either hanging around or at a session he dropped in on. "All I know is from the very first downbeat, I knew there was something very special going on," he says. "The great drummers we worked with over the years all have one thing in common: They are in total control, and they dictate—in the best possible way—the tempo, the feel and the vibe of the song. And when it's right and they're good at what they do, everything falls into place. It's almost like you're floating on a rhythmic cloud. You can expand your playing and your musicality in a way that you can't when you don't have that. Weak drummers, mediocre drummers are just following along and making noise. People like Jeff Porcaro are in charge of the groove—and when someone's in charge of the groove and you trust them, good things happen.

"Jeff Porcaro was one of the unbelievably amazing drummers. He was a student of what he did. There are a number of videos where he explains (his approach), and there's one where he explains the half-time groove he did on 'Rosanna.' He says he got it from Bernard Purdie, but his skill level and technical expertise took it to a whole other level. I'm really happy we got to play with him; I just wish it had been under better circumstances."

BURTON CUMMINGS

After **BURTON CUMMINGS** disbanded the very successful Guess Who in 1975, he embarked on a solo career in 1976. It was not until his second solo album, *My Own Way to Rock,* that producer Richard Perry brought Jeffrey into Cummings' orbit. Porcaro played on eight of the nine tracks on the album (with Rick Shlosser on the ninth), cut at Studio 55. Jeff also played double drums on two tracks with Ollie Brown. Cummings knew of Jeff, how good he was, how many records he had played on and how sought after he was but had never met him. He was excited to work with him. "Jeff was a very tuned-in L.A. musician," Cummings says. "He was a very busy musician and one of the best studio drummers in L.A."

Cummings says the title track of that album is one of the greatest tracks with which he's ever been associated. "It's just tremendous," he exclaims. "Jeff played different rhythms and his drum fills were amazing. The whole feel was just incredible on that song." "Come on By" features both Porcaro and Ollie Brown on drums. Cummings liked the two drummers playing together because it made the feel heavier. "They were both pounding away pretty hard," he says. "I remember when we did the song 'Charlemagne' and the two of them were both drumming, it became heavier and heavier because of the two drums."

Both Ray Parker, Jr. and Randy Bachman played guitar on "Come on By." Jeff recorded Bachman's entire 1978 *Survivor* album and Bachman contributed this comment about Jeffrey: "I was thrilled to get the opportunity to work with Jeff Porcaro and the rest of the band that backed Boz Scaggs on *Silk Degrees* and at that time were working on the first Toto album. He was my kind of drummer. He got the groove of the song immediately and literally became the spark plug to drive and guide the band. I cut 22 band tracks in five days, and they were all great. Many of them became my *Survivor* album. Jeff had the magic and shared it with everyone. I was one of the lucky ones."

Jeff only recorded three tracks on Cummings' third album, *Dream of a Child*, which Burton assumes was because Jeff was focused on Toto, while Cummings was also putting together a band of his own at that time. The three tracks—"Hold on I'm Comin'," "Guns, Guns, Guns," and "Roll with the Punches"—were all double-drummed with Rick Shlosser. "'Guns, Guns, Guns,' is one of my most favorite songs I ever wrote," Burton says. "That was Jeff and Rick. I like lots of drums. What's not to like? It's a heavier beat; the backbeat is reinforced by two drummers. It just makes it all heavier. I like caveman, Neanderthal drums. I like a big, big 2 and 4 backbeat, and when you've got two drummers, you've got lots of that. Jeff and Rick really locked in together."

Later, Porcaro played on Cummings' entire 1990 album *Plus Signs* (with brother Mike on bass on some of the tracks). Porcaro held together the six-plus minutes of "Boring Dreams" with his steadfast groove and innovative performance. “He did some interesting adlibbing, some fills a little behind the bar count, stuff that Jeff was very good at, that a lot of drummers wouldn't have even thought of,” Cummings observes. He further explains that when Richard Perry produced the project, Perry would send demos out to the musicians to listen to ahead of time. Bassist Ian Gardiner co-produced *Plus Signs* with Cummings and wrote some charts for the musicians, but Cummings admits he doesn't read, so he didn't use charts much. He says he always welcomed the musicians' input.

Jeff's contributions extended to orchestration and tempo. “There's a song called ‘Bridge in Time’ where Jeff was very innovative with the percussion,” Cummings notes. “I recall that he played some African instruments, and he was very inventive. Jeff always knew exactly what you wanted. His intuition was tremendous; he always knew what to play. As simple as that sounds for me to tell you, he always knew what to play and how to make it sound tremendous.” Jeff's tempo sense also elevated the music. “On ‘Permissible to Cry,’ Jeff said, ‘Hey man, it's a good song, but got to pick it up a bit, ya know. It's got to be a little faster,’” Burton says, in his best “Jeff voice.” Thanks to this suggestion, they cut it a little faster, which changed the whole feel of the song. “Ultimately, he was right,” Cummings states.

On a personal level, Burton remembers Jeff as a big basketball fan. “When we were working on the stuff back then, it was the glory days of Michael Jordan. Once in a while, we would meet up in the studio the day after there had been a Chicago Bulls game and Jeff would be, ‘Hey, hey man, did you see Jordan last night?’” says Burton (in his best Porcaro voice again). “He was a big Jordan fan.”

IAN GARDINER'S RECOLLECTIONS

Bassist **IAN GARDINER** describes Jeff as kind, encouraging and as "a really good guy and always helpful." Although he isn't totally sure, he believes he met Porcaro on a Richard Perry session. "Richard produced Burton's (Cummings) first two records and you never knew who was going to be in the studio the next day—Keltner, Gordon and then Jeff came on the scene," says Gardiner. "I just know it was playing with butter. All these guys were. As a bass player I just loved it. Jeff was just beyond good; he was so easy to play with. The pocket was always there. That's what I remember most about him; how effortless it was playing with him. His time was so good, but I remember once he told us, 'My time sucks!' (laughs) Maybe it was in his head, but not in anybody else's head. He'd play wherever he needed to be in a particular song."

Ian also worked on Randy Bachman's *Survivor* album with Jeff. "It was Randy and I and Jeff, and I think Burton played some piano on it, but we rehearsed and Jeff's takes were always perfect, impeccable on the first take," Gardiner states. "The rest of us would have to punch in parts, but Jeff wouldn't even have to hear the song and it was good right at the beginning; he knew just what to play. His whole family was amazing—his dad and Mike. I worked with Mike on the last album I did with Burton called *Plus Signs*, which I engineered and mixed. Mike played bass on it, and I was transitioning into engineering and producing. The whole family was amazing."

Jeff invited the band members up to his Laurel Canyon home one night after one of the sessions for the second Burton Cummings album, *My Own Way to Rock.* Gardiner and keyboardist Mike Rowe ended up going. "We had a great time," Ian says, commenting on how warm and generous Jeff was. "We had all come down from Winnipeg, Canada, and we were all a little out of our element. He was probably the premiere session drummer at that time, along with Jim Keltner and Jim Gordon. I remember he played us a lot of the Steely Dan *Katy Lied* record without vocals on it. He had it all on cassette. That was exciting. But he was always encouraging and gave great advice."

Just after Gardiner moved to L.A. in 1978, he got a call to do a session for a soundtrack for a movie called *California Dreamin'* with Jeff, Skunk Baxter, and Michael McDonald. It was the title track: the Mamas and Papas song "California Dreamin'" with McDonald on vocals. In the end, Gardiner says manager Irving Azoff squashed the song because McDonald's voice was everywhere, and he was worried about his client becoming overexposed. The band America re-recorded the title song. They did end up on the album, though.

Ian vividly recalls some advice Jeff gave him regarding the sometimes not-always-kind producers: "'One thing is, you don't have to take any abuse from anybody.' I've had that in my brain ever since."

LABOUNTY LEARNS JEFF IS RIGHT, TOO

BILL LaBOUNTY grew up in Oregon and started going to Los Angeles to record in the late '60s, at about the age of eighteen. He and his band would record a few tunes and take them back to Oregon, where they would press them. They were the proverbial "big fish in a little pond" at home. It was a time when they could take the records around to the radio stations, which would play them. "It was a much more innocent time," remarks LaBounty.

Although later LaBounty would be known more as a songwriter, racking up hits for such artists as Robbie Dupree, Lonestar, Sawyer Brown, Steve Wariner, Shenandoah and others, he started out as a solo artist. His first big session with a major drummer was Jim Gordon, and he recalls after putting the cans on his head and fooling around with his piano part, Gordon began to play along, and he says "it was almost orgasmic." "What eventually happened was Jim Gordon started not being as available and I remember him talking to my producer about how he couldn't make some dates, but he knew this young drummer named Jeff Porcaro," LaBounty recalls. "Somebody booked Jeff for a session I was doing and I was blown away by him. To me Jeff wasn't Jim Gordon; he didn't play like Jim Gordon, he played like Jeff, but playing like Jeff was another little orgasmic universe for me."

Bill says Porcaro could hear something once and not just play it, but completely understand it and do exactly what needed to be done. "I was young, and I would go into the studio with these preconceptions of how I wanted to do it and how I wanted it to sound, what was going to be right and what was going to be wrong and, of course, Jeff was the same way in spades, only better," Bill says. "I would write things like maybe I'd want something going into the bridge—an accent or a hi-hat pull." In the beginning they would listen to playbacks and LaBounty would say, "Would you mind doing this or that…" While Bill describes Jeff as very pleasant and polite, he'd say, "You really want another take?" "He'd get right in my face sometimes and say, 'Let's just listen to this.' Once Larry (Carlton) took me aside and said, 'Ya know Bill, we're first call players and stuff, but when Jeff plays something and he tells all of us that it's right, we just take his word for it. We'll go listen to it, but I've played enough with people that I know what's what so it might be better if you didn't hassle Jeff too much. If Jeff says it's right, it's right,'" LaBounty recounts. "I was young. I knew Jeff was great. It was a great learning experience."

But it really only applied to Jeff. "It only took a couple of sessions for me to realize that if Jeff is doing that little dance in my face, then it's right; we don't have to do another one," Bill says. "As much as a genius as Jim Gordon was, it wasn't like that with him. He was amazing and he had the skills like Jeff did, but I don't think he was as versatile. Either one of them would be anybody's wet dream on their session, but Jeff was like this walking drum machine with a groove."

LaBounty cut his first album *Promised Love* for 20th Century Records in 1975, and while Jeff recorded some tracks, none of them ended up on that album; they appear on the next one. In the meanwhile, to coincide with his first album, LaBounty made his live debut at the Roxy in Los Angeles, which Jeff agreed to play with him. Included in the set was an arrangement of Van Morrison's "Wild Night," which LaBounty usually did with his own band, of which he only had the sax player for this performance. While they were going over it in rehearsal at SIR, LaBounty explained to Jeff that the groove was like James Brown's "Cold Sweat." "We counted it off and of course he played it exactly like Clyde Stubblefield," Bill recalls. "Of course, I said 'Cold Sweat' but it wasn't exactly what I wanted for the arrangement, so I stopped the song and said, 'Is that 'Cold Sweat?' He stood up and said, 'That's 'Cold Sweat,' and I said, 'Okay, but we're not exactly playing 'Cold Sweat.' We're playing this arrangement I have.' The more I talked, the more steamed he got. I wasn't being obnoxious; I was actually kind of shy, but just the idea to Jeff that he wasn't playing 'Cold Sweat'… He just stood up, put his sticks on the snare and walked out the back door.

I ran after him. I said, 'Jeff, I don't care what you play,' and he said, 'Well, I'm playing 'Cold Sweat.' I finally talked him into coming back, but he was going to leave. Thankfully he came back, and we played the Roxy, and it was great."

With all that, LaBounty kept hiring him; he just chocked it up to "Jeff being Jeff." "If you had him on your date, everything was right; everything was special," he explains. "I loved Jeff like everybody else; everything about him. I knew what his temperament was, and I would put up with a lot from Jeff Porcaro."

Warner Brothers included "Crazy" and "I Hope You'll Be Very Unhappy Without Me," Jeff's tracks from *Promised Love*, on 1978's *This Night Won't Last Forever.* Earlier, LaBounty cut "This Night Won't Last Forever" as a ballad in 4/4 with Jeff on drums (along with Steve Lukather, who was still in high school), but when the version for the Warner Brothers album was cut, Larrie Londin was the drummer on the session, and he suggested a faster tempo. Bill says if he can find the Porcaro version, he's sure that Jeff fans would love to hear it.

When we began to talk about the cut "Crazy," Bill commented on how Jeff's instincts always kicked in to create the right part for the song.

On Bill's 1982 self-titled album, Porcaro played on four songs. "Dream On" and "Nobody's Fool" jumped out at me, and LaBounty comments, "Those are really Jeff-type tracks. At that point he was famous for having his own perfected version of the Purdie shuffle, and he played it on a lot of stuff. I wanted that kind of shuffle on 'Dream On.' I remember he was kinda upset and said, 'I'm not gonna play another Purdie shuffle,' but he did. He played a Jeff shuffle, and that was good enough for me. On 'Look Who's Lonely Now,' it's the same kind of shuffle. It's what everybody wanted back then." (Note: this session occurred around the same time as "Rosanna," but Jeff was already "shuffling" at 21 years old on Steely Dan's *Katy Lied*, and was known for his shuffles, getting called specifically to play them on many sessions—although he would continue to argue that he couldn't play them.)

ANOTHER STEELY DAN FAN

Jeffrey came into **BERNARD GRIMALDI**'s orbit on his first album with Bernard Zeiher in 1978, *Grimaldi/Zeiher*. Grimaldi, who hails from France, had been living in Los Angeles for five years. When the duo got signed to RCA, he asked to be able to record in L.A. "My template was anybody who had worked with Steely Dan, because I was blown out by them," says Grimaldi. "I was also very much listening to Michael Franks with John Guerin, so I was into American music, but especially Steely Dan. I really wanted to work with those guys. My friend Mark Gibbons, who played keyboards on both albums, helped me get in touch with (the musicians). They were all so wonderful." The kindness and humility of the musicians made recording *Grimaldi/Zeiher* and its follow-up two years later, *Récidive*, a dream come true for Grimaldi. They didn't have a big budget on the first album, and it was done fast, but "Jeff was right on the money every time."

The lyrics were in French, and Jeff wanted to know what the songs were about. "On the first album, I think I remember telling him when we did 'La Star des Couloirs,' it was about a street musician I had seen in the subway of Paris," Grimaldi explains. "It had a shuffle feel

I wanted. I chose Jeff on this one because of the shuffle he did with Steely Dan. He was incredible." He recalls that Jeff knew "Cite des Anges" ("City of Angels") on the 1990 greatest hits collection, *Toute Ressemblance avec des Personnes Ayant*, was about Los Angeles. "I told him it was about his town and the way I felt his town," Grimaldi recalls. (Note: The track is called "La Califusa" on *Récidive*.)

Grimaldi had already laid down the rhythm track with Jim Keltner, who he says is a genius drummer. "But there was a certain feel I wanted for this song," he says. "Jim's drumming was very simple, and for some reason I wanted to try something else. The whole track was already laid down; I had already even done some overdubs, but I asked Jeff if he would come and overdub drums, which is tricky. It's (especially challenging to overdub/replace) drums to a song that is already recorded with a rhythm track where all the musicians played together. When he did this, he completely blew everybody's mind that was sitting in the control room. He just nailed it immediately. I saw how much he was concentrating, and I could see what a challenge it was. Plus, he was playing over Jim Keltner, a drummer he absolutely worshipped. Jeff absolutely did something magical."

Grimaldi explains the track "Debout en Haut du Toit" on *Récidive* is about a criminal being pursued by the police. "The whole feel of the song is about that, so I am sure I gave him the idea of what it was about," Bernard says, adding that Jeff supplied exactly what the song called for. When Toto toured France in the early '80s, Grimaldi took Jeff and some of the band to the Eiffel Tower, which is a special memory for him.

ERIC CARMEN

(Note: I never spoke with Carmen himself, but emailed back and forth with Bernie Hogya, the lovely gentleman who runs his website, EricCarmen.com, and he gave me permission to use the many commentaries Eric has made about Jeffrey.)

ERIC CARMEN, a founding member of the Raspberries, had instant success with his first solo outing in 1975 (*Eric Carmen*), which contained the hit songs "All by Myself" and "Never Gonna Fall in Love Again." Unfortunately, his follow-up albums did not fare as well. On Jeff's extensive discography, it cites he played on three tracks on *Boats Against the Current* (1977) and three on *Change of Heart* (1978). Carmen produced both albums and talked about working with Jeff on the first one: "One of the things about being the producer is that you get to pick who would be right for each song. All the musicians I've worked with were hand-picked, because I thought they would bring something to whatever song they were asked to play on.

"Most of the time, they did. Sometimes they did not. I had to be ready to make up a guitar solo or a drum part if the guy I hired wasn't creative that day.

"I can tell you that my favorite session drummer of all time was Jeff Porcaro. He was, without a doubt, the most unbelievable drummer I have ever worked with (and I have worked with a *lot* of incredible drummers). Jeff just heard exactly what was in my head and played it without me ever having to say a word.

"The first time we worked together was on 'Boats Against the

Current.' (I wanted him on that song since I heard his drumming on *Silk Degrees*.) His drums were set up when I walked in; I asked him if he wanted to hear the song first, and he said no. On the first take, I kind of 'conducted' him, to show him where I wanted the fills, and what I had in mind. He had never heard the song before, but I realized I didn't need to say anything more to him. By the way, he was playing to piano and strings, with no click track—that's just about impossible for mere mortals. He learned the song on take one. He played very well on take two; I could have used take three, but I asked him if he'd like to do another one, and he said 'yes.' Take four is the one on the record. When I listen to it now, it's hard for me to imagine that we didn't play together at the same time. That's how perfect his time was."

Carmen then mentioned a cut that was not on either of the two albums listed in Porcaro's discography, which had me stumped: "We did 'She Remembered' the same way. As Jeff was walking out of the studio, having played to only my piano with no click track, he said, 'I really enjoy working this way with you. It's so easy for me to just play to your piano part. We should always work like this.' I can only tell you that I have worked with sensational drummers all of my life, from Mike McBride and Jim Bonfanti to Carmine Appice, Nigel Olsson and all the other terrific drummers I've known, but Jeff did things that no one else could ever do. He passed away, suddenly, very young, years ago, and I can tell you, I was devastated when I heard the news. He was, without a doubt, the most gifted drummer, and perhaps the most gifted musician, I have ever known."

After some investigation, I discovered that "She Remembered" was a stunning ballad on Carmen's 1984 self-titled album, but Wikipedia does not give Jeff credit. I asked Bernie about it; he told me it's one of Eric's favorites, and he sent me this excerpt from a biography he helped write for Carmen: "I was very excited to be at Geffen and I was excited initially to be working with Bob Gaudio," says Eric. "I've always thought the job of a good producer was to get the artist's vision on record. Obviously, there are lots of producers who believe their vision is better than the artist's.

"The very first day of recording, we decided to start with 'She Remembered.' Bob asked whether I would play it on a Fender Rhodes electric piano. I said, 'Well, I could. But would I want to?' He said, 'I'd love for you to try it.' Now, I hate the Fender Rhodes. It's a greaseball instrument. When I think of a Fender Rhodes, I think of 'Green Eyed Lady' and Styx. I couldn't imagine doing my favorite song on that whole album on a Fender Rhodes, and I sure couldn't imagine starting the session that way. But because I didn't want to cause any problems on my first day of recording, I said, 'Okay. I can try it.' We recorded a version that Bob fell in love with, and which I thought was a catastrophe. From that point on, everything that he wanted to do was on that version of the song. I started to lobby (Geffen A&R executive John) Kalodner to let me work with the demo. I told him that I could add a bass player and drummer to the demo and Kalodner said, 'Well, Bob thinks his is better.' So, essentially, we had Bob's version and Eric's version. We wrote the string charts to Bob's version, and I tried to affix it to my version. Bob had his drummer and I hired Jeff Porcaro to come in and play on mine. Bob did his mix and I told Kalodner, 'Give me any engineer you've got and one afternoon and I will convince you that my mix will blow his out of the water.'

"He gave me an engineer named Michael Wagener who worked with the band Dokken. I drove down to Redondo Beach, into some God-forsaken studio filled with skinhead heavy-metal guys. We loaded up the tape, started to mix and four hours later we were done. It was perfect. I loved it. I drove back, took it into Kalodner's office and played it for him, and he said, 'It is better than Bob's. Maybe I ought to let you mix the whole album. Ha, ha, ha.' This is the kind of thing I was fighting the entire record.

"Don't get me wrong, I love that track! I mean, I really love it and I don't feel that way about too many of the things I've done. Let me tell you why, in order: One: It's a one-take piano and voice demo that I cut at Beachwood Studios right after I finished writing the song. In other words, I just went in, sat down at the piano and sang it once. It was so fresh I hadn't had time to wear it out by playing it countless times in a studio with a band. Just me and the piano. Straight through. No punches, no edits, no second take. Straight from the heart. Direct to tape. No producer. Just an engineer and me. I love how my vocal isn't perfect; it's a little vulnerable at times and then toward the end it's pure emotion that takes over. It reminds me why I do what I do, and actually makes me think about doing it again.

"Two: Jeff Porcaro's drumming was overdubbed to my voice and piano. That means all Jeff heard in his headphones, and all he had to play to, was my voice and the piano. There was nothing else recorded at the time—and remember that Jeff and I had worked the same way on 'Boats Against the Current.' He played to piano and voice. For those of you who may not be musicians, it might be a bit hard to comprehend just what a superhuman feat this is. For most drummers, it would be literally impossible, because I never play to a click track, and my tempo may slow down or speed up a hair from time to time in order to create the feel that I'm going for. In musical terms, that's called *rubato*. In any case, his playing is not only so incredibly spot-on with me that it's ridiculous, but it's also so perfectly 'sympathetic' to my piano that I can't imagine how it could have ever been more perfect. It's as if he could read my mind and heard every nuance of the drum part I heard in my head and then had the technical virtuosity to actually play it so perfectly that you can't imagine the two of us weren't playing at the same time. And he did this in four takes. In other words, the first time he heard the song and played along, was take one. The drum track you hear on the song came three takes later. The whole exercise probably took less than forty-five minutes. That's absolutely amazing.

"Finally, three: The bridge. It's just such an odd little time signature thing going on, but it was completely organic to the song. I just wrote it the way I felt it and the strangeness made it great. You can't plan stuff like that (I wish I could). It just happens."

JAMO MEMORIES

PAUL JAMIESON's first session as Jeffrey's drum tech happened to be for Eric Carmen at Sound City, after he and Jeff met in 1975 through their girlfriends. As told in *It's About Time*, Jamo not only worked for Jeff, but they became best friends. During their friendship, Jamo racked up a lot of memories.

On tour with Boz Scaggs, Jeff played L.A.'s Universal Amphitheater for seven nights. The rest of the band was Steve Lukather, Scott Shelly, Mike Landau, Mike Porcaro, Lenny Castro, Randy Kerber and Steve Porcaro. "The band just kicked ass," says Jamo, the tour's drum tech. "I think it was opening night. I drove him to the gig, and at the time I had a 1960 Corvette. It was summertime and we hung out after. It was probably 12:30 at night; we were driving out of the back of the Universal Amphitheater and I 'accidentally on purpose' made a wrong turn. We ended up driving in my Corvette, smoking a joint, on the back lot of the Universal tour. Nobody was there. We drove over the bridge and the giant *Jaws* shark jumped out at us; we went by the *Psycho* house on the hill, and we drove through that swirling ice tunnel. That's one of my fond memories."

* * *

Larry Carlton snapped this photo while Paul Jamieson was helping B.B. King tune the legend's guitar Lucille during a Carlton session. (Courtesy of Larry Carlton and Paul Jamieson)

A great session memory happened on Larry Carlton's *Friends,* released in 1983. Jamieson recalls that both he and Jeff were excited that legendary guitarist B.B. King was to be in Carlton's home studio, Room 335, to cut "Blues for TJ," which King co-wrote with Carlton. Jamieson was particularly thrilled, because King was his favorite guitarist, and he had seen him perform many times, even meeting him on one occasion. "B.B. shows up dressed in a three-piece suit," Jamo recalls. "We played the track down. It was one take. And at the end of the take, B.B. said, 'That sounds so good. Can I ask a favor please of you guys?' And everybody is going, 'Yeah, sure, B.B., anything. What do you want?' He goes, 'It felt so good. Can we just do that one more time for me?' They played it again. I don't know which take they used for the record. We're standing around listening to everything and Jeff says to B.B., 'You didn't have to get dressed up for our session.' B.B. looked at him and said, 'When I play I want to look like I'm going to the bank to get me a loan.'"

* * *

In 1980, when Jamo came up with the idea of a drum rack, Jeff helped him design it, and then funded the prototype. They took the rack to Japan later that year, on Toto's *Hydra* tour, and Jamieson says the Japanese Pearl reps went crazy taking pictures, even drawing pictures of it. "Besides the toms and cymbal stands, all the microphone stands came off the rack," says Paul. "Then there was a wire loom that went across the center rail, down the right-side rail to the back leg, and then down to the junction mic box for the P.A. It was the cleanest thing you ever saw. There weren't any cables flopping or whatever. So Jeff was doing his deal with Pearl and they wanted to make the drum rack. They didn't want to pay us a royalty; they claimed it would be too much trouble with accounting. Instead, they wanted to do a flat rate deal with us."

On a day off in Tokyo, Jeff and Jamo had the rack taken over to the Pearl offices. The two of them met with about fifteen Pearl executives and engineers, and Jeff handed over the presentation to Jamieson. With the language barrier, Jamo felt they probably understood about 30% of what he was saying, so he decided to make it very dramatic and visual. He took a regular Pearl boom cymbal stand with a cymbal on it and kicked it. It fell over. Then he threw away the tripod base. He explained that a complete boom stand was $75, but with the rack, they only needed the top part, which was $25.

Next, Jamieson stood on the rack and did a tightrope walk across it with the bass drum in it. He also illustrated what an easy correction it would be if you broke the bass drum head during the show. "I moved the bass drum mic out of the way, put in the spare bass drum, put back the mic, and said, 'Instead of stopping the show to fix the bass drum head, we're still in the race 30 seconds later,'" Jamo recounts. "I set the whole thing up and showed them how nothing moved when you played. If you're the opening act and it's time for the set change, you unplug the mics from the box, grab the rack, and walk off with it. The only things you have to move are the floor tom, bass drum, toms, snare, hi-hat and throne."

All the Pearl folks were impressed. They ended up making a deal to make a prototype and bring it to the following Anaheim NAMM show. About nine months later, Jeff and Jamo went to NAMM and headed straight for the Pearl booth. "We go, 'Where's the drum rack?' and they say, 'Over at the hotel,' and we say, 'Well, we want to see it,'" Paul recalls. "We drive with them about five miles away in this rental station wagon to a motel, and there's their version of the rack. They took our concept and cheaped it out as much as they could. Truthfully, though, the one I had was built by a Hollywood set builder and it was overkill times five. The Japanese Pearl executive says, 'We will do a marketing survey.' And we looked at him and said, 'What are you talking about? Put it in the NAMM show across the street, where there are 10,000 drummers and ask them! Why would you pay Madison Avenue $300,000 to tell you what these guys can tell you in one day?' So we take the rack in the back of the station wagon and set it up in their booth at the show, and it was the hit of NAMM!"

Another funny story from that same NAMM comes to Jamieson's mind: He recalls that he and Jeff bumped into Lloyd McCausland from Remo, who told them that Remo Belli wanted to meet them. They made their way over to the Remo booth where McCausland introduced them to the man himself. Jamo recalls that Remo thanked Jeff for being part of "the team," and then he said he wanted to show Jeff his newest creation. "He had a little closet in the booth and goes in and comes out with this set of bongos and hands them to Jeff and says, 'Check these out,'" Paul remembers. "Jeff sits down and puts them between his kneecaps and starts playing on them and he tells Jeff, 'The shells are made out of compressed paper. It costs me $11 to make these. What do you think?' And Jeff says, 'How cool. You can go to Guitar Center, buy a pair, play on them all day, get drunk and at the end of the night throw them in the fire,' and Remo got insulted like he was saying they're a piece of shit and you should burn them, but Jeff was just joking that they were so cheap, you could afford to do that. Remo didn't know what to say."

Mostly, Jeff couldn't walk two feet at NAMM without being stopped by someone who wanted to shake his hand, tell him what

Jeff in Tokyo, Japan, 1982. (Courtesy of Barney Hurley)

his playing meant to them, or snap a photo with him. Jeff always made time for everyone. "For being as badass as he was, he was such a humble guy," Jamieson says. "I noticed that when these people would say, 'You're so great, I love this, I love that,' he'd say, 'Thank you,' and then he'd ask them about them and try to turn the conversation onto them. It wasn't 'me, me, me.' It was one of the beautiful things about the guy and his character. Only the people who knew him knew that part of him."

* * *

On the road, Jamieson did it all, even carry and light Jeff's cigarettes. "My buddy was addicted to Marlboros," Jamo says. "Every time we went through customs, he would give me a carton of Marlboros to take through customs, because he could only have so many with him to take into a country, particularly Japan. I harped on him about quitting cigarettes. I hate cigarettes. His thing was he'd only smoke them halfway—like that was going to help."

When he wanted a cigarette on stage, Jeff would give a signal, and Jamo would light a cigarette and either hand it to him or (if he was already playing) put it in his mouth. Halfway through the song, he would give Jamo a nod to take the cigarette out of his mouth. One night, after a couple of years of this, it didn't go so well. "He gave me the nod and I went to take the cigarette out of his mouth, but he turned his head and the hot part of the cigarette stuck to his sweaty face," Jamieson recalls. "It burned the shit out of his face."

That was the end of that arrangement.

* * *

Jamieson had a Yamaha drum machine plugged into Jeff's

monitors. Paul had a set list with each song's exact starting tempo on it. Sometimes Jeff would turn around and say "click," and Jamo would hit the drum machine to give him a couple of seconds of time reference on the cowbell. "Jeff would then wave it off and count off the song. Never once was the machine going while he was playing," Jamieson says.

One night, Jamo says, a keyboard section was dragging, and Jeff started yelling, "Pick it up, pick it up." David Hungate was on the riser beside Jeff and thought Jeff was yelling at him. "Hungate's time was as good as Jeff's, but there's Hungate with the headstock of his Fender bass, hitting the crash cymbals on the wrong beat," recalls Jamieson, laughing.

A JAMO CONNECTION

Drummer **GERRY BROWN** met Paul Jamieson in 1975 and says he is very grateful to Jamieson for introducing him to Porcaro sometime that year, as Jeffrey became a mentor. At the time, Jeff lived on Hesby Street in North Hollywood. When Jeff built his studio at that house, Paul would invite Gerry over, and Brown remembers watching Jeff play. "I would sit there and marvel at his approach—how it was such a simplistic, yet such a happening way of playing. What came to my attention was, whatever the tempo was, he had this way of playing just slightly behind it, and in doing that, it just made the whole groove so round," Brown says. "Wherever the beat was, he had this knack for playing just slightly behind it, but it made everything so round and then it glowed. There were a few times when I did sit down with him where I observed and noticed how he was playing. For my own playing, I noticed that to get to where he was, I had to be very conscious, not only of my hand positioning, but where the stroke was, and my arm

Gerry Brown and Jeff, circa 1982. (Courtesy of Gerry Brown, photo by Paul Jamieson)

movement. When I could lock in on that, it was Jeff Porcaro. It was not him, but at the same time, that felt kinda like his feeling."

Before he closely observed Jeff, Brown had been using less of a motion and playing more "into" the drum. "There's a trick if you hold a pencil in between your thumb and your forefinger and wave it in such a way that it looks like rubber, that was what I was gathering of his strokes. It was so smooth and effortless," Gerry explains. "So that was what I ascertained from his playing style. To this day there are many times where his spirit and his influence make an appearance in my playing. There are people who watch the YouTube videos and such, but I was there, and I feel so blessed."

As Gerry began to get his footing in L.A. Jeff gave him much-needed business advice. "No one had ever sat down with me and said, 'You need to know what your value is; you need to be aware of that at all times,'" Brown recounts. "In 1979 I had gotten connected to the Brothers Johnson from a tour manager who is no longer here named Wilbur Terrell. I was with them for a couple of years, and they did their album *Winners,* the first album not done with Quincy Jones."

Gerry went to Europe to play for a short period and when he returned, he received a call from Terrell telling him that Lionel Richie was leaving the Commodores. When he officially became Richie's drummer, Brown enlisted Jamo as his drum tech. Jeff quickly got word to Brown (through Jamo) that he wanted to speak with him. "I gave Jeff a call," says Gerry. "He said, 'Gerry, congratulations. Remember that talk we had a couple of years ago?' I said, 'Yeah.' He says, 'Okay, man, what I told you, knowing your value, that applies right now. Stick to your guns. Just remember what I told you. You have to know your value, man. You're a bad mofo. And all the stuff you're doing, just remember what I told you. It's going to serve you well.'"

The Lionel Richie gig launched the pop career that Gerry really wanted, due to Jeff's influence, which ultimately included George Benson, Stevie Wonder and Diana Ross. Summing Jeff up, Gerry says: "There's groove and then there's this other groove."

ELLIOTT RANDALL

Guitarist **ELLIOTT RANDALL** recalls playing on a live TV concert show (it could have been "In Concert" or "Midnight Special"), backing Felix Cavaliere of the Rascals. There was another group on the show; while Elliott does not recall the name of the band, he'll always remember the drummer, because it was Jeff. "He was a young drummer; I think about seventeen at the time, and he totally blew my mind," says Randall. "He was already so great, as a teenager, and I made it a point to go and introduce myself. We chatted a while, because in my mind's eye I saw that we were going to be doing stuff together, because I'm a drummer myself. I'm a student of Bernard Purdie.

"We exchanged telephone numbers, and then I didn't see him again until a couple of years later, when I was back in L.A. doing session work." Elliott, who went on to do sessions with such artists as Carly Simon, the Doobie Brothers, Carl Wilson and Peter Frampton, as well as turning down many coveted offers to be in bands like Steely Dan, the Blues Brothers and Toto, says the sessions are not memorable. Although Jeff and Elliott appear on some of the same Steely Dan songs, unfortunately they did not record at the same time. Randall says he always overdubbed his parts—but he did know when he was playing to Porcaro. "Jeff's style was really, really unique," Elliott says. "There was an intensity to his playing and also a sheer joy behind the drums. And that joy comes through whether you were seeing him doing it, or just hearing him on a recording. He loved doing it."

Even though Jeff played on Randall's solo album (more about that later), the guitar player says most of his hangs with Porcaro were in L.A. when Elliott came to town to work on a few things and Jeff invited him to stay at his place in Laurel Canyon for a couple of days. It was around '77, about the time Toto was coming together. "They were in the middle of forming the group. David and Jeffrey asked me if I would fancy being a guitar player with Toto. I've turned down lots and lots of people but that's the one turn-down I've regretted," Randall admits. "To the day I'll die, that will be the one I will regret. I admired their musicianship and who they were so much."

Elliott says it was really comfortable staying with Jeff. "We might have smoked a doobie and talked about, 'Look at the sky, man…' You know how kids talk about the universe and the Milky Way and how we're all just a little speck. He was kinda into all that spiritual stuff," he laughs. While he and Porcaro didn't spend a huge amount of time together in their lives, Randall felt a great bond with him. He calls him a kindred spirit with whom he made some wonderful art, and with whom he was able to have some good laughs and philosophize.

A LIFE-CHANGING SESSION

The musical exchange was profound when bassist **NEIL STUBENHAUS** met Jeff. Both musicians were on the sessions for Tom Scott's 1979 *Street Beat*. Stubenhaus was honored to be included on this album, and it is still even a shock to his system. During the first few days in the studio, they cut "The Shakedown." "These were marathon sessions. These guys smoked dope and didn't pay any attention to time. It was like, 'Bring your suitcase, we live here,'" Stubenhaus says with a laugh.

Scott introduced the song as a slow groove with the changes. "Everyone hit Jeff's joint, then Tom's and we mulled it over and it went nowhere for about an hour," says Stubenhaus. "We sat around kinda stoned, and I started playing it much faster in a different style, and Jeff kicked in immediately with that Caribbean beat he did on the Fagen tune 'The Goodbye Look.' It took off and we were killing it. Tom just lit up; he just loved it. And we just started playing the tune. It was a completely different groove and I take some credit for it because I started it, but Jeff just made it sound like magic. It was sensational."

It gave Stubenhaus, who was a "newbie" at the time, instant credibility. "I was a nobody. I was sitting with Jeff Porcaro and he jumps onto my groove and it turns into this six-minute tune and just takes off," Stubenhaus explains. "It was a new musical experience for me, having something that magical happen, being recorded on tape and the pride of being a little bit responsible for it—and Jeff turning it into magic. He turns magic into times ten. What he did was so perfect. It's not describable when it's happening in real time. It's not like he had to fish around for what to play. It was just instinct that happened instantly. There was no hesitation, there was no trepidation. He just hopped on that groove and went.

"Jeff just turned it into gold within a millisecond; there was no thought. That was really the turning point in my understanding of how this worked. My revelation was that, 'This guy's a pro. This guy just plays music. It's not about him. Then after it's done, it kinda is, but not because he drew attention to himself, but because he took a piece of coal and turned it into a diamond.' That was my first experience with something that amazing in terms of intuition. I did a bunch of other sessions with Tom with other musicians who didn't kick it into gear like that. After all is said and done, Jeff is underrated. As huge as it is, it is still underrated because only the serious pros who are in the room while it's happening really know how it's put together."

Neil feels that even the listener can't fully understand the magic of Jeff Porcaro. Only those in the moment, engaged within the music with him, truly know his genius. Everyone in the booth was going nuts. The incident gave Neil a shot of confidence, and he became someone Scott came to rely on. Neil then introduced Scott to guitarist Carlos Rios, who ended up on the track. Then Stubenhaus introduced Tom Scott to Vinnie Colaiuta. In fact, Neil invited Vinnie to the studio one day and it was Jeff and Vinnie's first meeting (discussed in *It's About Time*).

Later, Stubenhaus took Jeff to check out Vinnie at a Frank Zappa rehearsal. "About an hour and twenty minutes after watching Vinnie, Jeff was so overwhelmed he said, 'We gotta go.' There was so much to absorb," Stubenhaus recalls.

Neil also remembers a session for Livingston Taylor's *Man's Best Friend,* with Jeff Baxter producing, that he says defines Jeffrey. Baxter had hired another drummer—a really good drummer—on the session for this particular shuffle tune ("Sunshine Girl"), but after three hours of working on it, "it didn't happen," says Stubenhaus. "The next day there was another good drummer, but still no track. I said, 'Please hire Jeff.' Jeff Porcaro came. One take, phenomenal! It was sensational. He just killed it."

The quintessential Porcaro story that Stubenhaus shared, though, was on a Randy Crawford session for a Carole Bayer Sager tune, "One Hello," for the film *I Ought to be in Pictures.* Neil recalls it was a 10 a.m. call, not to go later than 1:00 p.m. "Marvin Hamlisch had just left Carole Bayer Sager for Steve Garvey's wife Cyndy," says Stubenhaus. "Carole walks in at about ten 'til 1:00, and we already have a track with Tommy LiPuma. Everybody's happy with the track, but now they're pissed because they have to leave. We had to be done at 1:00, and everyone has a 2:00 session. Carole listens to it and says, 'No, I don't like it, I want something different here and there.' Everybody is looking at her like, 'You've got to be kidding.' They don't want to go into overtime, but we're starting another take, and now it's overtime. Jeff counts off the song. Remember, it's fresh from Marvin Hamlisch leaving her for Cyndy Garvey. Jeff says, 'A-one, a-two, a-one, two, Cyndy Garvey.' Just like that. He could do anything. No consequence. It was so stunning. The brilliance was we played it again and we didn't do another take; that was the genius of Jeff."

COMING UP WITH FOZ

While some thought that was genius, others, like **DAVID**

FOSTER might call it a little bit of a pain in the ass, even while chuckling at the same time.

Keyboardist/composer Foster doesn't recall the first time he met Porcaro, but he remembers being aware of him during Jeff's work with Boz Scaggs, which was in 1976, because it was such a coveted musical experience, and he was jealous of the musicians involved. Foster and (guitarist/composer) Jay Graydon hired Jeff for the group they formed in 1980 called Airplay. When I was writing *It's About Time*, I asked David Paich if Jeff had ever mentioned any particular projects of which he was proud. One that Paich recalled was Airplay.

"I would give Jeff great credit for shaping the sound of Airplay, which is an album that didn't do well in America, but sold hugely in Asia. People still talk about it and still ask us to go over and tour," Foster asserts. "I know Mike Baird played some drums on Airplay, but Jeff was the primary drummer." Explaining what he means when he says Jeffrey helped shape the sound, Foster says, "You write a song, but you don't really know how it's going to turn out until you hear it. Everybody knows the foundation is the drums. If you remember Dick Clark back in the day with 'American Bandstand' and how he would play a new record and then interview kids to say what they thought, they'd always say, 'It's got a good beat.' That's what they noticed. The average person hears the drums and the vocal, and nothing else. The drums are obviously so important and when you get somebody as musical as Jeff, it really helped our sound. And I remember he was really quite involved. I mean we paid him like a session player, but he would hang around and help."

Foster and Graydon also wrote the music to Al Jarreau's 1983 hit "Mornin'," to which Jarreau wrote the lyrics. Both Graydon and Foster played on the track; Graydon was the producer and he hired Jeff. "Who else could have played that feel? That funka-shuffle, or whatever you want to call it, just fit perfectly for what we had in mind," Foster asserts. "But Jeff would make Jay crazy." Foster says while Porcaro was incredible as a musician in the studio, "he was hard to deal with because he didn't really want to conform to what you wanted. Most of the time he would give you something better than what you thought you wanted, but he would play two or three takes and when he'd had enough, he'd had enough. When you'd want to do it again, he'd go, 'No I'm done,' and he'd just disappear, and it would just really aggravate me. He didn't do it all the time, but he did it enough that I remember it 30 years after the fact." Foster feels that as incredibly as Jeff played on so many sessions, that he played best on the Toto records. "Maybe because he was invested in it."

Foster brought up the infamous Porcaro/Graydon gig bag incident, which is told in *It's About Time*. Foster says it was awful, but never knew why it happened, so I tried to explain it to him the best I could from what I've learned about this incident. It is sometimes represented as a prank, sometimes humorous and sometimes dark, but was definitely payback due to Jeff's sense of loyalty to Vinnie Colaiuta, and his feeling that Graydon was hurting Colaiuta's reputation.

For Colaiuta, it's all water under the bridge; he's had an unbelievable career since that episode. At the time, though, he says he was thinking that he was part of the band Pages and therefore he was going to do the entire record, so he didn't understand the philosophy of Graydon using multiple drummers on the project. The band had rehearsed all the music and was a self-contained unit in Colaiuta's mind: "Later on, as I started doing more sessions, I started to realize how that whole game worked and that sometimes producers cast different musicians. I can look back at it now and laugh at it," Colaiuta says today.

Jeff felt the same way back then, as he stated to Vinnie at the 1990 *Modern Drummer* L.A. studio drummer roundtable: "You were in the band," he said. "Before this album went down, you were rehearsing with that band and the buzz around town was, 'Wait until that album comes out because that shit is progressive and cool. Dig this cat.' Vinnie was already the hero of every musician that had heard him. Regardless of how many sessions he had done, everybody already knew about him. You had already seen him on 'Saturday Night Live' with Zappa with a yellow Gretsch set going, 'What the fuck is that shit?'"

To Graydon, it was completely out of the blue and unmerited. According to Jay, he had issues with the young Colaiuta's playing on Page's third album (called *Pages).* He was producing, and in his estimation, Colaiuta "hadn't quite gotten it together yet. There were some tracks he played on that were real good, but there were some that weren't making it, so I hired Jeff on it," Graydon says, explaining that as he was in the middle of an overdub solo during the recording one day, he felt a presence to the right of him. "I look over and Jeff is pissing in my gig bag," Graydon recalls. "I put my guitar down, I grab him by the neck and I'm shoving him into the back wall of Sound Labs, screaming at the top of my lungs." Graydon was furious. He says Porcaro cleaned it up for more than an hour. The story still conjures up negativity in Graydon. According to Paul Jamieson, Porcaro felt that Graydon was trying to ruin Colaiuta's career, which Porcaro was trying to help at the time: "Jeff was a payback kind of guy," Jamo says. "In fact, one of our favorite songs was James Brown's 'The Payback.'"

I had never spoken to Steve Lukather about this until recently. He remembers the incident as a joke gone wrong: "Jay was doing an overdub, probably a solo after we got the take of whatever session that was," Luke recalls. "I don't remember the artist, but I do remember the event. We were watching through the glass. I think Jeff was just having a laugh that got out of control, 'cause once you start peeing—for guys anyway—ya can't stop. It was very *out* when it went down—funny and also disturbing. The only thing that stopped Jay from totally losing it was he knocked over the new vintage guitar I had, a 1951 Fender Esquire, and gashed it a little. That calmed him down because he felt bad for me, but I didn't care. I was glad it helped diffuse the situation, which was a prank gone out of control."

Graydon says his relationship with Porcaro was never the same again, although he worked with him and hired him, of course, because of his playing. Some of the artists Graydon produced for which he hired Porcaro include Al Jarreau, Manhattan Transfer, Dionne Warwick, Kenny Rogers and El DeBarge. "He's a great drummer," says Graydon. "There's nobody who has ever played like him. Shannon Forrest comes the closest. Jeff was a fucking outstanding drummer. Why do you think I used him on everything I could, and why do you think he played on tons of records? He didn't think he could play a shuffle. The song 'Nothin' You Can Do About It,' on the *Airplay* album, is a shuffle. It's kind of what I call a funk-a-shuffle and 'Mornin'' (Al Jarreau) is the same groove. It's kind of a pop-jazz feel, a triplet feel that is in the league of a shuffle. There are a hundred variations of shuffles, and he never thought he was any good at them. I told him he was out of his mind. 'Rosanna' is the same groove."

Foster admits that he was a "bully" when he came into the *Chicago 17* project as producer in 1984. "I came in like a wrecking ball. I played all the keyboard bass and all the piano. Bobby Lamm was not really around. Danny (Seraphine) was an amazing drummer. In my opinion—and I've apologized to him since—he was limited in what he could do, and the more I was hard on him, the worse he played," Foster explains. "If you're hard on someone, it's just the opposite of building someone up. Poor Danny. I sent him a long e-mail apologizing to him. I called guys like Jeff Porcaro and Carlos Vega to play on Chicago records, which annoyed the fuck out of Danny."

I remark that I had heard a rumor that Danny had come down to the studio with a gun at some point. Foster cleared that up, explaining that it never happened. During the "You're My Inspiration" session with Carlos Vega, the manager called to say, "You'd better leave because Danny is on his way with a gun," but Foster has no idea if it was true or not. "The two main thrusts of this story are that I have profusely apologized to Danny because he is a great drummer and I treated him unfairly," Foster admits, adding he was a huge fan of all the Chicago music growing up. "I had Jeff play on the opening track of *Chicago 17*, 'Stay the Night' and you can't imagine how many people have sampled that snare—like hundreds. Jeff played the shit out of that song.

"One of my most exciting moments was when I started working with Earth, Wind & Fire," David continues. "As in awe of the Toto guys as I was and still am, I knew I had one-upped them, because everyone loved Earth, Wind & Fire. I would sneak into the Earth, Wind & Fire studio, because I was working there at night, and I'd go in there and get the tapes and play them for people. I'd make cassettes of a couple of the funk songs, and I'd go over to Jeff's house. David Paich was there, and I'd play these songs for them and they, of course, couldn't help but love them with Fred White on drums. I remember Jeff loved them which made me feel really good, because we're all looking for that approval."

Porcaro got to play on one Herbie Hancock track called "Paradise," written by Foster, Graydon, Bill Champlin and Hancock, which Graydon produced. It's on Hancock's 1982 album *Lite Me Up*. "I remember the sound was not great," Foster recalls. "In fact, when we heard the playback I said, 'Where's the kick drum? I just hear a tom-tom.' Jeff just looked at me and shrugged, 'I don't know.' The sound was so weird. But the session was so fun because it was Jeff and Jay Graydon and Herbie—but we made Herbie sing, which was really a big mistake. He's one of the greatest jazz pianists on the planet, and we told him to sing this little pop song."

George Benson's 1985 hit "Turn Your Love Around" was written by Bill Champlin, Jay Graydon and Steve Lukather. Foster, who played synths on the track, recalls calling Arif Mardin at Atlantic Records and telling him he found a hit song for him. Mardin loved it and let Graydon produce it. "It's a great record and Jeff (who programmed Linn Drums) sounds amazing on it," says Foster.

CHAMPLIN

"Back in the day, I thought being a good record producer was about hiring great musicians," says Foster. While that's one component, he explains, it really is more about the song. "I wasn't as zeroed in on the song as who I was getting to *play* on the song. Not to say that Bill had bad songs, because he didn't; a lot of them were very good. I always wanted to get the best players. One of the very first albums I produced was for a woman named Jaye P. Morgan in 1978. The album never came out, but I had Jeff Porcaro, Harvey Mason and every great musician you could imagine."

On singer/songwriter **BILL CHAMPLIN**'s 1978 album *Single,* Foster hired Porcaro to play on five tracks. It was a year after Champlin had moved to Los Angeles from Northern California. Champlin would later win a Grammy for writing Earth, Wind & Fire's "After the Love is Gone" with Foster and Graydon; co-write George Benson's "Turn Your Love Around" with Graydon and Steve Lukather; and become an in-demand session vocalist. He wrote several songs for *Chicago 17,* and he would end up joining Chicago in the '80s. But all of that was later. The recording of *Single* with Jeff was at the very outset of what would be a prolific career.

"We had a piece on there which was kind of a double piece with a big intro that was kind of insane—a kitchen sink and then some," says Champlin. The song was "Keys to the Kingdom." "It was a very hard piece of music. Foster got the chart written and I remember walking into Davlen Studios and on the first run, Jeff read this thing flat out, straight ahead, all the pushes and everything. I remember going, 'Whoa, I'm in another group of people here!' The guys playing on it were Hungate, Paich, Luke, Jeff and Foster." The song felt almost like a symphonic piece to Champlin. "Jeff played it blind. Any good drummer in Los Angeles could have played the verses, but the intro on it was nuts," Bill asserts. "Foster went totally apeshit on (the arrangement) and we actually had to get Marty Paich to come in and conduct the strings."

During the *Single* sessions, Jim Preston, the drummer who had been with the Sons of Champlin since 1972, was visiting. He came over to Davlen while the band was on a lunch break, and the receptionist told Champlin he was there. "I walked up these little stairs to the office to get him," Bill recalls. "I said, 'Jimmy, do you want to meet Jeff Porcaro?' He said, 'Oh my God, awesome. That would be great!' Jeff was having a sandwich; I brought Jim over and said, 'Jeff, I'd like you to meet the drummer with the Sons,' and Jeff went, 'Jim Preston?' I said, 'Yeah, Jim Preston, this is Jeff Porcaro.' And Jeff got on his knees and did that 'Salam, Salam, Salam' to Jimmy because he had listened to him for a long time and loved his playing. It made Jim's life—not his day, not his week—it really blew his mind. It was so sweet. Then they went over and talked drums. It was a real soulful thing that he did."

Actually, Champlin had played with Jeff before he moved to L.A. In 1977, Champlin was called to overdub the lead vocal to Lee Ritenour's "Isn't She Lovely," with Porcaro on drums. Through his relationship with David Foster, Champlin overdubbed on Foster's two earliest productions: the Keane Brothers' self-titled album in 1977 and Jaye P. Morgan's self-titled album the year before. "Jeff played on both of them, so before I even met the guy, I had recorded with him," Champlin says with a laugh. They also played live together briefly, when Champlin went to the club Donte's to see Larry Carlton. Jeff was playing drums, and Bill sat in on a couple tunes. "I thought, 'This feels great,'" he remembers.

Walking around the Sherman Oaks Fashion Square in the San Fernando Valley one day (when it was still just an outdoor mall),

Champlin encountered Porcaro. "There were shops on both sides and in between there were benches you could sit on. Jeff was sitting there playing his knees and floor, working on a thing," Bill says. "I snuck up behind him and listened to him for a second. He was working on some kind of 9/4 time signature. I said, 'Sounds like a single there.'"

He recalls both of them appearing at an early morning "Mark and Brian Christmas Show" in Hollywood one year. "I think Jeff and Keltner were playing that show; it was at some God-awful time that I would refer to as shit-o'clock," Champlin says with a laugh. "At one point Jeff and I were sitting together, taking a break, and Mel Torme came in to sing 'The Christmas Song.' Both Jeff and I were crying like babies. I looked at Jeff and said, 'I got you,' and he said, 'You, too, man.' We were just going, 'Man, this is the real deal. This is the guy who wrote the thing. He sang it before Nat King Cole did, because he wrote it.'" Mark and Brian did a New Years show one year in Santa Barbara with (as Champlin put it) "every name in the book" in the band, including Paich, Jai Winding, Russ Kunkel and Jeff on double drums, and Mike Porcaro on bass.

Champlin says he probably sang on a hundred songs that Jeff played on, but didn't know it, because Champlin was mostly overdubbing vocals. There is one session he recalls, where Steve Cropper was producing the cartoonist Garry Trudeau (the 1977 album *Doonesbury's Jimmy Thudpucker and the Walden West Rhythm Section Greatest Hits)*. "I was playing organ, Steve was playing guitar, and Duck Dunn was playing bass," Champlin recalls. "The chart was a little slow and David (Foster) was in hurry to get to another date, so he said, 'Let's just make this easy. Me and Jeff will put our parts down, and you guys can overdub.'

"I also had Jeff on one song called 'Without You' on my *Runaway* album, and that's what he did," Bill notes. "All I did was bring up the click track a little faster for the tag. Jeff and David just put the track down—piano and drums."

RITENOUR

LEE RITENOUR recalls while growing up in Los Angeles, trying to break into the music scene as a guitarist, that the Porcaro family was royalty. He knew of Joe Porcaro at the foreground and then, as he calls it, the "wunderkind of sons." Jeff was already royalty from his work with Steely Dan, Ritenour says, not to mention the other records.

Ritenour does not remember on which session he met Jeffrey, but he does recall they both were probably 18 or 19 years old. "It was so cool to see him work. He was already a pro at such a young age. He was very cool. It's funny how the young players get attracted to one another as they're coming up at the same time," Ritenour muses. "He loved good players and good songs. Jeff was interesting because he was already a mature drummer who respected the arrangement and the song. He wanted to make the record always better. I, myself, wanted to make sure I fit in with the music and the players and that the session went well. Jeff and I were alike in that way."

They were doing a lot of sessions together, and when Ritenour began doing his own projects, he hired Porcaro to play on them. In 1977 Jeff played on two cuts off Ritenour's *Captain Fingers*. The words that come to mind about the drums on "Isn't She Lovely" are buoyant and joyful. Ray Parker, Jr. was also on that session. The funny side story

Lee tells is that he met Ray Parker, Jr. through arranger Gene Page on a previous session. "Ray turns to me and holds out his hand, and with that big grin of his says, 'I'm Ray Parker, Jr., the greatest guitar player in the world.' I held out my hand and said, 'We'll see about that,'" Lee recalls with a laugh. "Then we were fast friends. Jeff had that same confidence, humor and maturity that that story reflects. And then there's a young Bill Champlin singing that song and David Foster shows up on the scene, so it was an interesting crowd."

In the late 1970s, Ritenour traveled with a group of session players to Criteria Studios in Florida to work with Barry Gibb. The other musicians involved were Jeff, Lee Sklar and Richard Tee. "They wanted the track perfect," says Ritenour. "It was all these great players, and Barry was incredibly detail oriented. We started off with the band and pretty soon we were playing along with the demo of the song. Little by little he said, 'Let's simplify things and let's take out the percussionist, we'll add that in later,' so the percussionist went out into the hallway to play billiards," Ritenour recounts. "Then we worked on that for a while and then he said, 'Ok, let's leave off one of the guitars,' so Barry's guitar player—good player—exited. Then we played for a while longer and he said, 'Ok, let's just do it as a trio, so Lee, you wait, too.' Then it was Richard Tee, Leland and Jeff. Pretty soon Richard Tee walked out into the hallway, leaving just Jeff recording to the demo. Finally, Jeff walks out and we're laughing. 'What? Did we all get fired?' Jeff says, 'No, man, you gotta check this out. It's incredible.' We all walked back into the studio, and they had brought in this mechanical thing that was playing the snare drum. It was a precursor to the LinnDrum. They worked on that for something like three days. If Steely Dan wasn't bad enough, the Bee Gees took it to another level."

In 1981, Porcaro played on two songs on Ritenour's record *Rit*: "Good Question" and "Mr. Briefcase." Ritenour relays a story he heard about when Toto was working on an early album at Sunset Sound and hitting it hard, burning the candle at both ends for weeks, sleeping in the studio. "In love with the music, in love with hanging with each other," Ritenour says. "Jeff is asleep on the couch at Sunset Sound in Sunset 2 and it's 10:00 in the morning and the lady at the front office says, 'Hey, your mom and dad are in the lobby. They came down to listen to some tracks, remember? You guys gotta get yourselves together.' Jeff says, 'Yeah, yeah, ok.' Jeff gets up and goes out into the little outdoor area connecting all the studios where there is a little basketball court, and his parents are walking across the concrete basketball court toward the studio. Jeff says, 'Hey good morning,' and Joe looks at him and says, 'Hey, you might want to take that pizza off that's on the side of your head and clean it up.'"

Ritenour always knew a session would be good if Jeff was on it. "It all starts and ends with the drums," Lee asserts. "There can be a lot of lousy tunes, which we've all played on, but as far as the tracking and making the producer, the songwriter and artist happy and making sure we got the best out of whatever we were working on, it really started with the drummer. And Jeff always had a great sound, and when the drummer had a great sound, that helped the production from the beginning; the bass sounded better, the keyboard sounded better, the guitar sounded better. Everything sounded better."

JIM MESSINA

Around the end of Loggins & Messina in 1976 or 1977, **JIM MESSINA** recalls one day meeting Jeff with David Paich, although he can't recall where it was. Paich approached Messina because he had played on the duo's 1974 album *Mother Lode.* Messina recalled really liking his playing but observing that he was very "square." ("I like square people, though," Messina says.) They asked his advice on management, and he told them who the manager had been for Poco and for Loggins & Messina—but also told them management was always a very personal preference. He gave them two suggestions; Toto did take one of them: Larry Fitzgerald, who was partners with Mark Hartley as Fitzgerald Hartley.

Messina had very little occasion to hire an outside musician, but after his first 1979 solo album *Oasis,* when it came time to do *Messina* two years later, he was rehearsing the material with a drummer that wasn't working out. His secretary/assistant Ivy knew Jeff and suggested Jim use him. He thought it was a great idea, but said they would need to rehearse. "She said, 'Jeff never rehearses,'" recalls Messina. "I said, 'Would you ask him?' She goes, 'You want me to ask Jeff if he's going to rehearse?' And I said, 'Yeah.' She got back to me and said, 'Well, I asked Jeff if he would be willing to rehearse and he said yes.' He could only do a couple of dates, but Jeff showed up, God bless him, and It was just him and me. I said, 'Jeff, I just want to walk through these arrangements because we've spent a couple of months getting to where we are now, and I don't have the finances to spend three weeks in the studio recording, so if you would be kind enough to walk through these with me.' So he did. I think we got through it in a day. He took his notes; he showed up for the album with his notes and we recorded the album."

Jeff asked Messina whom he had in mind for percussion. Milt Holland, Messina's usual choice, wasn't playing anymore, so Messina had not decided. Jeff said, "What about my dad?" Messina said, "Do you think he'd do it?" Jeff said, "Oh yeah." Then he added, "And Victor Feldman also plays piano." So Jeff got both his father (who played on "Whispering Waters") and Victor Feldman to join on the project. "Those two additions to the album, just made the music unbelievable," Messina exclaims.

"Jeff was just such a great supporter," continues Messina. "What I didn't realize until later was that Jeff was such a huge star as a recording drummer, but I don't look at people as stars; I think of people as musicians—craftsmen—and would he be a good personality and instrumentalist on a session? There are some musicians that eat up more time than necessary with their bullshit, and Jeff was very unlike that. It was just all go. I remember one time we were doing 'Lovin' You Every Minute'; we had done two takes and both were spectacular. We could have used either of them, but I wanted to do one more. I said to Jeff, 'You played the parts exactly as we talked about them. I'd like to do one take where you express it where there's anything you'd like to add or subtract where it makes it your own performance, without any consideration to what I asked you to do. Could we keep it at the same tempo? I liked the energy you had.'"

Messina cut the talkback and asked the engineer to time Porcaro to see how close Jeff got to the original tempo he cut. He laughs as he reports that it was 1/100th of a second off. "His abilities blew my mind," says Messina. Jeff's final take is the one they used. "It felt right because everybody was having a great time, and if you listen to it, it's very tight. What's interesting is you don't think about Jeff being a Latin player, but after the take, I knew there wasn't anybody else I would have wanted to play it."

Everything was cut live, including the percussion. (Messina says he always cut live on every project.) Observing Jeff and his father Joe working together, Messina says, "He was very respectful of his father, and they were pals. And his father respected him, too. You could feel the mutual respect. It was a very comfortable session and there was a lot of laughing going on. Victor Feldman was hilarious."

Messina says one of the things he admired about Jeff's character was that he was not afraid of the drum machine. "He was always inspired by something new, and he had an inspirational attitude. He wore those big glasses, and his eyes would open so wide, and they would be magnified with excitement. For such a small guy, he had such a big voice, just whoa! He was just a very inspired musician; no fear. It was a blessing."

On the album, Messina wrote: "Thank you Jeff Porcaro for bringing my music together. Your attitude and professionalism brought joy and inspiration to all of us."

MARC JORDAN

Living in Toronto at the beginning of 1977, **MARC JORDAN** was signed to Warner Brothers Records. The label was so eager to get him into the studio that before the ink had even dried on his record deal, producer Gary Katz threw him into the deep end. It was early on in Katz's relationship with Porcaro. Jordan arrived to the first day of recording for his debut album, *Mannequin,* and met Jeff. Marc was intimidated, not just by Jeff, but the fact that the room was filled with superstar musicians: Steve Lukather, David Paich and Victor Feldman.

"Jeff was the lightning rod in the room," Jordan says. "He was the big personality. He was very funny. I remember one thing he said, and if he hadn't said it in a funny way, I probably would have had a nervous breakdown. I had never really made a big-time record before, so I wasn't really in the pocket as much as everyone else. By the time I finished that record, I was like a session singer. I understood what the parameters were, but I didn't coming in. Probably in the first hour of the session, he said, 'Get Jordan's guitar out of my headphones!' I was probably all over the place time-wise. I'm sure I was. I know I was. But he said it in such a way that it wasn't insulting; it was funny; everybody laughed. I knew in that moment who Jeff was. I'm telling you, he could have made it very uncomfortable, because I was still learning and he was in his prime.

"The week before that, I was playing a bar by myself in Ottawa, Canada in a blizzard," Jordan recalls with a laugh. "It was a major transition. Jeff was amazingly kind to me. He could have been a prick because I was so green and it took me a little longer to do things than he was used to, but he was very kind. He talked to me and he was like a pal, which helped a great deal with my confidence. And confidence is a big deal in the studio because you've got to feel like you can say things and get your ideas out there, and he made that possible. It was Jeff, and to a certain extent Lukather, but mostly Jeff who made me feel included," Jordan says, adding that at the end of the day, Porcaro put his arm around him and said, "I love your voice."

With Jeff and the other players, Jordan learned a great deal about groove, and it made a mark on his singing style. The demos from which they were working were made with a Toronto band nothing like the musicians who were in the studio. Jordan says his history really was as a folk musician: "I arrived in L.A. like a folk singer, and I left like Boz Scaggs." After being exposed to the likes of Katz's crew, Jordan and his music were "funkified." "I loved it, but it was shocking," Jordan admits. "It was a big learning curve for me, and that all came from the drums and the bass to a certain extent."

Jeff played on the whole album except the song "One Step Ahead of the Blues," and his performance was a revelation to Jordan. "I was so blown away by his articulation and the incidental—I don't even know the proper language—rhythmic 'flotsam and jetsam' that was going on between the 2 and the 4," says Jordan. "There were so many grace notes and so many almost percussion-like moments, in order to propel the track forward. Jeff was propulsive. That's why people used him—because when he was on a track, it moved. He had a momentum in his playing that was undeniable, and it made everybody a little better."

Jordan has other vivid memories of his time making *Mannequin*, among them Jeff and Lukather's dinner banter making him feel sorry for second engineer Lenise Bent (who was the only female in the crew), and recording "Lost Because You Can't be Found," thinking it was a great track as it went down. "Marina del Rey" conjures up memories of Jeff playing with Robert Greenidge, who was on steel drums. "He could play bebop on these pans," Jordan recalls. "I remember him and Jeff jamming a bit; we were just all amazed at what this guy was doing. They were getting off on each other, and we were all amazed that this guy could play jazz on these pans."

Porcaro came to play on Jordan's next album, *Blue Desert,* the following year because Jay Graydon produced it. Jeff played on three tracks: "I'm a Camera," "From Nowhere to This Town" and "Release Yourself." "It was hard to get Jeff in those days because he was busier than a one-armed paper hanger," Jordan says. *Blue Desert* was made at Seals & Crofts' Dawnbreaker Studios with Jordan feeling more confident than on the first record: He had a tour under his belt, he had gotten used to L.A., and he knew the studio musicians this time around. All of this led to a higher comfort level.

One funny recollection Jordan has is on a session that David Foster and Jay Graydon were producing. "Jeff lit his drums on fire," Jordan remembers, surmising that it was because Jeff was not digging the session. "I think it was for an artist by the name of Mel somebody." Jay Graydon thinks it was a Mel somebody, too, but can't recall the name either. Graydon says: "Jeff did that a few times. He sometimes used paper towels to semi-mute the toms. Either that or he put the paper towels on with tape to intentionally light. I think I saw him do it twice, and at least one time it burned the heads a little bit. You never knew what Jeff might do."

THE WISDOM OF GREG MATHIESON A LA JEFF PORCARO

(Note: For some reason I had trouble catching up with keyboardist **GREG MATHIESON,** who would write great posts about Jeff on Facebook. I was eager to talk to him about working with Jeff but seemed never to be able to connect with him. I finally messaged him and just asked if I could use his posts in the book, so more people than just his social media connections could have the benefit of seeing them. He said I could, so here they are!)

Jeff at the Baked Potato, circa 1980. (Courtesy of Barney Hurley)

A LESSON FROM JEFF ON WHAT MAKES UP A GROOVE

"Jeff and I and a bunch of the greatest musicians in L.A. got this call for two weeks of triple dates. We were grooved because we were going to make some money and we were going to hang with the cats for two weeks. But then there was this catch! After we got the master take on the first song, we found out that we had to duplicate the master take one BPM faster and then one BPM slower. Then they wanted us to do all three master takes one half step above the first original key and then all three master takes one half step below the original key. That means nine master takes per song. This means it would take all day to record one song—and after you play this song that many times you never wanted to hear it again in your life. *Bad vibes.*

"So about the third day, I get bored, so I decide to play my whole part behind the beat or click, back where Jeff put his snare drum. Well, they didn't like that take and so they gave us a break. I was out in the lounge getting coffee and I heard Jeff running and yelling my name. Now there are two things wrong with this situation. Jeff never ran at someone, nor did he yell at anyone, so something was up because Jeff was always just 'cool.' He gets to me and says, 'Greg don't ever do that to me again!' I say, 'What man, what's going on?' He says to me 'Don't ever play on the backside of the beat again because I will have to play even further back and that messes everything up.' I promised that I would never ever do it again and everything was cool. Then he said, 'Here's what makes up a groove…' and so this is the lesson that I learned from Jeff that day:

"'Here's what makes up a groove. Greg, you play it where you feel it, which is center time. That's cool, Greg. I dig that. The bass player will play it with his time, and the guitar player will play it with his time, and the percussion will play it with his time, etc. and that lets me put my snare drum on the backside of the click. See, it's how all our different combinations of grooves or the way each person feels time weaving around the click that comes together as 'one' that makes a groove. It's how all of our different grooves from the different players weaving around the click and the 'push and pull' against each other that makes up a groove.' Man that was some great advice! I've been thinking about it ever since.

"So to me, after all these years of thinking about it, grooving hard is not perfection. It's not us playing perfectly together. It's when a group of musicians get together and agree on the tempo. After they agree on the tempo, they play with their own sense of time or their own personal natural groove. That 'magic groove' happens when all of their personal different natural grooves merge (some on top, some center, some behind the beat) and there is this magical 'push and pull' around the agreed tempo. That's when the groove happens. It's the 'push and pull' of everyone's natural groove around the tempo that makes a groove. Now, you have to have the right musicians to make this happen. But they are not playing exactly in sync with each other. They're playing off each other, listening to one another weaving around the tempo, setting up this magical 'push and pull' that makes the groove. Not all musicians can do this. You have to practice, listen, and be able to adjust to the players around you. Also, this is why some rhythm sections sound better than other rhythm sections. The rhythm sections that are listening to each other and have that right balance of 'push and pull' are the ones that groove the hardest. All it takes is one player in the rhythm section that won't listen or won't adjust his playing to stop the section from grooving.

"Then you know what? Sometimes the tempo changes. (Did I just say that out loud?) Man, I've played to a click my whole life. I can do it my sleep. But I say, 'Who cares?' Who made the rule up that the verse couldn't be a little slower, so when the chorus happens it 'pops,' and when you get to the second verse, you take the edge off the tempo so it settles down? *Music is supposed to breathe.* It's alive! Who made up the rule that you can't speed up just a little bit in someone's solo, just to make it exciting? Then it might come down for the next solo. I want to know who started the click or 'tempo police'?

"Have you ever quantized a whole track, listened back and thought, 'That's perfect, but something is wrong?' What's wrong is that it's perfect. It's 'stay pressed.' You just got it back from the cleaners; all the soul has been squeezed out of it. Now, this is even better: I'm sitting behind the console in the studio. I'm listening to something, and I say to the second engineer, 'Something doesn't feel right.' He says, "No, it's perfect, just look at the waveforms on Pro Tools. They're perfectly aligned.' See, that's the problem. We're looking at waveforms and not using our ears. We've stopped listening.

"OK, I've gotta stop raving… I'm off topic. I use Pro Tools plus Logic, and they're great tools, but we can't forget the lesson that Jeff taught me. We have to let music breathe a little. The genie is out of the bottle, but I wish we could find a better balance between technology and the natural groove that lives in our hearts. Let music breathe a little. I'll end with my favorite quote from my brother Abraham Laboriel: 'Let the music win.'

"As I told you we had to get nine master takes per song, so it took a whole day to record one song. The only fun part about the sessions was the cats on the record dates. They were the best and fun to hang out with.

"There was this big stack of music on the acoustic piano. It had all ten songs in three different keys. One day I was looking through it to see what kind of songs were coming up. I came across a chart that was totally written out like a classical piano piece. I thought to myself, 'I'm the wrong piano player for that song.' I could have played it, but to do all nine versions they should get a piano player who reads really well that does a lot of movie dates. I didn't want to put myself through it. I'm a groove player and that's what people call me for. So on a break I start talking to the contractor. I tell him when they record that one, they should hire a classical piano player to read that chart, because I'm a groove player. The contractor starts to argue with me and says, 'No, it's ok, you can play whatever you want,' but I know the arranger is going to want me to play his part, so I keep arguing. Finally, I raise my voice and say, '*I'm not that guy, man!*' real loud. I hear Jeff drop his sticks and start laughing really hard. Apparently, Jeff had been listening to the whole conversation. He thought that me saying 'I'm not that guy' was just real funny and so did the other cats.

"So they record that song with another piano player. I ask how it went and they say just ok. I guess I didn't miss anything. So now we're on the last song on the last day. The way we're set up in the room, when I play acoustic piano I'm looking away from Jeff, but when I'm at my keyboard rig, Jeff is on a riser directly in front of me, so I can see his face. On this last song they're really putting Jeff through the mill. 'Can you play the hi-hat like this? No, use a brush. No, try a beat with cross stick. Try cross on 2 and snare on 4'—you get the idea. I'm looking directly into Jeff's eyes and I'm thinking, 'Any moment he is going to snap.' I'm thinking, 'Jeff, it's the last song, man, hang on.' Finally, they ask Jeff if he can play a foxtrot. 'A what?' There is absolute silence. I think, 'Oh no.' I am waiting for him to freak out on them. I close my eyes and think, 'Here it comes.' I look up and Jeff is looking straight at me with a big grin. He stands up and throws his drums sticks down and yells, '*I'm not that guy!*' real loud. The whole band just starts to laugh for what seems like five minutes. It was so, so great! It was better than freaking on them.

"For the life of me I don't remember what happened next. I know we finished the song, and everything turned out ok. Well, that's a story you don't forget. The big grin on his face and him looking me right in the eyes as he said, 'I'm not that guy' is burned into my head forever."

SMOKE GETS IN YOUR EYES

"We're up at Larry's (Carlton's) house in the Cahuenga Pass in his home studio, and we're cutting the *335* album. This day we are going to cut the track to 'Nite Crawler.' We've played this song live a number of times, so Larry's not going to play on the track. He's going to be in the booth. It's me on Rhodes, and I'm looking straight at Jeff Porcaro on drums, and Abraham Laboriel is to my right. Larry's cousin (we call him cousin Steve) comes out to move a mic on the drums. Jeff had just rolled this big fat joint and lit up. Larry said the tape was rolling and told us to start to play. I forget who counts it off, but we start the take. Now, Larry doesn't know that cousin Steve is still right next to Jeff, and that Jeff has this big fat joint in his mouth. We start the take. I see cousin Steve sit down on the floor next to Jeff. The tune is grooving, but as we get into the song, the smoke from the joint starts to go up into Jeff's eyes, but it doesn't affect the groove. Looking at Jeff, I felt bad for him, but in a way, I thought it was funny. We make it through the take, and guess what? That's the take that's on the album."

THE SPUD

The original Baked Potato "Spud Band"—Mathieson, Jeff, Lukather and Pops Popwell—would always start their set with "All Blues," according to Mathieson, because Jeff wanted to warm up before they played "Bump Me." When the Greg Mathieson Project would play there, the last song in the set would be "The Spud Shuffle." He explained in a Facebook post: "We always ended the set with this song.

At least ten times, Jeff came up to me after the show and said, 'Man, I can't play a shuffle.' I'd look at him at and say 'Jeff, get out of town. We just burnt the place down. I'd play a shuffle with you any day of the week.'

"See, for you drummers out there, Jeff was human like us all. We're all musicians trying to get better!

"Someone just commented (on the FB post) that a great drummer lays down a 'pocket' for everyone to play to, and that's why they call it a 'pocket.' A great drummer lays down where he feels the time and that is his 'pocket.' But…he is aware of and playing off the time of the other musicians in the rhythm section. He is constantly adjusting his 'pocket' to what's going on at any given moment or any given bar or beat to make the 'groove' happen. If you're a drummer and you don't listen to the bass, guitar or keyboard player and only listen to yourself, you're not a great drummer!

"When I played with Jeff, he listened to me and adjusted to my groove, and I definitely listened to his groove and adjusted to him. That's the way it works! When I played with Carlos Vega at the Spud it was the same thing. Hell, listen to the live album with Vinnie at the Spud. We're adjusting to one another every other bar!"

Mathieson recalls producing an album for David Roberts called *All Dressed Up* at the beginning of 1982: "I was still playing with Jeff and Luke at the Spud. When I finally did hear his material, I realized that all I had to do was switch Pops (Popwell) to Mike Porcaro and I had the rhythm section from Toto, minus David Paich. Toto was doing their fourth record at Record One, working at night. They were past cutting tracks, so it was way cool. Plus, David Paich, Mike Porcaro and Steve Porcaro were hanging at the Spud every time we played. So were Joe Porcaro and his wife and Jeff and Mike's sister. We were all family. See, neither David Foster nor Jay Graydon would have pulled this off so easily. I was using Toto's band. David Roberts had hit the lottery!

"Sometime in late January I flew to Toronto, Canada to listen to all of David's songs. We narrowed them down to about ten or twelve tracks and talked about the schedule. David remembers me wanting to take a walk to clear my head, even though it was real cold outside. I dug the cold fresh Canadian air, and I felt great when I got back. I remember going to a McDonald's, and they put vinegar on their French fries (there). When in Toronto, do as the Toronto people do. I couldn't hang with it, but my wife still likes vinegar on her fish and chips. It's funny what you remember.

"When I got back to L.A I had a plan. I called Jeff, Luke and Mike and found out what week they were free in February. Then I booked studio 1 at Sunset Sound, which is where Toto 1 and 2 were recorded. Then I booked Humberto Gatica to engineer it and made sure that David Leonard (who was the second engineer that had just helped us mix the Baked Potato album) was available. The stars all aligned.

"David Roberts came to L.A. before we started the tracking session. I was living with my lady (that became my second wife—and we're still married). She had a house just off Coldwater Canyon. We talked about arrangements, but I had a 'secret plan.' When we played the Spud, I never told anyone what to play. That's exactly how I was going to run the sessions. I mean, do you really think I should tell Jeff Porcaro what to play? Tell Luke or Mike? See, once again as an arranger, I wrote out the lines and hits and maybe a suggestion of a bass part, and then said to the guys, 'Make me look good, cats.' I let everyone jump in with ideas like it was a band, and you can hear that on the record. I told the cats it was a loose noon start. (We never started until 1:00pm). As long as we got two or three song tracks a day, I was cool. Sometimes we worked until 8:00 and sometimes we hung out until midnight. Everyone in Toto knew we were cutting tracks, so people were coming by to hang out. It felt like a party. I bought a couple cases of Corona and a bottle of Tequila and stuff. The key is once you get the cats there, you don't let them leave, so you have to feed them or do whatever they want. But here is the deal: Not one of us drank or did anything, because we knew that everything that we played was going to tape and needed to stand the test of time. Our names were going to be on this record, so we demanded a lot of ourselves; we couldn't be messed up and play sloppy. We had a few beers at the end of the night when we'd listen to the playback and everybody said, 'Greg you should do this or that.' Maybe Luke would say, 'Let me go double that part.' It felt like a band. You can hear that on the record!"

DAVID GARFIELD

Keyboardist **DAVID GARFIELD** (Cher, Smokey Robinson, Larry Carlton, Brenda Russell, Michael Bolton) has a lot of stories and memories dating back to the first time he met Jeff around 1978 at the grand opening of the Leeds Rehearsal facility where Garfield was performing with his band Karizma.

David Garfield with Joe Porcaro and Jeff's boys. (Courtesy of David Garfield)

For the NAMM show in 1987, Jeff was asked by Paiste to play at their booth and for a company cocktail party. He brought Garfield and brother Mike along for the gig. "Jeff had hired me to do this NAMM show gig with him. We were up in the room at the Hilton, and he was going, 'How in the hell did I get roped into doing a cocktail gig?'" Garfield recalls with a laugh. "He had no idea what to do or what to play. I remember Erik Paiste came to the room, and we were all sitting around. Jeff was going, 'I never do this, I can't do this, I can't do this,' and Erik said, 'No, no, no, it'll be fine, just play for half an hour.' But that's what he liked about me; I could come into those situations and pull out songs. I'd write out charts on hotel stationery; little chord charts for Mike. I'd pick something with a nice groove. I remember one tune I picked out was a David Sanborn song, 'Theme from Love Is Not Enough.' Jeff had a ball.

"Jeff, Mike and I did three shows a day in the Paiste booth that year, and then one night we had a show with Larry Carlton, Lukather, and Terry Trotter—it was like Larry Carlton's band and Lukather's band all together. I remember John Robinson was there; he sat in, and I watched Jeff and him interact. Jeff was so gracious to the up-and-coming guys. J.R. was a new guy at the time, and Jeff let him play. I remember that year the three of us really bonded."

In 1988, Garfield performed on Jeff's instructional drum video. "We all went down to Bill Schnee's studio, and I remember sitting out in the hallway and Jeff said he wanted to do 'Babylon Sisters.' I had no idea how to play it; there was no music. I had brought the CD with me, and I listened to it and tried to write out a chart, but it was complicated, so I remember that day being disappointed that I couldn't pull that song together for him," says Garfield. (Remember that this was pre-internet and visual aids. As a result of this, when Garfield put the *Tribute to Jeff* CD together after Jeff died, it was very important to him to include that song.)

David remembers one day at the Porcaro home on Valleyheart Drive in about 1988 while he and Jeff were working on the song "Big Bone" for the *Los Lobotomys* record. They went into the garage/studio to work on the groove, and then Jeff showed him a cassette of an instrumental song that Donald Fagen wrote for him to record. David says he may be the only person who knows about this. "Donald thought Jeff should make a record, and he wrote him a song," David reveals. "Jeff wanted to be a side guy; he didn't want to make a record, but Fagen thought he should. Jeff said, 'Check this out,' and he played me the cassette; it sounded a lot like a Steely Dan song. Jeff said, 'Donald wants me to record this and make my own album,' and I remember thinking, 'Oh great, I would love to help you make a record.' Jeff said,

'I have no interest in doing a record; I'll never do my own record.'"

While they were recording *Los Lobotomys* at the Complex in 1988, David had planned out who was going to play which song. There was an orchestration of who would play the drum kit, and there was a second kit that was a hybrid of electric toms and pads and then a percussion setup. Jeff was in the middle, Carlos Vega was on the left and Lenny Castro on the right. "On this one song that Lukather wrote called 'Smell Yourself,' I had put down Vinnie was going to play that song. We were at the rehearsal and Lukather got all bent out of shape because he wanted Carlos to play it," Garfield remembers. "I had carefully orchestrated who was going to play on what song, they were paired up and had to move. It was a set list, and it was a thing that made sense to me, but because Lukather wrote the song, he started to give me a hard time. Luke was kind of tearing into me, and then Jeff—this was classic Jeff—goes, 'Hey Luke, no, Vinnie should play that one,' and shut him down. He defended me—and the thing is, that song has become legendary and Vinnie's performance on it is awesome. It was the perfect call. After that, I realized Jeff was the one guy who could rein Luke in. Jeff really knew how to cool him out, so when Jeff died Luke didn't have that mentor, that big brother."

In about 1990, Jeff was playing with Garfield at the Baked Potato. Jeff had just recorded with Bruce Springsteen. Bruce wanted Jeff to go out on tour with him, and he had offered a million dollars. "We were sitting in his car out back, and Jeff was telling me that he wasn't going to take the Springsteen gig because Toto was starting to make money. He didn't want to jeopardize Mike because Mike had just bought a house," David recalls. "I was privy to the fact that he didn't want to take all that money because he didn't want to do that to his brother."

Garfield recalls another night at the Baked Potato when Jeff's drum rack was taking up lots of real estate on the stage. "There was a framed picture of Lukather right behind Jeff," David says. "Jeff was playing and did this flamboyant fill at the end and threw his hand back up, hitting the wall and breaking the frame and glass. His hand came down. The glass had cut his hand and we didn't know what happened, but at the end of the song, his hand was full of blood."

Garfield says playing live with Jeff was "the best." He says he was extremely solid, tasty and he put his whole heart into it.

Jeff had the pulse of the politics of the moment, according to Garfield. When they were flying down to New Orleans to do the New Orleans Jazz Festival in April 1992 with Boz Scaggs, the high-profile Rodney King case—the African-American man who had been beaten by LAPD officers—had been tried and was in jury deliberation. "When we got off the plane in New Orleans, just as soon as they opened the door, Jeff looked at the faces of some of the skycaps that were at the gate and immediately knew what had transpired," Garfield recalls. "I remember Jeff being so attuned. He was walking right next to me, and he saw the skycap and said, 'Oh my God, I bet they decided a not guilty.' He asked someone and they confirmed it. And then the riots broke out and we actually stayed a couple of days longer in New Orleans because of that."

They rehearsed at Sea-Saint Studio for the New Orleans show and Carole King was on the bill. Garfield notes that somehow Slash ended up playing guitar with her, and Jeff was compelled to get in line after the show to get an autographed photo of Slash for one of his kids.

When Garfield recorded the *Tribute to Jeff* record in 1996, he wanted to involve Jeff's kids. Jeff's nephew Chase (Joleen's son) had taken up the drums, so David invited him to play on the record. It came to his attention that Jeff's boys were playing drums, too, so they came to L.A. and he organized a day for them to come to the studio to play snare drum on the song "Twenty-One Drum Salute (So Many Drummers, So Little Time)." Their grandfather Joe Porcaro coached them. David says the kids were really excited because they knew the project was an effort to remember their father.

MICHAEL OMARTIAN

Back during the Steely Dan *Katy Lied* days, keyboardist/producer **MICHAEL OMARTIAN** would see Jeff quite a bit on sessions. He describes working with Fagen and Becker as a "very different thing." "We used to joke about it all the time because the one defining thing about those guys was it didn't matter how proficient you were at what you did, you seldom knew where you stood," Omartian explains. "It was just always their M.O. We would just always joke, 'Well, I don't know if we'll ever know whether this was right or not.' We'd go to the studio together and all of us cats would play—Dean Parks, Chuck Rainey and Jeff, whomever—and we just wouldn't know. Of course, working with Jeff was always a pleasure because not only was the music great, but he was also such a great hang and good vibe. It didn't matter what we were going through, he always had a good thing going. It always felt comfortable with him, and it was a friendship.

"Coming into those sessions, a lot of times we would cut a

song, like on *Katy Lied,* more than once with different components. Jeff would usually play the drums on whatever, and they would try a different guitar player or bass player. Cutting with Fagen and Becker, you'd walk in and listen to a playback; you know Jeff, he was the groove-meister—he was back there moving and grooving, smiling and going, 'Yeah!' and you'd look over at Fagen and he was just staring at the console. You got nothin' back. Jeff's going, 'Yeah!' and Fagen's going, 'That's pretty good,' And you're going, 'Pretty good? What the heck are you talking about? That's *really* good!' It was our inside joke: 'Who knows if anyone will say we did anything right?' It was like a drug, though—there was a challenge to it," Michael admits, explaining in comparison, that there were definitely those sessions that were the other side of the hip coin.

I mention to Michael that while Jeffrey usually didn't believe tracks required more than a few takes, Steely Dan was the only band in which he found it worthwhile to be worked to death. Omartian concurred. "You never went out to a meal with them; you took a lunch break, but they were never with you. It was just weird. It was a very different experience; they just weren't effusive or outgoing. I mean they were geniuses, but I don't know. Jeff and I would go out to lunch," Michael says. "He had a Volvo P1800. I was into cars at the time, and we would talk cars; he loved that car. We didn't do a lot of socializing outside of the studio, but I considered him a friend just like I considered Hungate and Lukather, but there wasn't a lot of hang time. I was married and had kids."

Omartian recalls they joked around quite a bit, and Jeff was always drawing. "He'd be in there and you'd see these naked caricatures of people," says Omartian. But in the studio, his recollection of Jeff was he never had to be told what to do. "He'd hit it and the most you'd have to say was, 'Give me a hit or a foot push at this bar, but I don't remember ever saying the groove isn't correct. His instinct was always correct, and that's what made him so incredible. With Jeff it was just innate. You didn't have to tell him what to do. He'd have the thing right from the jump and then he'd elaborate; he'd make something more out of it. That was meaningful to me because that was one component I didn't have to deal with when we were doing stuff that I was producing. He was always on time, always prompt, there for the duration, and he was good vibes with everything. I don't ever recall thinking, 'Oh God, I gotta deal with him today because he's got a bad attitude,'" Omartian says, adding that it was quite the contrary if Jeff heard a song that really jazzed him. He would get really excited and couldn't wait to get at it.

Mentioning the common knowledge that Porcaro enjoyed his pot, Omartian recalls a short moment in time in the late '70s when Jeff decided he was going to stop. He thinks it lasted a couple of weeks. "I've got to be honest, the feel wasn't quite the same and we would all comment to him, 'Get back on it.' We all talked about it."

When Omartian would see Jeff sitting at the drums, he knew the groove would be great. "That's what is so tragically missing from today's music; today everything is coming out of one head, one person's idea at a computer," Omartian states. "What we had was different personalities, different vibes, different talents that would come together, and it was about picking the right part that would interface with what the other person was doing and not get in the way but be complementary. Everybody had played on so many things that it was second nature to listen to what everybody else was doing.

"One of the biggest tragedies was when Jeff called me, pretty late in his career and said, 'Omar, I'd be happy to come down and just put some hi-hat and maybe some crash cymbals on drum grooves out of the box.' That's how bad it got. Seriously. I mean, Jeff Porcaro is playing hi-hat and crash cymbals with a drum machine? What a tragedy."

THE CHRISTOPHER CROSS/TOMMY TAYLOR/PORCARO SAGA

During July 1977, in San Antonio, Texas, drummer **TOMMY TAYLOR** joined a band with Andy Salmon on bass and Rob Meurer on piano and synths, with an unknown guy named Christopher Geppert handling guitar and lead vocal duties. The musicians believed they were a band until right before Geppert was to sign with Warner Brothers Records. That's when they found out only he was being signed.

According to Taylor, they were told that it would not change the band members' positions in the unit, and it was "only a formality." "That's certainly not what happened," Taylor explains, adding that it impacted the musicians financially in a big way. According to the last conversation with management and the numbers he was given, they were all slighted $2,501,980 due to the success of the album. They were not kept in the loop on decisions or even pertinent information. In fact, Taylor says, it wasn't until sometime in the middle of the recording of the first album that the label decided Geppert would be known as Christopher Cross. "The first time I heard about that was when I read the liner notes," says Taylor.

Creatively, there really was no obligation to the musicians.

Tommy Taylor and Jeff. (Courtesy of Tommy Taylor, photo by Rob Meurer)

Taylor says he met Jeff while they were recording the debut album. "We were a bar band," Taylor says. "We were a casuals band. Chris wrote the songs, and we worked up the arrangements and recorded them, but we weren't seasoned studio players like Jeff and Steve Lukather and those guys. We were band guys. We were the Beatles; we weren't Hal Blaine. Even Omartian—he was the guy who made the choice, or we wouldn't have been on the record at all. He could have hired all those guys."

As producer, Michael Omartian liked the band vibe. "I was very happy with that. There's something to me that I like in certain situations when musicians are playing at their limitation, because a great band brings something to the table because of not how much they know, but actually the things that they don't know, so they are playing at the top of their abilities and you get something unique," explains Omartian.

Cross' debut album contained the hits "Ride Like the Wind" and "Sailing." "We were cutting tracks and 'Sailing' came up," Taylor recalls. "Honestly, 'Sailing' was just another one of Chris' songs; we never cared that much about it. We never would have dreamed that song would have done anything like it did—we were sure Warner Brothers was trying to kill our career when they put it out as a single. When we had 'Ride Like the Wind' and it blew up the charts, it was fantastic—and then you're going to come out with *what*? You really don't want us to do another record.

"'Sailing' was in a slow tempo, and I wasn't used to playing with click tracks or metronomes or anything. The demo is pretty steady, and I don't think we were getting the part exactly. Michael wasn't completely sold on what we were playing. I was just basically playing what Rob Meurer had shown me, because he was a drummer too, and I really wasn't a ballad player; I came from more of a rock angle. The feel was a slow 16th-note 2 and 4. It wasn't anything really earth-shattering, but they weren't happy, so they decided to bring Porcaro in to play it, and also have him play 'Mary Ann' which was slated to be recorded."

It was bassist Andy Salmon who mentioned to Taylor that they were calling Porcaro. Taylor recalls that Meurer and Salmon were not thrilled with the idea. Omartian had already taken over on piano early in the sessions, and Meurer was moved over to Rhodes and synths. Taylor acknowledges that although Omartian is great, they were all

Both top and left: Jeff at Warner Bros. Studios, Burbank, California, during the recording sessions for Christopher Cross' debut album, 1979. (Photos by Rob Meurer)

feeling somewhat displaced, since they were supposed to be a band. Taylor says there was a lot of pressure; all the Warner Brothers heads were in and out of the studio constantly.

"I came into the studio (Amigo) the night before everybody played," Taylor recalls. "Carlos Vega's gear was still set up. He had a 14″ x 24″ kick, 10″ x 14″ and 12″ x 15″ toms, 16″ x 18″ and 18″ x 20″ floor toms; and I've got a 14″ x 18″ bass drum, 5″ x 8″, 6½″ x 10″, and 8″ x 12″ toms and a 14″ x 14″ floor tom, all miked from the bottom, doing the single headed thing. Everybody looked at the drum set like, 'That's not going to work.' Chet (engineer Himes) and I had been working on this drum sound for a while. Chet miked the drums up, we ran the faders up and everybody's freaking out. Every day one of the cats from the record company comes in and points to the drum set or the speakers, shakes their head and walks out. After the record came out, the woman who ran the studio said she got calls every day asking what kind of drums they were, what kind of heads I was using, what sizes they were, how they were miked, but I kind of got lost in the shuffle.

"Rob and Andy brought it up that they were concerned that they were bringing Jeff in," Tommy continues. "And Jeffrey came down. He agreed to play my kit to keep the band sound; on the second record Steve Gadd played my kit so it would sound like they were Christopher Cross' drums. But Jeff was great. He came down and played 'Sailing' and 'Mary Ann.' I was there, and Jeff was so wonderful that I don't recall it being uncomfortable. He was a huge star. I mean, we weren't that far apart in age, but he had done a lot by the time he was in his twenties. I'm a huge Steely Dan fan and *Katy Lied* was a huge pinnacle for me. I didn't really draw a lot from Jeff, other than from osmosis, but I loved his playing. I thought he was really cool, just one of those guys. I thought Jeff had joined Steely Dan; I really didn't know what a session player was—I was really naïve. Here's a guy who has gold records, Toto and everything else, and he was totally respectful of me and my position in the band. He was, 'Hey let's see what we got,' and 'I dig your kit, that's really cool, that's an interesting sound.' He sat down and played the track, and what he played didn't really fit.

"Maybe it was on 'Arthur's Theme' or something, but Chris told me later that Jeff and he were listening to a playback and Jeff turned to him and said—and this is paraphrased—'Man, why don't you use Tommy? He's in your band, he's a great drummer, why don't you use him?' Chris responded, 'But he's not Jeff Porcaro,'" Looking back on those sessions, Taylor wonders if Porcaro was trying to purposely *not* get the track to hand it back to Taylor. "I can put forth that assumption way after the fact, judging by the way he treated me. What he played was great, but it was just a little heavy-handed for the song," Taylor notes. "They weren't happy with that either. So it was, 'Well, you just had your number one guy come in and he didn't get it, so now what are we going to do?' 'Well, you're going to get another shot.' So I was remembering what he played and those big flams he played in the middle of the chorus. We had had that same kind of part, but they were just single kind of hits, so I made a combination of what I had learned from Rob and took those flams from what Jeff had done and played them more with the attack that I would play them with, and that's the track you hear. After the fact, everybody was really happy. Chris could turn from not being a team player to being a team player; he came back and congratulated me, and all of a sudden, we were a band again."

Taylor was using a Rogers pedal, and Porcaro told him he used to use the Rogers but was now using a DW. Jeff suggested he try it and left his for Taylor. Jeff added that he had a whole locker full of Rogers pedals that Taylor was welcome to. "He was totally approachable," Tommy says. "That's one of those things I regret: I could have asked him anything in the world, but I was so insecure in those days. Jeffrey was holding out his hand."

"ARTHUR'S THEME (BEST THAT YOU CAN DO)"

Cross won five Grammy awards for his debut self-titled 1979 album. Omartian surmises that for Cross, coming from Austin in the '70s and then going to Los Angeles he was like a kid in a candy store full of the musicians whose names on the backs of albums he had seen growing up. Suddenly he could hire those same musicians to play his music. During the making of the second album, *Another Page*, Cross approached Omartian with the idea of using studio musicians.

"At first, I thought, 'Ugh, this is going to be a little uncomfortable. I don't know how you're going to break that to (the guys in your band)," Omartian remembers. "Please don't make me do it, because it's not my job.' The first thing Chris said was, 'I've always wanted to work with Jeff Porcaro.' 'Ok.' 'I've always wanted to work with Lukather,' 'Ok.' 'I've always wanted to work with Hungate,' 'Ok.' So what happened was that the first album was finished, and then we got the call from director Steve Gordon, who said he would love to have us come look at the movie *Arthur* and maybe do a theme song. We went to Warner Brothers for a screening and laughed our butts off. Then Peter Allen, Burt Bacharach, Carole Bayer-Sager and Chris wrote 'Arthur's Theme (Best That You Can Do).'"

They cut the song at Lion Share Studios and nailed it in three hours. Among the musicians was **MARTY WALSH** on acoustic guitar. He was in a booth that had a window and a door that opened into the studio. "I recall that the door was next to the entrance," Walsh remembers. "There I am, tuning up my acoustic guitar and it was like these doors blew open and here comes Luke, like a fricken tornado, 'What's up cats?' and he sits down at the piano which is right in front of me and proceeds to play this classical thing and he is ripping it up. I had never met the man and I'm going, 'Shit, I'll just sit here and strum this acoustic guitar, man, and you can go be Lukather. You're blowing me away, and I don't even know what to say.' It was just crazy."

The ease of cutting the track, in comparison to the time it took with his band, was not lost on Cross. It was not a hard decision to move forward with session musicians. "Of course, he idolized Jeff, so he was just on the moon," says Omartian. As a producer, Omartian says when it came to feel, Jeff was always his choice, but not always available—he recalls that sometimes Porcaro wasn't available for an entire month. With some of the more MIDI-involved music, Omartian often hired Paul Leim, and he remembers hiring Mike Baird for Donna Summer's "She Works Hard for the Money" because of how hard Baird hits.

The memory of "Arthur's Theme" for Tommy Taylor is pretty messed up: One night he was invited to Cross' house for a dinner party. Taylor showed up and when he didn't see Cross, he just assumed he was at the grocery store getting a last-minute item. He asked Cross' wife where he was, and she "turned white as a ghost," Taylor recalls. "She said, 'He didn't tell you?' 'Tell me what?' She said, 'He's in L.A. making a new record.' I said, 'How can he be recording a Christopher Cross record when we're not there?' She said, 'He's recording this new movie theme for a movie that's coming out with Dudley Moore. He wrote it with Burt Bacharach and Carole Bayer-Sager.' He never told anybody in the band he was going to record a song, basically under our name, with other people. She was so mad: 'I can't believe he didn't tell you!' We never knew it was being cut until it was done!"

MARTY WALSH

The first time guitarist Walsh heard the name Jeff Porcaro, it was from a trumpet player he played with in a band. It was one of those, "Have you heard of this guy…?" Walsh hadn't—yet. Marty was just nineteen when he met seventeen-year-old Jeff. Walsh was in a band whose manager had a rehearsal facility in Burbank. The manager said to Walsh, "I'm going to have a jam session and I'm going to invite this guy Jeff Porcaro to come." Walsh remembered the name that his bandmate had mentioned.

"I said, 'Great, I want to meet this guy. He's supposed to be great,'" Walsh recalls. "So we got together one evening at this rehearsal place and played together. I forget who else was there, but we hit it off. It was pretty apparent that there was this groove thing going on. At the time, I mean, I could play, and my time was pretty good. He pulled me aside afterwards and said, 'If you'd like to, I'd like you to come and jam with this band I have.' A few days later, he invited me to this jam session with Kerry Morris on bass, Scott Shelly and Steve Edwards on guitars. (We played) above a doggie-bed manufacturing company in North Hollywood where they'd been given this loft where they could jam. The band had all their gear set up there; I dragged all my stuff up and we played. It was cool, but it was kind of like a band because Scott and Steve were great guitar players. I think Jeff just brought me in so we could do a little playing together."

A few years later, on a tour bus with the DeFranco Family, drummer Tom Drake said, "'Have you heard this new Steely Dan record? Jeff Porcaro is on one of the tracks, 'Night by Night,'" Walsh recalls. (Actually, Jeff was also on "Parker's Band" with Jim Gordon.) "We all knew of him, so we were all over this track and that's all we listened to. That was, 'Oh my God, Jeff is on this song—he got on a Steely freakin' Dan record!' We thought that was an amazing feat."

A few years later Walsh got the gig with Seals & Crofts, playing alongside Ralph Humphrey on drums and Bobby Lichtig on bass. In '76 they recorded a live album, which was the first album on which Walsh had ever played. That year, Lichtig left for a period of time (when his wife had a baby), and Marty recalls Mike Porcaro filling in, which is when he says he got to know Mike well.

Three years later, Marty played on a demo of "Love Pains," co-written by his brother Dan and intended for Yvonne Elliman. Producer Steve Barri hired Jeff and Mike Porcaro to play on the track, with Michael Omartian on keyboard and Jay Graydon on guitar. They called three other guitar players, but no one was available on that day. Since Marty had already played on the demo, Omartian had already written Marty's guitar part into the chart.

"They were going to hire somebody to read my guitar part that was going to be on this record, and it's totally featured," Walsh says. "So I get this call, and I show up and there's Jeff. Wow! Mike's there; we had just been on the road together, so we're palling around. And Jeff remembers me! So we do this session. It was about three of the best hours I ever had in the recording studio. I had just gotten this new amplifier: a Roland JC120, which had two 12″ speakers and a chorus effect that moved from speaker to speaker—and every guitar player at the time was playing in mono. I knew the studio and I knew the engineer, and I had enough balls to say to the engineer, Joe Bogan, 'Put two mic's on this thing, pan it left and right, and you're going to pee in your pants.' So we cut this track and everybody comes into the studio to listen, and my guitar is blasting through the speakers in stereo. Everybody is going, 'Wow, what is this?' All of a sudden, I'm a cat. That session put me on the map."

In the early '80s Walsh was on a two-day record date where Jeff could only make the first day. An unnamed drummer was on the second. "The first day the arranger gives me a chart and says, 'I need you to play this eighth-note guitar part as a setup in an intro that I'm going to build; I need you to give me four bars of this thing.' There's no click track, so Jeff goes, 'Ok, you ready?' I go, 'Yeah.' He counts it off: 'One, two, three, four,' and I start playing. I've got his hi-hat on one side of my headphones, and I'm on the other side. He's playing a hi-hat part, and one bar in I'm saying to myself, 'Oh, Jeff's playing my right hand.' It was like I had to play his time. His hi-hat part wasn't going to be on the record, but he was essentially giving me a click track, (but instead of a click, it was) a groove that was so strong that I remember consciously thinking, 'Wow, this feels great.'

"The next day it starts out the same: Arranger, give me the setup, four bars, drummer, count off: 'One, two, three, four,' and I get click, click, click, click. One bar in, I go, 'This isn't Jeff. Now I gotta fend for myself.' I gotta play my time to essentially what is a click track, which is not easy to do. Playing to a click without any type of groove is not easy to do. I tell that story because it really demonstrated to me what differentiated Jeff from everybody else. It was, 'Even when I'm giving the guitar player a click, I'm going to give him the baddest-ass groove I can give him.' It was that important to Jeff to give me that groove. For the next guy it was, 'Well, this is just a click track, so who cares?'"

Walsh says every time he'd walk in the studio and see Jeff's drums, he knew it would be a good day. He recalls a session with Porcaro for a Japanese production. "I remember being at Bill Schnee's studio one time, cutting with him. He was looking at me with those glasses and smiling; his tongue was sticking out and we were grooving, and the feeing was just, oh geez…" Walsh struggles to find the words. "He had that way of looking at you when it was good, like, 'This is fricken cool.' We cut a track and I forget exactly, but I think we went in to listen and the producer asked Jeff to stay on the drums. I was sitting on the couch and the producer had Jeff out there fixing stuff. I was looking at Jeff sitting at the kit and listening to this guy talking behind me and thinking, 'Do you know who you're talking to? This guy just gave you the greatest track you could possibly get, and you're making him think about it and go fix things?' You don't do that with Jeff. And it wasn't like the whole band had to go do it again; it was like, 'Everybody's parts are cool, but Jeff, you have to fix this.' It was so surreal."

Walsh saw Jeff every now and then, and one of Walsh's fondest memories was in 1989 when he ended up on a session with him for an album (*Perfect)* with contemporary Christian artist Benny Hester. The musicians on the two days of tracking were Porcaro, Walsh, Neil Stubenhaus and Aaron Zigman. On the second day of tracking, Walsh was early and so was Jeff. When Jeff arrived, he said to Walsh, "Hey, have you heard this band Living Colour? There's this song called 'Cult of Personality,' man, that's great." Walsh told him he hadn't heard it, and Jeff left the studio. About twenty minutes later, Jeff came back in. "He walks right by me, doesn't say a word and drops a cassette (of Living Colour) right on my music stand," Walsh remembers.

Talking about recording that project, Walsh observes: "Jeff didn't play on the click necessarily; he moved ahead, he moved behind, he moved the time kind of around the click. He wasn't into being totally metronomic. He was into being musical, so if it needed to be a little bit back, it was back. If it needed to be front, it was a little in front. But I recall there was one moment where we hit the bridge of one of the tunes and this click track is going—because there were sequenced parts to this project—and all of a sudden, I'm going, 'Wait a second, Jeff is pumping way ahead of the click here.' He was getting somewhat dramatically ahead. Of course, I'm playing with him, I'm not playing with the click track. The whole band is going with him. It's an eight-bar bridge. We get to the eighth bar and what he's done is worked it musically, so he had extra time to stretch this fill out to be a long and most perfect fill. Many drummers would have gotten ahead of the click and gone, 'Oh no, what am I going to do?' And they would have played something to try to get back into the click and it would have sounded clumsy. But I think he did that on purpose so when he got to that last bar, he had this time and he wound that fill up and it was something to behold."

In 1991 Walsh got a call from Michael Omartian's office to play on a track for an artist named Ramone Carter. There were two days of tracking; the band was Jeff, Mike Porcaro and Lukather, but

Luke could not do the second day, so Walsh was called in his place. He hadn't worked with Omartian in quite some time, and when he arrived, Jeff said, "Yeah, I told Omar to call you." From then on, Walsh began getting calls from people he didn't know on sessions with Jeff, and Jeff would say: "I told the producer to give you a call." "I started doing dates that he recommended me for, which was the most validating experience I had as a musician, bar none," Walsh declares. "I played on fricken hit records, and they're just another day in the life, but the fact that Jeff would recommend me validated me as a player. He wouldn't do that if he didn't like your playing. So he liked playing with me enough that it was, 'Yeah, get this guy, I dig playing with him,' which meant everything to me."

Walsh says when Jeff passed away, knowing that there was no possibility of working with him again changed the overall aura of the music scene. He says he played with every great drummer on the scene, but there was nobody like Jeff. "There was something so special about his persona," Marty states. "I tell people I played guitar so differently when I played with Jeff. I thought of different things; I literally thought differently, I thought of different ways of playing guitar. It was like when he walked into the room this magic dust floated around and my brain went, 'Oh, how about doing it this way,' and I wouldn't have necessarily thought of doing it otherwise. It was the most incredible sensation. I guess it was because of his personality, who he was and his dedication to his craft. That sounds so trite, but it was contagious."

STEVE KHAN

Guitarist **STEVE KHAN** (Brecker Brothers, Billy Cobham, Billy Joel, Bob James, Aretha Franklin, Lou Rawls, Michael Franks,

Diane Schuur) met Porcaro and Lukather at a Columbia Records convention in London in the late '70s when they were playing with Boz Scaggs and he was playing with a singer named Marlene Shaw. "I remember they were really, really great and we hung out for a little bit," Khan recalls. "It was very frantic and very quick. Recording 'Gaucho' with Jeff was probably next." Recalling the early portion of the evening before Fagen and Becker left the studio throwing up their hands, Khan says if it had been his record, any one of Jeff's performances would have been perfect. "Jeff Porcaro played his ass off," Khan says. "Jeff gave it everything that he had, and on every single take!"

Khan mentions that Fagen and Becker did throw out four songs on *Gaucho*, although somehow a few songs in unfinished forms did make it online, such as "Kulee Baba." The internet credits Rick Marotta, but Khan insists the version posted is Jeff. "Those people are wrong," Khan tells me. "I'm sure that we did a version of that tune with Rick and maybe one with Purdie too, but that's Jeff. Also, *listen to that count-off—the sticks clicking*—Rick doesn't count-off like that."

Continuing to speak about "Kulee Baba," Khan says, "When I listen to that, in the choruses, there's something that I play, it's just a rhythm part, but it's some rhythm I play that I've tried to sit around here and duplicate, but I can't do it. I think there is something about the way Jeff was playing that made that possible. When you listen carefully to the track, it sounds like Chuck (Rainey) is still fishing around for what he should be playing. He's playing very minimalist through a lot of it and of course Don (Grolnick) is playing these big, beautiful chords, so most of the rhythm is coming from Jeff. But that was typically my experience with him: He just played so great."

In 1981 Khan worked with Porcaro on two Bobby Colomby-produced tracks on Pages' self-titled album. He reveals that when he flew out to Los Angeles from New York, he knew nothing about Pages' leaders, Richard Page and Steve George, but soon grew to appreciate them. "When I found out Jeff was playing, I would have flown myself out there to do it," he says with a laugh. "As always, Jeff was great, completely solid. He knew exactly the right thing to do. He made everybody else's job really easy. I think those are two fantastic tracks," Khan says, referring to "You Need a Hero" and "Come on Home."

Khan and Jeff worked together again on Randy Goodrum's *Fool's Paradise* in 1982. When I comment on the feel of "One Step Ahead of the Bad News," Khan says Jeff's double-time groove might have been over the top for another artist, but Goodrum and (producer) Scheiner loved it. "When he was playing that, it made me play something that I probably never would have played if he were not playing double time," Khan says. "Sometimes when you are playing a rhythm part, you obviously want all the pieces to fit, but I think I played, for some reason rhythmically more 16th-notey stuff, because that's kind of what Jeff was doing and it seemed to lock in with that. I would never have been the one to play double time while Jeff was playing straight time."

ROB MOUNSEY

Keyboardist **ROB MOUNSEY** met Jeff on the infamous "Gaucho" sessions. "All of the takes sounded so perfect. They were all to a click, by the way. I was reading something like a seven-page piano part that Donald had written, which was notated pretty completely, and we were focused so hard on being accurate and correct. Jeff was just amazing that way, because he had such total independence of two hands and two feet. His stuff was so unbelievably accurate. It felt great, too, but it was almost machine-like. He amazed me, the way he played that stuff. It's not just about a steady tempo, it's about all these figures and parts being really, really accurate. Everything is really in the exact slot. I really miss playing with rhythm sections like that," says Mounsey, who has played with the likes of Paul Simon, Aaron Neville, Carly Simon, Brian Wilson, Chaka Khan, Eric Clapton, James Taylor, Diana Ross, Natalie Cole and Rihanna. "Everything really becomes one big animal when everybody is finding the center of the pulse and all that; it's quite wonderful," Rob continues. "We felt like we had twelve perfect takes. We didn't know what was wrong with any of them."

Rob is astounded to find out that Jeff knew all along that all the performances except the drums were going to be erased; that all that work was being done to get the drum track. He says he's glad Jeff didn't let them in on the secret. "It's especially astounding to me because all of Jeff's performances sounded so correct to me," Mounsey declares. "I don't know what they were hearing that they didn't think was not quite there. That's a mystery."

In 1989, Mounsey worked with Porcaro when the keyboardist produced a record in L.A. called *There Were Signs* for a songwriter named Bill Gable. Gable knew Jeff and was able to get him to overdub on a couple of tracks. Mounsey points out one of the cuts, "High Trapeze:" "Jeff was playing all these crazy Rototom sort of things; sounds like boobams. It kinda sounded like a whole lot of tuned bongos played with sticks. It's very cool. It's one of my favorite kind of songs—sort of fast and slow at the same time, so there's sort of fast-tempo percussion streaming by, but it's sort of light and then there's kind of a broad, slow melody across it. That's one of my favorite things: both fast and slow happening at once."

ABRAHAM LABORIEL, SR.

"Did you ever hear about the time Jeff broke up a fight in the studio?" **ABRAHAM LABORIEL, SR.** asks me.

No, that's one I never heard. He proceeds to tell me the story, choosing to leave out incriminating names, but wanting to share it to demonstrate the kind of person Jeff was.

The argument was between a notable artist and notable engineer. The artist was nervous, and the artist asked the engineer if he was recording digitally or analog? The engineer said it was analog, direct to disc. "The artist said, 'You are a liar. You're a liar because I only prepared my voice to record digitally,'" recalls Laboriel. "We had been recording most of the day and everyone was tired. The engineer said, 'Don't call me a liar, and especially not in front of all these people; you cannot do that.' And the artist said, 'Man, I am not prepared to sing analog today.' Then they were about to come to blows. Jeff got off the drums and ran and stood in the middle of them and said, 'Guys, guys, guys, we are here to make music. This is ridiculous. Let's everybody play the music; let's everybody get the take and then everybody go home.' I was very impressed because he just ran and stood in front of these people that were about to hurt each other."

Laboriel moved to Los Angeles on July 4,1976, and met Jeff shortly after that. It was on a session produced by (then Elektra staff producer) Greg Prestopino for Gabe Kaplan ("Welcome Back Kotter") that resulted in a single called "Up Your Nose." Laboriel knew

Prestopino from Boston. The session had Jeff on drums, Fred Tackett on guitar, Bill Payne on keyboards, Doug Livingston on pedal steel and Little Feat percussionist Sam Clayton. "We had the time of our lives," Laboriel recalls. "And it was an instant love affair with Jeff."

Abraham says he was blown away that Porcaro knew who he was from the get-go. Laboriel had played several songs on Boston artist Andy Pratt's self-titled debut album, which contained a minor hit, "Avenging Annie." It was his very first recording session in the United States while going to school at Berklee. "When I met Jeff, he immediately said, '"Avenging Annie!" That's my favorite recording in the whole world,'" Abraham recounts. "That was the encounter. He made it clear from the beginning that he knew who I was and that he already loved me." (Although I can't find confirmation of this, apparently Jeff told Laboriel that the record was in violation of the RIAA for being too loud, but he had been able to get one of the few copies before they re-mastered it to conform with RIAA regulations.)

"To make a long story short, I was brand new in town, and Jeff started to recommend me," says the bassist, who would go on to be a first-call session player, recording with the likes of George Benson, Al Jarreau, Barbra Streisand, Elton John, Herbie Hancock, Dolly Parton, Michael Jackson, Madonna, Stevie Wonder, Paul Simon, Quincy Jones, Billy Cobham, Larry Carlton and Donald Fagen. "It took about two years before I started to be trusted in Los Angeles by people. But what happened as a result of that encounter with all of those musicians when we were recording for that Kaplan session, Greg asked me if I wanted to do a demo for Elektra as a solo artist." Laboriel re-assembled all those musicians for that demo, which he says was incredible. "Jeff was a ringleader, and for the first three months in town and on every session they had for other people that I was a part of, he would ask everybody to please jam and rehearse my charts so that when the time came to record, everybody would be prepared," Abraham recalls. "That's how it started. We didn't know each other from anybody."

One of the surprising conversations Laboriel had with Jeff was how Jeff really didn't care about playing drums as much as he did about being an artist. "He said, 'The best hands in the Porcaro family belong to my brother Mike,'" Laboriel recalls. "'And he also didn't care about the drums.' I said, 'Come on Jeff, you must be putting me on,' and he said, 'No, it's true.' So I asked Mike and Mike said, 'Yes, I have the best hands of the whole family, but I don't want to play drums.'"

Laboriel got choked up a couple of times during our talk. Once, as he told me about conversations with Jeff's father Joe: "Joe said, 'Because Jeff became so successful at such a young age, his bones were still developing when he was performing every day at the top of his ability. Because of that, he was chronically in pain.' The idea that all the enjoyment that we drew from hearing him every day, he was giving it to us while ignoring some pain," Laboriel says tearfully, "Joe said he believes that was the reason he was chain-smoking marijuana: to manage the pain to the best of his ability."

While Jeff never really spoke of the pain, it was common knowledge that he didn't like to do a lot of takes. He was outspoken when he believed the take had been gotten. Laboriel recalls a story where they had played a song once in a session with producer Tommy LiPuma and artist Randy Crawford when Jeff spoke out to preserve his energy. "We started to play, and Jeff says, 'Hey Tommy, we are going to do a whole album, right?' And Tommy says, 'Yes.' And Jeff says,

'You have other songs, right?' And Tommy says, 'Yes.' And Jeff says, 'Well, why don't we put this song off until some other time,'" Laboriel recalls. "Tommy says, 'This is going to be one of the singles; I really want to do it now.' And Jeff says, 'Tommy, this song doesn't want to be played right now.' That's a quote I remembered my whole life. I never heard anybody say the song does not want to be played. Isn't that amazing? Give us another song and then we will come back to that. I don't know if it had to do with his pain or a special wisdom of his that we were going to do a whole album of ten or twelve songs. Eventually we recorded the song, and everything went fine."

Laboriel says on another session he heard Porcaro say, "Catch me in another space. Right now, I cannot play this. I need to be in another space to play this."

Playing live with Porcaro at the Baked Potato in Greg Mathieson's band was "out of this world," says Laboriel. "Greg and Jeff really loved each other a lot, and it was because of Jeff we ended up doing Larry Carlton's *Room 335* album." He describes Porcaro's playing at the Baked Potato as effusive. "He would just stand up and play with his drumsticks against the wall behind him," Laboriel recalls. "He would say to Greg, 'I don't want any solos, I want to play the music, I want to play the song,' but he would stand up and play the wall and then sit down and continue to play the groove."

The main difference between playing with Jeff in the studio and live, says Laboriel, was that in the studio Jeff never lost track that the purpose of being there was to create a record environment; the music needed to sound like a record—as opposed to sounding spontaneous. "That's the reason everyone wanted to hire Jeff," Laboriel asserts. “Because as disciplined as he was, he'd also sound spontaneous, so each time you'd listen to the take it would put a smile on your face.”

When Laboriel talks about playing with Porcaro, he says he created a cushion. “Every beat felt huge, like you had all the room in the world to find where you were going to put your personal attacks. Jeff had a way of making it seem just huge, whether it was fast or slow, because each beat was enormous. That was something he coined and owned. It defies explanation how he discovered the way he played like that, giving everyone so much room.”

On an Al Jarreau session with Jay Graydon producing, Laboriel overheard Graydon ask Jeff about playing with the click: He said, ‘Jeff, I wanted to ask you, sometimes you are right perfectly with the click and sometimes you are behind the click and then you go back to the click and then you go ahead of the click and then you go back to the click. How can you do that?’ Jeff looked at me and rolled his eyes,” Laboriel remembers. “He said, ‘Jay, if you want me to play with the click, hire anybody else. The moment you hire anybody else, you'll know I will prefer the music over the click.’”

One of the high-profile Jarreau tunes on which Jeff and Laboriel played together was “Mornin',” released in 1983. “That song was composed by David Foster to fulfill a publishing commitment he had in Japan. We were all really excited to play it. It was really hard to believe it was something that David wrote to fulfill an obligation. At the most we played it three times,” Laboriel remembers. “The moment we started to play it, it had a lope and a strength and commitment that was undeniable. One of the things Jeff would always do was he would see if they had demos and listen to the demo. If they did not have a demo, he would start playing and creating a feel, and the minute the producer would approve, he would say, 'Start rolling tape.' He had a lot of authority because, in retrospect, we now know he was in a lot of pain. And on the breaks, Jeff was very astute. He would say, 'Let me hear it and when I tell you, punch, but I don't want to do the whole song again.' He was a tremendous asset to recording because he was constantly resolving problems."

One time, Jeff was so pleased about getting Abraham a particular gig that he wasn't even on, that he insisted on picking the bass player up and taking him to it, staying and taking him home. It was for Donald Fagen's song "New Frontier" on *The Nightfly*. "He called me and said, 'I recommended you and they said yes, so I'm going to pick you up, I'm going to drive you and stay.' After four hours Donald and Gary Katz were happy, and they said they were done. Jeff said to me, 'I've never seen them do anything that fast, ever,'" Laboriel recalls. "That is another song in my memory of my very special relationship with Jeff."

Jeff also had a special relationship with Abraham's children. Laboriel fights tears again as he relays first, how Jeffrey treated his youngest son, making the point that it was even before Jeffrey had his own children and really knew that kind of connection. Then again, I remark to Abraham that Al Schmitt told a similar story in my first book, and all you had to read about was Jeff's relationship with his younger sister Joleen to know that he had an affinity for children way before having his own. "He treated him like his own child," Abraham says of his youngest, Mateo. "Mateo would be hanging with us in the studio. Mateo was young, maybe six or seven years old, and Jeff would say to him, 'I have an amazing collection of toy soldiers and I like to reenact wars, so you and I will get together, and we'll do that together.'

And Mateo no longer felt like he was my son, but he felt like he was Jeff's friend, and that was so important to him, that people would acknowledge his existence. Jeff was sensitive to that."

Through the years, Jeffrey was there for Abe Laboriel, Jr. "He and Abe, Jr. really hit it off, and when it came time for Abe to go to Berklee in Boston, Jeff called his father and said, 'Dad, I want you to give my drum set to Abe Jr. to bring to Boston.' Joe said, 'I cannot do that because it is the drum set I use to teach.' Jeff said, 'No, no, no, I want you to give that drum set to him. I will order you another kit and I will have it sent to your studio,'" Abraham recounts. "Jeff sent my son to Boston with the set he had learned to play on. He said to Abe, Jr., 'Day or night, no matter when, anytime you want to talk about anything, I am here for you.'"

By the time Abraham and I ended the conversation, we were both crying.

ANKA'S ACCOUNT

Porcaro played on three of **PAUL ANKA**'s albums, starting with *The Music Man* in 1977. Although Ed Greene is listed as another drummer on the album and the internet does not specify which players are on which tracks, Anka says Jeff recorded most of the album. In fact, Anka says he often scheduled his recording dates around Jeff's availability. It was very admirable to hear an artist of Anka's stature talk about how the whole team—the musicians and the engineers—is important to making a project.

Anka's own success began at age sixteen with his hit "Diana," and he swiftly became a teen idol with such songs as "Lonely Boy" and "Put Your Head on My Shoulder." Not everyone realizes Anka composed the "Theme for the Tonight Show Starring Johnny Carson" as well as Frank Sinatra's signature song "My Way."

Anka does not recall how he first came to be in touch with Porcaro but explains that the good players were always on his radar; as soon as Jeff's reputation as a drummer began to spread, he became aware of him. "And just to watch him come in at noon, and in most cases light up a joint…" Anka says, to which I interrupt, "Even on your sessions?" "Why not? Who am I to stop his creative process?" Anka responds. "I'm not angel-squeaky clean. As long as he played well, and he did, I was fine with that."

In 1983, Porcaro cut three tracks on Anka's *Walk a Fine Line.* Anka explains that he has always been hands-on in every aspect of his career, including the hiring for his projects. He says the producers would confer with him—after all, he was writing most of the songs and knew what he wanted the music to feel like. "Anytime we could get Jeff, we would want him for all the sessions for continuity, a vibe and sound, which he was amazing at," Paul declares. "His time was incredible, and like all great drummers, he knew how to tune his drums. The criteria for me, even to this day, is to get the same drummer on the whole album if possible, so that's what I did in meeting him and ultimately some of the rest of Toto who also played on my albums. They were on there, as was David Foster, who was a session player at the time. I brought him down on my plane from Vancouver and ultimately got him his green card.

"The drummer is key," Anka continues. "Even live. The

drummer and the bass player can really mess up a band. You want the best dynamic in terms of drums. We very carefully selected the band to accomplish what we wanted."

1989's *Somebody Loves You* was only released in Germany, but Anka managed to get Porcaro on six tracks, including one called "You and I," a duet with Dionne Warwick. Anka says he always cut basic tracks live with a rough vocal and in this instance brought Warwick in to overdub at the end. "In the case of Jeff, when you're a great drummer as he is, Jeff's time, his sound, his vibe, his passion in the way he played were paramount," Anka states. "In the hands of the wrong drummer, time, sound, vibe and passion, you're dead. It's a technical thing to where, if you don't have him on that session, any contribution from someone else just doesn't work. He just got it. He was just exceptional. And what a sweet guy and a great disposition!"

Anka recalls that Jeff also offered creative input. He sat around the piano and listened and would say, "Here's the way I hear it. Here's the tempo, here's the vibe." "Nothing else works until you lay it down with your basics with your drummer and your bass player," Anka reiterates. "You're absolutely nowhere without your drummer and your bass player."

BECOMING ROOMIES

Guitarist **DAN FERGUSON** came into the circle through David Paich. His father, Allyn Ferguson, was a jazz and film composer and had a close working relationship with Joe Porcaro and Marty Paich. Dan remembers going to sessions with his father at age twelve and seeing Joe and Emil Richards. Ferguson also remembers that the Paich

Family lived right down the street, and they would get together for family dinners and such. He and David, who was a few years younger than Dan, became friends.

"David and I played together and listened to records frequently and also recorded at the home studio of a French horn player named Bill Hinshaw, who even had built an echo chamber under his house!" Ferguson recounts. "David and I did our first recordings there. I was fifteen and Dave was twelve or thirteen. We listened to everything on the radio and the records our dads brought home from sessions. My dad arranged for Sarah Vaughan, Andy Williams, and conducted for Johnny Mathis, who is still a friend. Mathis gave me a one-hundred-dollar bill for my twelfth birthday and I bought a Schwinn ten-speed. When Johnny came over next, he rode the bike but didn't know where the brakes were and crashed the bike. Nobody got hurt."

On one of Dan's breaks from college, David got him an audition for Sonny & Cher, who he was playing with (thanks to Jeff) when there was a sudden guitar vacancy. He auditioned with the band but didn't meet Sonny or Cher until ten minutes before his first gig with them in Indianapolis in front of 20,000 people. Dan had met Jeff a couple of times prior to playing with him on that stage, but the Sonny & Cher gig is where they cemented their friendship. Ferguson says he and Jeff got along famously from the start. What that means to Dan is that they had a similar sense of humor, and he describes Jeff as welcoming, outgoing, positive, full of love and mischief.

When Dan's roommate moved from the Wonderland Avenue rental house in Laurel Canyon in 1975, Jeff suggested he move in. He lived there for close to a year. "It was a wild house," Ferguson says, remembering the interesting multi-level layout of the house. "Jeff had the downstairs room, the lowest point in the house. It was really an odd-shaped house. There were a couple of steps up to the living room, which had a little alcove and the kitchen off of it. Then there was a whole flight of stairs to an upper level that was my bedroom; it was like a turret at the top of the house with a little balcony. It was almost like going to the basement to go to Jeff's room, which was a big room. It was like making a voyage going down to his room, or him coming up to my room would be special. We'd go out on the balcony."

Ferguson says Porcaro was particular about making his room nice and beautiful. "What I knew about him from being on the road and in the next hotel room was he always set up his room in a really nice way so he could groove," Dan recalls. "He either had a little lamp or something so he could make the light special, and he had little rock collections and his art placed around the room. So he made this downstairs bedroom very special. Jeff loved beautiful things, and he made environments for himself wherever he was," Ferguson says, comparing it to the way Jeff also dressed intentionally with statement every day. "It wasn't that he was particularly stylish, but he had a style," Dan remarks. "He looked up to Jim Keltner and you can see it in the way he dressed, with the leather vest and white shirt. And he always had that giant shit-eating grin on his face; that cat who ate the canary."

Dan says as roommates they weren't too domestic. Cooking? Well, Jeff might have brought some food from home and Dan might have done the same. He doesn't recall them being very tidy in the kitchen. In fact, he says it became such a disaster that his sister came over and cleaned it, which took a whole day.

The only time he ever saw Jeff in a crabby mood, Ferguson says, was after a shitty session or a relationship went awry. He said mostly he was very even-keeled and upbeat. He also mentions his talent for making people he liked feel so welcomed and vital. "Some people call it charm, but if he didn't like you, he didn't bother," says Dan. "I loved his excitement at playing music, and he knew how to enjoy people. He made you feel so special. He wanted to be with special people."

Later, after they lived together and Dan was buying a house in Sherman Oaks where he and his girlfriend (and wife-to-be) Adrienne Andros (who performed under the name Dede) were going to live, Jeff played on several projects in the studio Dan built. At Jeff's Hesby home studio, Dede recorded the vocals to the 1986 mini-series "Master of the Game," to which Dan's father wrote the score.

KENJI SHOCK

Until I saw a Steely Dan forum mentioning the album *Kenji Shock* from the artist Kenji Omura, the record was just another in Porcaro's huge discography. But someone on the forum touted his playing, so I dug deeper, listened, and sure enough, it was classic Jeff. Lo and behold, I discovered it was produced by none other than the wonderful drummer **HARVEY MASON, SR.**! Mason produced the album in Los Angeles in 1978 and decided he didn't want to play on the entire record, as he wanted to focus on the production. He did play on two tracks but hired Porcaro to play on the remaining six. As soon as the record company sent him the music to listen to, he thought about what players he wanted. "I come from the Quincy Jones School," Mason explains. "It's like a movie: Who are you going to cast? Who is going to best handle this and have it be as painless as possible?

Immediately I knew I wanted it to be Jeff, because I loved the way he played. He played so sensitively, he played with groove, and he didn't play any extraneous junk. He was really my only choice."

Harvey says he knew Jeff pretty much from the time he moved to town in 1970. He knew Jeff's father Joe and had heard Jeff's playing. "I heard a couple of things he did and loved his groove," Harvey recalls. "I loved the way he played, and I loved his spirit."—so if Mason wasn't going to play on Omura's record, it was definitely going to be Jeffrey "because I could just hear what he would bring to the record."

Mason says the songs were great, from a terrific artist who died far too young from a drug overdose. Jeff really cooks and gets to stretch out on the first track, "Left-Handed Woman." Although it's not something he did on every session, Mason sensed given the opportunity, Porcaro would thrive. "He just needed to be in the environment," Harvey says. "People like to pigeonhole musicians, but great musicians have a wide scope; I knew he would love the chance to get to do that. There was no question in my mind that he could handle that—I didn't have to say anything. He just heard the demo and went to his place."

Mason says he never had to give any kind of direction to Jeff. "I hired Jeff because I didn't have to say anything to him. I didn't have to say like, 'Maybe you want to do this,' or 'Maybe you want to do that.' When you get great talent, you trust them to bring what they're going to bring to it. That's how you end up getting the best. That's what works the best. Jeff was wonderful and easy to work with," says Harvey, adding that Porcaro would have ideas and offer suggestions as well.

Mason says Porcaro was not in the least bit intimidated by the fact that Harvey, a notable drummer, was producing him. "Jeff was very secure with who he was. Jeff was just a very cool guy, cool in the sense of being a very cool guy, so even if he was intimidated, you would never know it, because he was so cool," Mason says with a laugh. "But he had been around a lot of great musicians and playing with a lot of great musicians. He wasn't intimidated. I knew what he would bring to the project, and I certainly understood about leaving the playing to the musicians and that I could hire him and not have to say anything."

Mason says Omura was very pleased to be in the room with the talent Mason chose. "He was pretty quiet," Mason says. "He didn't speak a lot of English, but he was ecstatic about the record."

STRANGERS IN LAUREL CANYON

Sometime around 1975, a nicely-attired Jeff was driving up Laurel Canyon in his flashy car when he spotted a long-haired guy making his way up the hill on foot. He stopped to see if the stranger needed a ride. **STAN LYNCH**'s van was parked at the bottom of the street, at the Country Store, due to a broken transaxle. "I hear a car pull up behind me, and I figure it's probably pulling into its driveway, but then it pulls up beside me and the window comes down—electric window, by the way. This is all like a miracle to me," recounts Lynch. "It's a black; pretty sure it's a beemer—it's just a different universe. I may as well have been abducted by aliens (laughs). I see this cool dude with a real shirt, and he's got beautiful shades. There are cool tunes playing, and he says, 'Yo, need a ride?' And I say, 'Well, yeah, I do.' I'm thinking, 'Whoa! What is this weird encounter I'm having that I'm not sure I should be having?' Within two seconds he says the magic words: 'Are you a musician?' 'Yeah!' (The magic word in 1975.) 'What do you play?' 'Drums.' He says, 'I'm a drummer. I play.' I'm thinking, 'Whatever he's doing, it's all working for him.' I didn't even understand the rules of the game. He's about a year older than I am, but he's in a whole different league—everything about him. I think I was working at Peaches Records on Hollywood Blvd., so everything was wrong."

Leaving his Gainesville, Florida home at sixteen, Lynch moved into a house with the members of Tom Petty's band. When they left for California, he was still in high school, so he couldn't join them, but he eventually quit school and made his journey west in a van with his drum set and P.A. At the time of this odd meeting with Jeff, Lynch was living in a basement without running water and auditioning for bands through the then-popular Musician's Contact Service.

Lynch recalls that Jeff lived right off the main drag of Laurel Canyon and Porcaro invited him to hang out. Lynch couldn't believe it when they pulled into the driveway of an actual *house*—not an apartment. "It was beautiful; it was decorated, and it had style," says Lynch. "It wasn't Playboy magazines and an ashtray full of butts, which was closer to my reality. He had floor-to-ceiling electrostatic speakers; he basically had a reference playback system in his house, complete with a Revox two-track, I think MacIntosh power amps; everything out-of-the-catalog of cool. Now I'm taking stock of this guy and going, 'So, yo, what are you working on?' And he says, 'I just did a session last night. You wanna hear it?' I'm thinking, 'A session? What?' We were probably working on the first Petty album, and we didn't know they were called sessions. We were just recording. I'm pretty sure he spun a rough of 'Black Friday,' and it sounded stunning. I remember we smoked a bunch of his weed and it was amazing, and I was smoking his

Marlboros—real cigarettes—and we were sitting in his beautiful place and just listening to this.

"I probably could have asked him some questions, and he would have had all the right answers if I had only known the right questions. I wasn't grown up enough to know the right questions. I was probably asking, 'What kind of drums do you play? What kind of sticks do you use?' I was greener than shit, and he took it like a champ. He asked where we were working, and I told him we were working at a little place called Shelter Records. He said, 'I think I've heard of Shelter Records,' probably because Leon Russell and Jimmie Lee (Keltner) and Jim Gordon were all into that Shelter camp. Maybe I dropped one breadcrumb that made me appear not to be a complete dildo. But he was so cool and so kind. I remember talking about my band and telling him we were from Florida, and then he took me back to my crib. I remember going upstairs and there was a singer living there who was a little further up the food chain in the music business, and he said, 'Nice car you just got dropped off from.' I said, 'Yeah, it was a guy named Jeff Porcaro.' He said, 'Oh, wow!' And then he gave me chapter and verse: 'Here's what you just left—you were swimming in the bigs.'"

Of course, one day Tom Petty and the Heartbreakers became huge, and there came a time when Stan and Lukather began writing together, and Lynch did sessions. Notable guitarist and songwriter Danny Kortchmar hired Stan, and Lukather was in that circle. "When I ran into Luke, one of my first questions was, 'Tell me about Jeff Porcaro,'" Lynch recounts. "And Luke, as you can imagine, would almost fall to his knees when he would talk about Jeff. 'He's just the coolest guy in the world, the Porcaros are everything to me, I love them,' and if anyone was dumb enough to ask what Jeff played like, all he'd say was, 'Just the most amazing thing you'll ever hear.' Luke and I became friends, so he invited me to sessions that I think Toto was doing, although they might have been his sessions and Jeff was there. And now we're meeting."

Then Lynch started working with Kortchmar, and Luke said he should be writing songs. One day Stan came into the studio with a lyric for "Kick Down the Walls." "Jeff was the arbiter of anything that went down on a Toto record. Everything went through Jeff," Stan explains. "So when I came in, Luke said, 'Give it to Jeff. He needs to read it.' Jeff knows who I am at this point, I sat on the couch, he read it and quoted a couple of lines. One in particular I remember was where I made reference to a 'big old human clock,' and he said, 'That's cool.' Then he looked at me and I said something like, 'You know, we've met and we have a few things in common. I've been in your orbit for a long time, all the way back to '70-something when you gave me a lift home.' He kinda gave me a look sideways and went something like, 'That was you?'

"I'm pretty sure I was there when he cut 'New York Minute' because of Danny and Don, and I couldn't believe it. He was obviously, from my perspective, the finest musician I ever saw play live in the studio. I never got to see anybody of that level. That quick study of his was amazing," Lynch states. "I was in a band that would do sixty takes. We would literally play the same song for three days. We were that insane with crazy producers: 'Now we're going to try it with you standing on your head.' Jeff was the height of professional class. When you're in a room with cats like Luke and Kootch and Henley and Porcaro, you know the kindest thing you can say is, 'Anybody need coffee?' I would sit and watch Jeff's process. He would listen to a demo, and I didn't see him make a note on a piece of paper, ever. I'm sure he did, but on this stuff, he didn't. He just intuitively knew. He seemed like he knew what he was going to play before he played it. He could pretty much play anything, so if he could think it, he didn't have any problem translating that into his hands. And it was all felt. Everybody talked about his groove, but the sound...," Stan pauses to find the words. "That's the thing that fucked my head up. I remember when he sat down to play, the sound of his drums, and it wasn't the sound of his drums, it was the sound of *him.* Anybody could have played Jeff's drums, but it wouldn't have sounded like *that.* It was *him.* It was a specific sound that came from his hands and his attitude and his pulse and the way he leaned into it and the way he talked to those drums. I mean he just pulled the sound right out of that kit."

When Toto actually was in the process of recording "Kick Down the Walls," Stan recalls the day Jeff overdubbed his part. (In *It's About Time*, Lukather recounted how Jeff nailed the song in one take, everyone was jumping up and down, and Stan was completely blown away.) "I remember feeling like, 'There's no way you can overdub to this,'" says Lynch. "That's what I was thinking as they were playing the demo. 'I don't know where you do this. I don't know where this is going to go.' And I just remember thinking Jeff had church bell balls. He listened to the track, he went out and on the first pass he was getting his headphones together. He'd play the groove for a couple of bars, and you'd see him point to the bass drum, his finger up or down, point his finger up or down to the overheads, talking through the glass in shorthand for about two minutes. Then Danny said, 'What do you think?' And I don't remember the exact quote, but Jeff said something like, 'Let's twist one,' some reference to burning a joint. It was something cool that Jeff would say like that. And there wasn't even a fuckin' count on the song. He just closed his eyes and played the motherfuckin' record top to bottom, four and half minutes of this deep groove and there wasn't a missed…" Lynch stops with amazement. "I could have spent a week trying to edit a track like that together. I couldn't have done it. And he did it top to bottom with such panache. The place went fuckin' mental. He got up, walked in, ordered a sandwich, threw on his cool man bag, and walked out of the room saying he had to do something, and he'd be back to eat the sandwich. His voice, the physical beauty of him. If the motherfucker hadn't been the greatest drummer on earth, he would have been the coolest voiceover guy and the coolest actor or male model. You put it all together and lightning strikes and you get Jeff fucking Porcaro. Even shirts hung on him right. I always wondered, 'How can this motherfucker tuck in a beautiful shirt and not look like a geek?' And the smile."

When Lynch saw Porcaro in the Toto configuration, he says he never saw such admiration for a fellow band member. "They were literally cheering in the room while he was playing, they were screaming," Lynch remembers. "Like Jeff would take a corner at sixty miles an hour, he'd take this beautiful corner, rhythmically, and come right out just beautifully—picked a beautiful line through the curve—came out and when he'd stick the landing, the guys would sound like little girls going over in a rollercoaster. And Jeff never looked up. He just did it. And that freaked me out, too, because they were in a band and they were successful, they were obviously at the top of their game, and yet, they still loved each other—which was not what I was experiencing in my band at all. I was experiencing very bizarre behaviors; there was a lot of envy, posturing and false bravado—and I walk into a Toto session, and it was like boys in a sandbox playing with their trucks."

Lynch felt the love. While Lukather was playing a solo, he made Stan stand right next to him. "He didn't want me on the couch. He wanted me hip-bumping with him," Lynch says. "I dreamed that's what it would be like when I was a little kid; that I'd be in a bar band and I would grow up and all these guys would love me and it would be wonderful and we'd play this great music—and they were actually doing it. They were doing everything at the pinnacle. They were still high-fiving and smiling, and they couldn't wait to light each other's cigarettes. It was extraordinary. It was beautiful. I don't think I'll ever see anything like that again. It was pretty much without guile, without ego. It was stunning."

On Toto's *Isolation* tour, 1985. (Courtesy of Barney Hurley)

CHAPTER THREE

The Eighties

ANOTHER DRUMMER: HENLEY

(Note: I was able to connect with Henley, but only via a one-time emailed list of questions through his manager. I asked for as much detail as possible, but in these situations there is no control, hence the brevity of his comments. It is always difficult for a journalist to conduct an interview in an email, when it is not possible to follow up an answer with a question to further the information. The answer gets left at a sentence in that format, whereas in a telephone conversation there is the opportunity to further the story and recollections by additional probing. Either way, I am grateful he consented to participate.)

When **DON HENLEY** decided to cut his first solo album in the early '80s, the Eagles—the band of which he had been a founding member in 1971—had already been mega-successful with such hits as "Take it Easy," "Lyin' Eyes," "Take It to the Limit," "Best of My Love," "One of These Nights," "Heartache Tonight," "Hotel California" and more. What is now known as the beginning of a fourteen-year "hiatus" was seen in 1980 as a breakup, so the band members were all on their own.

Henley says prior to his first solo endeavor, *I Can't Stand Still,* he believes he met Jeff briefly once. "I think I met Jeff in 1981, at some club in Westwood, where some kind of fundraiser was being held," he wrote to me through his management. "I didn't know anybody there, but Jeff introduced himself and invited me to sit down with him in his booth."

When it came time to make his album, Henley says he believes it was Danny Kortchmar who brought Porcaro to the project. Kortchmar confirmed that in a phone discussion: "Yes, it was my idea," Danny says. "And why not? Everyone was hiring Jeff. He was the best. That was what I was there for. Don really didn't know any of those guys; that wasn't the world he lived in. Of course, he knew of Jeff. Everyone knew of Jeff. And Jeff could play any kind of material; he could do anything."

The ability to "do anything" included playing seamlessly along with a LinnDrum machine, as in the case of "Dirty Laundry" on Henley's inaugural solo album. As discussed in *It's About Time*, when I asked Jeffrey about his work on the hit song, he said simply, "'Dirty Laundry' is just me laying it down. It was an electronic track, meaning it was sequenced. That Farfisa organ part is a sequence going down, so I was just bashing. I played 1 on the bass drum, 2 and 4 on the snare. I'm just pounding. It's just a groove." I thought I'd get Henley's take on what Jeff brought to the track, and in my written question I told him what Jeff had said to me about it. His answer was: "I think that there might have initially been a LinnDrum machine on Danny's demo track, but Jeff brought life to that track. He brought groove and attitude."

Porcaro played four tracks on Henley's *I Can't Stand Still* and both Kortchmar and Henley agree that Jeff's versatility led them to pick him to play on "New York Minute" from Henley's third offering, *The End of the Innocence.* "I think he was the obvious and unanimous choice of both myself and Kootch," Henley asserts. "Jeff had jazz chops and parts of that song are a little bit jazzy. Jeff also knew how to not 'step on' the lead vocal. His playing was always tasteful, and his time was perfect."

Danny says Porcaro's choreography between the sticks and brushes was astounding; that he changed between the two without missing a beat. (Note: For complete details, see *It's About Time*.)

When asked if he had any specific memories of spending time with Jeff, Henley's response was: "I remember Jeff as a great human being; an incredibly thoughtful man with an enormous generosity of spirit, a sharp sense of humor, and an enthusiasm that could lift any recording session or live performance to another level. His talent and his love of music were deep."

Kortchmar and Henley are of the same mind. "It was great being around him," Danny says. "Look, we're still talking about him all these years later. There will never be anyone like him. There are other great players; three of my best friends are drummers. But there will never be another Jeff Porcaro."

IVAN NEVILLE

The first time **IVAN NEVILLE** met Jeff, the singer/songwriter was in his early twenties. "Something came up where there was a song that I had written and performed with my dad and my uncles that Boz Scaggs was interested in recording and those guys worked with Boz. I was called to go to the session, which was taking place at Jeff's house. It was all the Toto guys and Boz, and they cut a track based on a demo I had done. It was a song called 'One Thing,' which never made it on the record," says Neville, who sang background vocals with Jim Gilstrap. "Then after that session, I got a call saying they wanted to re-cut it based more on my demo. I went back over to the studio and ended up playing some things, and I was fucking insane, playing with these guys on this song I wrote. It was a dream come true. I remember one day we had Popeye's chicken; they knew I was from New Orleans. And one day David Paich even had a Neville Brothers shirt on. I was like, 'Oh my God!' I knew the song 'Rosanna' had a Bo Diddley, New Orleans vibe about it and all of that. That was my initial introduction to Jeff and all those guys. It was so cool." Although Neville recalls being in awe meeting all of them, "They were the sweetest guys to me," he says.

Ivan and Jeff crossed paths at various places. When Neville was working with Rufus, who was managed by Fitzgerald Hartley, he ran into Jeff from time to time, since Toto was also on their roster. Once in a while, they'd run into each other at Jeff's favorite market, Gelson's on Laurel Canyon in Studio City. "It felt really cool that the guy knew me!" says Ivan. "I thought, 'This guy played on *Thriller* and all these records—and I know the guy!'"

In 1987, Ivan was about to record his first album, *If My Ancestors Could See Me Now,* with Danny Kortchmar as producer. They were discussing who would play on the record; of course Danny was going to play some guitar, and Ivan was going to play a lot. They hired Porcaro to cut most of the drum tracks (Steve Jordan plays two songs: "Money Talks" and "Primitive Man," with Porcaro on Latin percussion on the latter. Jim Keltner also adds some electronic machinery on "Primitive Man."). As Neville recalls, all three drummers played together. "Those three guys so respected each other," he remarks. "They were in awe of each other."

Neville says probably his favorite cut on the record is "Not Just Another Girl," but "Sun" is also a favorite. "That song has that weird turnaround, and I had no idea how someone would interpret that or how they would play to that," Neville says. "Jeff couldn't have played something more perfect and fitting than what he played. What I got from him was he was arguably one of the four greatest drummers, along with Charlie Drayton, Steve Jordan and Jim Keltner (in no particular order), just depending on the day and what song and who else was playing. There's just a thoughtfulness and unselfishness in Jeff's playing when he was contributing to a song; he made the song something it wouldn't have been without his contribution. 'Sun' is an example of that, and so is 'Not Just Another Girl,' because I couldn't imagine that song feeling the way it did until Jeff played on it. I played bass on that song and that's one of my favorite things—I played fucking bass with Jeff Porcaro! The way that song built and the way it made me sing—especially toward the back of the song—is amazing. He did this one drum fill that was so signature. He did it one time in the song. It was a fucking drum roll, and he went to a ride cymbal thing out of that, and it took that song somewhere I never imagined. You're talking about a song that has some loopy shit in it and sequenced keyboard shit going on in it. It wasn't stiff because of what he did and us playing to it; what he did made that song build the way it did. I remember playing that song live and I wanted whoever was playing with me to capture what he played. You had to make it your own but have Jeff's mindset if you could. Over the years I've played it differently myself."

Neville also mentions "After All This Time." "It's a ballad and Hutch (James "Hutch" Hutchinson) played fretless bass. I think he's probably pretty proud of that song. That song has a signature flam kind of fill on the tom-toms. I've heard him do similar things on other songs like on Toto's 'I Can't Hold You Back.' And my dad is on that song, too, so you get the fucking voice of Aaron Neville. When I think about making that record…" Ivan's voice trails off.

"Another song that comes to mind is 'Another Day's Gone By.' Jeff did one of those classic drum fills to open the song up," Neville recalls. "Such a great group of people came together to make that record, and I felt so honored. Randy Jackson played bass on that song, and J.D. Souther sang harmony with me. How cool is that? Bonnie Raitt is on 'Falling Out of Love,' which was based on a LinnDrum pattern that I had come up with; Jeff put a beautiful groove on that with the machine still playing. Keltner put that silly electric drum on it that he carried around. He had this little machine with all these sampled weird sounding things that he was experimenting with, and he put some shit on some songs.

"The thing I most recall about Jeff doing those sessions was he was just so kind and cool toward me," Neville continues, "I just get choked up thinking about him and how nice he was. He just made me feel so cool. I'm a kid from New Orleans and I hadn't played on a bunch of records. I mean I was on the scene, but he always made me feel so fucking cool. He would share stuff with me. Everyone knew who he was. We were recording at A&M Studios and he'd pull up in his car. I remember he had that Mercedes with the license plate SODIGIT—he'd always say that: 'So dig it.' So, the way we were making the record, we were playing everything to these killer drum tracks—and Jeff was there the whole time. He just chose to be there the whole time, even though I'm sure he had other things he could have been doing. After the drums were done, he kept showing up. That meant the world to me."

When he listens to that album, even to this day, Neville feels Jeff's soul. "It's so rewarding to me." He then chuckles as he recalls, "Jeff had this walk about him. He had this little strut. As cool as you knew he was because all the stuff he recorded on—fucking Steely Dan, 'Rosanna'—he was just as friendly and sweet and as nice of a guy and made you feel special. I can picture his walk. It was so badass. But he was the most humble fucking dude. You felt good that he knew you and respected you; you really felt that much better about yourself."

Neville remembers one day driving down Porcaro's block and seeing him outside. He pulled over just as the managers, Fitzgerald and Hartley pulled up. They had just fired Bobby Kimball. "It was a hard day, I'm sure," Ivan says, remembering that Jeff excused himself, telling Ivan he had to go talk to them because there was some "shit going down."

Neville later did more recording with Jeff that was to be his second record, but it was never released. "I remember at that time Jeff telling me that Miles (Davis) recorded with them, and Jeff was smiling from ear to ear, he was so fucking proud."

The last time Ivan saw Jeff was on Jeff's last sessions, Paul Young's *The Crossing*, where Neville was called to play organ on "Cold Sweat." Neville says he was in a dark place at the time. He recalls that his car had been in a wreck, and he hadn't gotten it fixed, so he had to take a cab to the session. His ex-wife and daughter were with him. "I didn't have a ride home. I was going to catch a cab, but Jeff gave us a ride. I was living in North Hollywood at the time, off Tujunga and Burbank," Ivan remembers. "I was really in a bad place at the time. That was the last time I saw him."

Around seven years later, around 1999, Neville—now in a better frame of mind—was attending a friend's housewarming party on

Hesby Street. "The only other person I knew who had lived on Hesby Street had been Jeff Porcaro," Neville recalled at the time. "I never put anything together about the location of his house. There were a lot of people at the house; it was evening time and it was getting dark. My friend had the backyard lit up pretty nice and the vibe was cool. She brought me to this back little garage, into this certain area and said, 'I want to show you this because you're a musician. I rent this out to musicians who want to rehearse in this little spot.' I go into this little back shed area and it was so surreal. I look around and think, 'Fuck, I've been here before.' It was fucking Jeff's house! I said, 'I think this was my friend's house.' It was so weird."

LUIS CONTE

LUIS CONTE says the instant he met Jeff (and Joe) Porcaro, he felt like they were family. "Jeff treated me like I knew him forever," Conte says. Luis was in high school the first time he saw Jeffrey play at a big drumming event. "It was a big deal; I had no idea about anything, I was just a kid in high school, and I went by myself, but I heard people talking: 'Jeff Porcaro is going to play later.' Jeff Porcaro, who is this guy? I didn't know who he was. It had to be around '71. And there he was. He came in and played with a band, and I can't tell you who they were, but it was, 'Yeah, whoa, I saw that guy play, he played great, that's Jeff Porcaro.'"

Much of the time in the studio, Conte would overdub percussion to Jeffrey's drum tracks, but there were times they got to record live together. Conte recalls, "Some song for a movie I can't remember, but it was at A&M and I remember the one thing about playing with Jeff, I turned the click off and just played with him. His time was just so unique. If I listened to the click and played with him and listened back, it just didn't feel right, but if I just played with him, it felt right. The only other drummer that happened with, for me, was Steve Jordan."

Luis was on the session discussed previously by Abraham Laboriel, where friction began between the artist and engineer, and he concurs that Jeff had the ability to smooth things over between people. "If shit was coming apart, he would figure out a way of getting it together," says Conte. "He was a peacemaker."

In 1988, Jeff called Luis because Lenny Castro was not able to go on the upcoming Toto tour. "He said, 'Hey man, Lenny can't go on this tour. Can you recommend somebody?' I went, 'What's the tour? When is it? How long?' I said, 'Shit! I'll do it.' He said, 'Really? Oh man, I didn't want to ask you because I didn't think you'd want to go. But you're on the gig!' I talked to their managers, and it was six weeks

Luis Conte and Jeff. (Courtesy of Luis Conte)

in Europe and a little bit in Canada. I am so blessed that I was able to do it in hindsight now," Conte says. "I'm so glad I did that tour, in every way: musically, friendship-wise. If I hadn't done it, it would have been a huge regret."

Even the best of musicians wanted to tell Porcaro how they felt about his playing, but Luis says Porcaro did not enjoy receiving compliments. Still, Conte seized the opportunity one day on the train going somewhere in Europe. "He's sitting across from me in this little compartment, just he and I alone," Luis recalls. "I thought, 'Man, I gotta tell Jeff how I feel about him and his playing,' so I said, 'Man, your feel, and the way you play, and just your feel when you play and your groove and your shuffles and all that stuff you're so great at,' and he just stopped me and said, 'Stop! That ain't me, man. That's John Bonham and Bernard Purdie. Don't even tell me.' He was that kind of cat."

"Africa" was in the tour setlist, of course, with the live version featuring drums and percussion playing a feature together, without the band. Conte didn't realize that Jeff didn't like to solo. "There's that percussion moment, so I said to Jeff, 'We're going to do this thing. Are you going to play?' He said, 'No, no, no, I just hold the time down, man, you do your thing, I just hold the time down, blah, blah, blah.' Well, Lukather told me later that I was the only guy who ever made him stretch out even a little bit," Conte says. "After the tour got going and we kept playing 'Africa' and started opening the shit up, Jeff started to open up just a hair. I mean he wasn't quite doing a drum solo thing where everyone stopped or anything, but he started stretching out a little bit. Playing with him was amazing and I'd be the first one to say that my playing improved after playing on that tour with him, in some way. I don't know how; I just know I was a better player after I finished playing with him for those months."

Jeff and the guys loved their pranks (a few are recounted in *It's About Time*) and Conte recalls a great one Jeff played on their road manager, Martin Cole, on the last date of this tour, which was at the Hammersmith Odeon in London. "Martin was from London, so Jeff said, 'We have to figure out how to bust him.' You know how Jeff loved to draw; he drew a caricature of Martin, but as a cross dresser," Luis recalls with laugh. "Then Jeff and Luke kept building on it and brainstorming—'And then we're going to do this, and then we're going to do this…' and they came up with this whole thing. It got so deep that they ended up printing up big posters that you put up on light poles in the streets, and they paid somebody to put these posters all over the route we would take from the hotel to the Hammersmith Odeon. The slogan on the poster said: 'Vote Gay, Vote Martay.' It was hilarious." According to Luis, Jeff was as excited as a little kid on Christmas morning as they rode to the venue and he anticipated seeing the first poster. "Jeff yelled, 'There it is!'" recalls Conte. "Martin's head went down and all he said was, 'Oh my God, my mother is going to see this.'"

In early '92, Jeff called Conte again to talk about the *Kingdom of Desire* tour, but Conte had just signed a contract to tour with a French artist with Abraham Laboriel and Steve Gadd. He didn't know a lot about the artist, but he had recorded the album, and it was a good job, so he had already committed. When he told Jeff this news, Jeff said "Oh wow, bummer, man. What's going on?" "I explained to him what it was; that it was a French artist named Michel Jonasz," Conte recalls. "He said, 'Who's in the band?' I said, 'Abraham is in the band. Gadd is in the band and Brad Cole.' He was quiet for minute and then he said—I'll never forget this—'Hey, let me ask you something. If your son needs some shoes, who's gonna buy the shoes?' 'Well, I am.' 'And your daughter, right? You're gonna buy her shoes, right?' 'Yeah right.' 'Well then, you have to go on that tour. Don't worry about it, man. When you get back, we'll play again.' That was Jeff. It was amazing. It was just, 'Who's gonna buy the shoes for your son? Then you gotta go do that tour, man. I'm sure it's a whole lot better tour than ours.'"

As fate would have it, Jeff would not make the Kingdom of Desire tour, either. "We continued the conversation," recalls Luis. "He was on his way to Florida, and so was I, because my family lives in Clearwater. We tried to hook up to maybe see each other in Florida, but it didn't happen. Jeff went home early. After I arrived in Clearwater, I was having dinner with my uncle. The TV was on, and (the news reported that Jeff had passed away). I couldn't believe it. I thought, 'I am never ever going to play with a drummer like that.' There was only one Jeff."

The last time Luis actually saw Porcaro was one day when he drove up to do a session at Capitol Records. He was parking his car as Porcaro was getting out of his. "I said, 'Hey man, are we on a session together?' He said, 'I'm in A with so and so.' I said, 'Oh, well I'm in B.' It's always super busy and usually I would go home after I finished, but that day I thought, 'Let me go over to A and see if Jeff's still there and say bye to him,'" Luis remembers. "He was actually doing an overdub session, so he was at the end of the room, back there, in the playing room, just overdubbing to some track. I got there and just waited there and was getting ready to walk out before he was finished, but I'm so glad I stopped. I thought, 'What are you doing? How many people would like to say they are in a studio watching Jeff Porcaro play drums, man? And you're leaving? I don't have anything to do. I can hang out for another half hour or whatever and talk to Jeff.'" Luis is so glad he stayed. It was the last time he saw and spoke with Jeff in person.

TOM SNOW

Prolific songwriter **TOM SNOW** has had his songs recorded by Cher, Melissa Manchester, Olivia Newton-John, Dolly Parton, The Pointer Sisters, Barry Manilow, Diana Ross, Bette Midler, Linda Ronstadt and a long list of others. He also recorded three solo albums on which Porcaro played various tracks.

On his first album, *Taking It All in Stride*, released by Capitol Records in 1975, Snow played and sang, with Milt Holland keeping time with a shaker. Then they put the bass and other instruments on the tracks, but the very last element was the drums. This is when Snow met Jeff, but Jeff only played on one track ("Everybody Lives Everybody Dies") on the album. On his second album a year later (the self-titled *Tom Snow*), Porcaro played on six songs, as did David Paich, and they were together a lot in the studio.

Snow recalls a period around 1979 and 1980 when he was co-signed as a writer with Richard Perry, and Jeff would do demos for him for free. "He and Mike would come out to a little studio Gary Brandt had in North Hollywood. When I would ask Jeff if he would play drums for me, he would say, 'Oh man, come on, let's do it. I'll do it for free.' He was an incredibly generous guy," Snow remembers, adding that one time they did three demos on a Saturday afternoon.

Snow says he often played on the songs he wrote for other artists, so he'd see Jeff in the studio on those sessions, too. On Diana Ross' "Getting Ready for Love," Tom says, "I remember sitting at the piano and looking over at Jeff with this great swinging grin on his face and cutting the rhythm track. That was a period when I was in the studio a lot on the songs I wrote, and when I saw Jeff in the studio, I always knew it was going to be a great track. I mean there were other great drummers, but Jeff was a piece of music himself. It was always great, and he was funny, and he was always high. And he had great instincts."

Tom also remembers a lot of the songs he wrote for Leo Sayer on which Jeff played, like "Thunder in My Heart." Probably Tom's favorite composition on which Jeff played was "You Might Need Somebody," recorded by artist Randy Crawford, and produced by Tommy LiPuma. According to Snow, Jeff brought the song to life. "I didn't play on it with Jeff, but Tommy told me about the session," says Snow. "When they were trying to re-create my demo, which was a straight-ahead rhythm feel, it wasn't working for Randy. Tommy told me that Jeff said, 'Hold on, just give me a second,' and he just immediately broke into a fabulous groove and boom, the song just came together. It went on to become a big hit in Europe. Jeff saved that one, and it probably wasn't the first one he saved, either."

Among Snow's other favorite Porcaro works are all Jeff's tracks on *Tom Snow*. "I was writing long songs and sort of stretching my compositional muscle, more than just writing songs, I guess you could say, and he was so right there and so into it. There's a song on that album called 'Rock & Roll Widow,' which had the most intensely slow groove and the fills on that…" Snow's voice trails off. "There's so much soul coming out of those drumsticks." Snow would come in with rhythm section arrangements and start playing the songs on piano. Usually, halfway through the first verse, Porcaro would start playing along. "He would just settle into a groove and then Wilton (Felder, bass) and Fred Tackett on guitar and David Paich on electric (keyboard) would come in, but usually the groove would be stated first by Jeff," Tom recalls.

Snow wrote "You Should Hear How She Talks About You" (Melissa Manchester) with Dean Pitchford. Tom was not in the studio when this song was cut, but he remembers Clive Davis calling him afterwards and playing it over the phone. "Clive had gigantic speakers in his office, and I remember hearing it and getting the chills, thinking, 'Oh yes, that's a hit,'" he says.

BRENDA RUSSELL

BRENDA RUSSELL can't remember exactly how Jeffrey came to be in her life with her ex-husband Brian, but he was there very early working with them on their demos—for free. "All of a sudden we were working on demos, and we had Jeff and we had David (Paich)," recalls Russell. "They weren't Toto yet. It was amazing. We loved them so much. Then my husband and I broke up, and they were forming a band of course, and I called Jeffrey because he became my favorite drummer. I'm pretty musical, and I love musicians a lot."

She calls Porcaro—and Steve Gadd—"the baddest." "Jeff was so badass. It was like watching a movie, watching that guy play," Brenda gushes. "He was so expressive and fierce. We would all go down to the Baked Potato when he would play with his buddies like Abe Laboriel. We would just jam into that little room and watch Jeffrey. It was so great to be in that room and watch him do his thing with these badass players. I'm excited just thinking about it."

Russell says she loved working with him because he was straight ahead about everything. "He was an Aries, and I'm an Aries, so I understood that. He just said right out what he wanted to do, and he was very serious about making the music and being on time and being present," says Russell. "No matter what shenanigans we were up to, we were always about the music. He liked my music and that was the biggest compliment ever because he was so musical, so brilliant and played with so many great people," Russell continues. "He really dug what I was doing and that really made me happy."

Porcaro played all the tracks on Russell's second solo album, *Love Life* (1981). On her third album, *Two Eyes* (1983), he played tambourine on only one track. Russell doesn't recall why he wasn't on the rest of the record and how he came to play tambourine on that one song. She says she loved his playing because he was very funky. "It was like he had the soul of a Black man playing," Russell says. "He had that groove that was unstoppable. He was like a metronome. He had every expression that he was feeling on his face, too. He was so marvelous to watch."

Russell was not only the artist and songwriter, but she was the arranger and producer. "At that time, there weren't many women artists involved in the production area of their records, so it took me a minute to get the respect I was due," Brenda explains. "Jeff was always respectful. He never said much about anything, except, 'That's great,' or 'It's not great,' or 'Let's do it again.' He was more about the business of music. He had some laughs of course; he had some great stories."

DAY-TO-DAY LIFE

If there's anyone who gets to know an artist pretty well, it's the road manager. **CHRIS LITTLETON** signed on for that position with Toto on day one. Toto's managers, Fitzgerald Hartley, also managed Rufus, whose production manager was Littleton. Early in '78, Littleton got a call from Fitzgerald Hartley requesting that he take Toto to the big CBS artist showcase in New Orleans. "I was still living in Marin County at the time, so I flew to L.A. and went to Ratz Studio on Barham Blvd. I walked in the door and the guys were jamming. I stood and listened for about five minutes and said, 'I wanna be with this band; these guys are great!'" Chris remembers. "We organized the gear and I drove a truck down to New Orleans to the CBS convention. I'm thinking it was something like April or May of '78. They got the deal with Columbia, and the guys were recording."

Littleton says it was a very exciting time. After completing the debut album, they flew to Kauai Resort Hotel, where Toto played two 45-minute sets a night for two weeks to prepare for their first big gig as the opening act for Peter Frampton at the Blaisdell Arena in Honolulu. Even though it was their major debut and Frampton had been at it for a while, Frampton confessed in *It's About Time* that they scared him silly; there was no way he wanted to follow them on stage that night. "The guys were on fire," Littleton recalls.

As tour manager, Chris was tasked with booking all the transportation, the buses, trucks, hotels and flights. He traveled with the band and looked after the guys. "We were pretty lean in those days, so I was also calling spotlights and doing lights on some of the gigs," Littleton says. "Everybody was doing three or four things just trying to

At the Littleton Studio City house circa 1979, when Jeff gifted Chris' son Brian a drum set. Both Jeff's brothers came to enjoy the celebration. Note Brian's artwork of the Toto sword logo in the background. (Photo courtesy of Chris Littleton)

make it work." Littleton says Jeff was cool throughout. "He was such a calm, laid-back guy. He was so on top of his music and craft," Chris asserts. "He was a great leadership guy in the band; he and Dave. They played off each other so well. In the middle of '78 I was still living in Marin County and Jeff came to me and said, 'We kinda need you to be here in L.A. all the time,' so the guys footed the bill and moved me to Studio City. I got my first house just a few blocks from Jeff's place. My family and I moved into this place in 1979 and at that point it was full time, every day, go to the studio, hang out, do whatever needed to be done."

One of those responsibilities was making sure Paich got up and arrived at the studio on time, because he was perpetually late. Littleton was the one who had to sail the ship smoothly. Jeff, known for his punctuality, was not always pleased with Paich's tardiness. Chris laughs as he tells one of his favorite stories that occurred during rehearsals at S.I.R. for the *Hydra* tour: "Dave was always late for everything. It was incredible. We were about three or four days into rehearsal, and Jeff and Luke and Lenny said, 'Listen, this has got to stop. We've got to start on time. This is crazy, so we're going to start fining people if they don't show up on time.' And I'm like, 'Ok, we're going to see how this is going to go.' So Paich comes into the studio a couple hours late and Jeff launches on him. He says, 'Listen, we're paying people to be around here, we're paying for all this stuff. We have to start on time, and if we don't, we're gonna start fining people for being late.' Paich stood there for a minute, looked at Jeff and said, 'Well, how much is the fine? I'll pay a year in advance.' And that was that!" Littleton says, laughing.

Littleton actually got in trouble with Paich once when he got the call times mixed up and accidentally got David to the studio on time. "Everybody looked at Paich and said, 'You're on time!' And he turned to me and said, 'Littleton, you lied to me about the time!' And I said, 'No, honest to God, man, I didn't.'"

Chris says Jeff never got angry, though. He'd just do a kind of freeze-out. "He never got super agitated about anything. He just got cooler and cooler when he got pissed. He would push his glasses up on his nose and just look at you. 'Yo, dick, this is what we gotta do.'"

Posing for press in Japan. (Courtesy of Chris Littleton)

Porcaro was happiest, according to Chris, when the "machine" was functioning at its best. The things that irked Jeff were when the artistic production details went awry. Littleton recalls during the first album, going to Clair Brothers in Pennsylvania. Leo Bonamy, their lighting director and production manager, was the creative designer for the set. "We had a very small budget at that point and we had these flats of trees that were supposed to stand on stage, designed by a scenery company somewhere near Lititz, Pennsylvania," Chris recalls. "We went into the studio to rehearse, and Leo had all these set pieces set up. Jeff just stood there looking at them. He looked at me and Leo and Paich, and finally he said, 'Jesus fuck, this is horrible,' and he grabbed a claw hammer out of one of the carpenter's tool boxes and just went bat shit crazy and smashed these things up. Oh my God, we laughed so hard. That was it. 'That's not what I was thinking, guys! The art department needs to start over.'"

Littleton recalls the sword episode in Japan in great detail: Jeff's concept was the sword through the rings to fly in and rotate as the centerpiece on the stage. Porcaro sketched it out and sent it to Japan. It made its debut at Japan's Budokan. "They lowered this thing down," Littleton recalls. "It had a motor in it so it would turn. It was designed so quickly and how it was put together that as soon as it started to turn, it started to oscillate and swing. No matter what speed you set it, it started swinging back and forth instead of actually turning in a nice tight circle. Well, Jeff didn't like that at all. So we ended up just keeping it stationary and lifting it in and out."

He describes Jeff as "the rock" who was always there on time for whatever needed to be done. "He was a punctual guy, he paid attention and was on top of his game," Chris says and observes that Jeff appreciated you the most when you were working as hard as he was.

In typical Jeff fashion, he bonded with Chris' nine-year-old son

On tour with Toto in Japan, 1979. (Courtesy of Chris Littleton)

Brian and gifted him a drum set. "We had a birthday party for him one time at the house, and I had a friend who dropped off a little miniature motorcycle for him. It had a small horsepower engine. I had a sloped driveway that went down to the street, and Hungate's house was across the street from mine. Jeff got on the bike and said, 'I'm gonna ride this,' and I said, 'I don't know if that's such a good idea,' and he said, 'No, no, I can do it,'" Littleton remembers. "We start the damn thing, and he goes down the driveway and across the street into the curb on the other side, flips over and lands on Hungate's lawn. We laughed so hard."

Littleton left Toto in 1986 because he wanted to be on the road more than the band was touring, but he was with Toto through the first six albums. Some of Littleton's best memories are what he calls the privileged moments that only a few humans ever experienced, when the band would be setting up for a session and just jamming. They'd be running a two-track while the engineers were getting sounds and Chris says it was some of the best music he ever heard in his life.

Toto and Jon Smith press conference in Osaka, Japan, 1979.(Courtesy of Chris Littleton)

On tour in Japan, 1979. (Courtesy of Chris Littleton)

DEEP IMPACT

Every reporter knows when he writes, he is tasked with answering the five w's: "who," "what," "when," "where" and "why"—up front. In this very important, poignant story, I may not be able to answer all the w's for sure, because the "who"—producer **JIM ED NORMAN**—is not certain "what," "when" and "where," but I will deduce. Given the fact that Norman only produced one album on which Jeff Porcaro played drums—Albert Hammond's *Your World and My World*—most likely that is the "what," which makes Producer's Workshop the "where" and 1981 the "when." I will get to the "why" this story is so profound in a minute, just after I give some context to who Jim Ed Norman was coming into this extremely open, soul-baring story.

During the '70s, Norman wrote string arrangements and contributed piano to some very successful Eagles and Linda Ronstadt albums, among others. Prior to Hammond's album, he had been producing for a few years, having notable success with artist Anne Murray. But as Norman recalls this story, he didn't feel as though he had been on the job very long. It's highly possible that that's just how Jeff made him feel in the moment. So I'll let him tell you the very profound incident in his life: As a producer, Norman says he discovered quickly that his responsibility was to hire the best person for the job. After a connection with Steve Porcaro's daughter Heather, it brought Jeff to mind when he was going to produce Albert Hammond, and he hired Jeff for some of the sessions.

"All of a sudden I found myself in the studio with Jeff Porcaro," says Norman, who was obviously very aware of Jeff's immense contributions to music. "As many know, along with being an amazing drummer, Jeff was also a visual artist. As we were working, every time we would listen back to a take and talk about it, the musicians would gather in the control room and Jeff would start doodling with a pencil on paper. He would go back out and do a take, and when he'd come back in, he'd add something to the doodle. The drawing he was doing was riveting to me, but it had a kind of angst associated with it that got my attention and began to bother me. I was concerned. 'Is this what he's feeling? Is this what's going on?' I absorbed that. Each time he came in, he added on to it, and at a certain point I was so overcome with my anxiety, as there was more talk of 'do this, change that, do more takes,' that I found myself at one point when they went out to track, picking up the pencil with the eraser and erasing the part that he had drawn that I found the most alarming; the part that was causing the most anxiety in me."

When Jeff returned to the control booth after the next take and looked at his partially erased doodle, he walked over to Jim Ed and said, as only Jeff could say, with no malice and maybe a little smile: "Oh, so you like to fuck with other people's art?" Norman was devastated. "He was absolutely right," Norman admits. "I didn't make any excuse about it because I had done it; it was bold-facedly right there. But it did create the opportunity for me to stop and reflect on what it was he was saying. I said, 'You know, Jeff, you've got an interesting point because I think to some extent that's a little bit of what has been going on between all of us here today. I'm obligated to comment and participate in a way because of the responsibility I have as a producer for this artist and what it is that we are doing, to be sure that I live up to the artist's expectations and the record company's expectations. To some extent, I think what you've landed on is the struggle that I have between the responsibility vs. accommodation, responsibility vs. revelation, responsibility vs. exaltation, putting you on a pedestal about what it is you're doing.' All of a sudden the drawing had become representative of what was going on in the room and as he had drawn that, what it had evoked in me, whatever anxieties came along with it because I was young and new. He created in that moment for me an internal dialog with myself that has never left me: 'How far do I go with art, letting it happen and staying out of the way?' For me, the objective was always to create the safest possible environment for them to work in to do what they do. I was really fortunate in that moment that that discussion was about a picture he drew and not his drum part."

Norman says this moment was something he never forgot. He has actually been forever grateful for the comment/observation Jeff made. What happened was so devastating in one sense, but in another, it opened him to a consciousness and something very spiritual and emotional. It paved the way for Norman to have an inner dialog with himself about the role of a producer—a person who is somewhat obligated to mess with a person's art; someone paid to have an opinion on someone's art; the balance of helming a project, letting those on the project be creative while being responsible to the artist and record company. Jeff's comment is something that he says comes to mind frequently. "It was an important moment and has stayed with me all my life as a creative person," Norman reveals.

MYRON GROMBACHER

You would think I would be accustomed to hearing about the generosity of Jeff Porcaro, but there are still stories that blow me away. In 1981, Ohio boy **MYRON GROMBACHER**, who had previously been in Rick Derringer's band, had already joined up with Pat Benatar but hadn't yet moved to L.A. While rehearsing for her *Precious Time* tour, Grombacher was staying at the Oakwood Apartments in North Hollywood and went into Guitar Center one day. As Benatar was already a MTV hit, the band had become well known for their hot videos.

"When I was in the drum department, I saw Jeff Porcaro. Every drummer knew of Jeff Porcaro," says Grombacher. "When I was first learning to play in Youngstown, I was in a band called Coconut and they were like an R&B band—I was in any band that would let me in—and they would do a couple of things from Boz Scaggs' *Silk Degrees,* so I had to learn Jeff's parts, which were perfect. Then, when I started to really get serious about playing drums, I'd listen to everybody, and Toto was an amazing band and Jeff was an incredible drummer. The whole family was good; anybody named Porcaro was amazing. It's like Wackerman: anybody named Wackerman, hire them (laughs). You don't have to hear them; just hear the name and hire them.

"So I see Jeff at Guitar Center and I think, 'Should I say something?' But then he heads straight at me and he says, 'Myron!' And I go, 'Jeff!' He knew me from the Benatar band. We started talking and I'm gushing about what an amazing drummer he is, and then he invites me to his house—which was when he was living in North Hollywood with the studio behind it. And I'm not doing anything, so I went the next day. We were just bullshitting, and he asks, 'What are you doing tomorrow night?' I go, 'Nothing really,' and he says, 'You gotta come with me to the union dinner.' I go, 'What?' I think it was like the annual musician's union Christmas dinner party. I go, 'Sure.' I met him there and then I met everyone—Rick Marotta, Lee Sklar, major producers, all the L.A. heavyweights. So from not knowing anyone in Los Angeles I went instantly to knowing fifteen or twenty guys, some of them heroes, like Rick Marotta, Russ Kunkel and Jim Keltner."

Three days later Grombacher's Oakwood Apartment phone rings and it's a producer on the line telling him that Jeff has recommended him for a session. "He hooked me up with the first session I did in L.A.," Grombacher recalls. "It was so long ago I can't remember what it was, but I just remember that not only did Jeff help me through the door, but he kicked me through the goal post. I was just starving to get notoriety and fame and all that bullshit that comes with it, and it was a good check; it was, 'Ok, this is how we should treat people.' And I try to do that in my life. Any chance I get to help someone, I do, because the karma thing is good that way. And still, when I do sessions and I'm not sure what to play, sometimes I think, 'What would Jeff do? Maybe I should let it shuffle a little more.' He had such an incredible swing feel."

Myron would see Jeff on and off. When Porcaro moved to Hidden Hills, Myron was close by in Woodland Hills and they would run into each other at Gelson's Market and various places. The last time he saw him was at Village Recorders where they were both doing sessions. "He was the same sweet guy: amazing smile. That was an ice-breaking smile. And his laugh. His voice and his bear hug," Grombacher recalls. "That picture of all of us at the NAMM with Alex Van Halen—we're all laughing at a story Jeff is telling. He was the funniest, smartest, most talented dude you could imagine; just a great life force."

Jeff having fun with esteemed colleagues at the PASIC Convention at Universal City, CA, 1985. From left to right: Myron Grombacher (Pat Benatar), Alex Van Halen, Jim Keltner, Paul Jamieson, Jeff. Seated: Jeff Chonis. (Photo courtesy of the Peter van Ham Archives)

SPEAKING OF STORIES…

Anybody remember the one about Jeff's trip down to Florida to record with the Bee Gees and then work on helping **ALBHY GALUTEN** and **KARL RICHARDSON** at an insane attempt to invent a drum machine? The story is told in *It's About Time* by Jeff himself (backed up by Jackson Browne and Vinnie Colaiuta, to whom he ranted when he returned from Florida). For this book, however, I was able to track down both Galuten and Richardson to get their takes on the adventure that had gotten Porcaro so wound up.

As a fan of Toto and Jeff's playing, Richardson and Galuten had met Porcaro prior to the trip to Florida. Richardson recalls that when it came time to record the Bee Gee's 1981's *Living Eyes,* they felt they needed some extra musicianship to push the songs over the edge.

Neal Schon and Jeff watching Billy Cobham at PASIC 1985, Los Angeles. (Photo by Rick Malkin)

The brothers were coming off *Saturday Night Fever* and all the hits it yielded, like "Stayin' Alive," as well as their smash follow up album, *Spirits Having Flown*, but Richardson admits the songs to be recorded for this project were not as strong.

At the start of my conversation with Galuten, he wanted to address Jeff's style, juxtaposed against some of the other main drummers of the day. "When you think about Russ Kunkel, he always has his drums tuned so they'll resonate as long as possible," Galuten assesses. "He wants to play as few notes as he can. The drums have to resonate a long way and he plays very, very simply. Steve Gadd is his opposite. You turn on the click and you see him nod and you just think, 'Ok, I don't have to worry about this guy; his time is good.' When he counts off against the click, he puts the click on the upbeat. That's brilliant because when the click is on the downbeat, if you're right in time, you don't hear it. You only hear it if you're off. Steve likes to play a lot of intricate stuff, so you can give him drums that were tuned in the factory and they were tuned brilliantly to resonate and ring and sound beautiful and he will find a way to hit them so they don't resonate at all, because he wants to be able to play a lot of stuff, and if the drums ring out, it sounds too messy."

Galuten says Jeff was the best of both worlds. "He has a great sound, he knows how to play complicated stuff at minus 20 decibels, so it sounds like a percussion overdub inside the track, but he also knows how to get a great feel, and he knows how to get a great sound."

As the story goes, they had created a loop for "Stayin' Alive," by splicing bars from the hit "Night Fever" into a half-inch four-track loop. "Barry Gibbs' time is immaculate," Galuten explains. "We would do 18 tracks of vocals with him, and he would do them without listening to the others. Unlike other singers, he wouldn't want to hear what he was doubling; he'd just do 18 tracks in a row, triple three-part in two octaves, and then you would put them up together and every breath, every actual click, every bit of timing would be right on the money. It was unbelievable. So we had done that loop and we were trying to figure out how to do more loops.

"I was very pleased to hear that Jeff came back from Miami and made the loop for 'Africa,' but what he did, which was so much more sensible, was they just played, which is where the original 'Stayin' Alive' loop came from, and then they just picked a great feeling couple of bars."

During his time in Florida, they asked Porcaro if they could sample him. Richardson says he felt Jeff's ambivalence: a little angry, but somewhat in admiration of the creative territory they were broaching. But both Richardson and Galuten remember the picture Jeff drew on his snare drumhead—Jeff's go-to outlet for his true feelings. Galuten says he'd give anything if he had kept it. "It said 'I thought the Loop was in Chicago.' And it had a picture of a hangman's noose (for a loop) and a drummer hanging there," Richardson describes. Galuten says the drummer in the drawing was Jeff, and he remembers the loop as being wrapped around him, so Galuten interpreted it as "he was trapped by the loop." Either way, it's pretty grim.

Richardson says all in all, Jeff was very good-natured about it, he believes, because they were breaking interesting ground, and all learning something new together. Although Karl does remember that as they were building the robot drummer, Jeff thought they were crazy.

That robot drummer was named Solly (Noid) in the back room—short for solenoids, created by a person named Seth Snyder. "We were using the studio more like a laboratory," Richardson admits with a laugh. "We were putting solenoids—or electromagnetic actuators—onto actual physical drums so we had a powerful power supply and a powerful electromagnet of this plunger actually smacking a bass drum and making a bass drum sound. But it kept getting too hot. We felt the sound of it for about five minutes and that was it. The thing almost blew up."

Richardson says they hired Jeff because of his impeccable time. "I loved Jeff. He was such a great musician, and he had a perspective on how he looked at life and the way things worked. I really respected Jeff. He should still be here."

In 1985, after Galuten moved to Los Angeles, he was working on a Clive Davis session for a Dionne Warwick track called "Whisper in the Dark." "Jeff was nice enough to give me drum samples," Albhy says. "He came in and gave me samples that I recorded, and we put together patches. This was not in the days of LinnDrum. I had dozens of snare samples and multiple hits on the same snare, so I could do the parts differently and subtly, and 16 different hi-hat patches with different kinds of hi-hats and where to hit them and how close you were to the bell and if it was open or closed, because it was back in the early days of sampling. Back then high quality was16-bit sampling. I remember when I was putting this track together, I was thinking of Jeff, and I had thought about which drum he would play with which hand and where—every turn and every feel and every bass drum dynamic because there were multiple bass drums because they would sound different when you hit them harder and they would sound different when you hit them softer."

Albhy recalls that Porcaro was there early and Jeff commented: "My God, it not only sounds like my drums, but it sounds like how I played them." "He sat down and was cutting the track and I'm listening to him play and I'm thinking, 'Oh my God, he's making more decisions in every bar with his hi-hat hand than I made with this whole track,' and I became brutally aware of how much more complex a human being is using their emotions and their gut and their feel and their muscle memory than you possibly can be when you use your intellect," Galuten recalls.

Between Florida and the Dionne Warwick recording, Galuten got the Synclavier (Note: a digital synthesizer and polyphonic digital sampling system, considered at the time to be the most advanced of its kind). "With a Synclavier you can look at the waveform of every groove and you can analyze them," Galuten says. "What I learned is that the analysis doesn't make any sense. You look at the 'Funky Drummer' thing and there are beats that I thought if you made the downbeat back by three milliseconds or 16 beats per minute tempo and the hi-hat back by a couple of milliseconds, we could create some nice feels that way, but they'd never have the lope of a real drummer."

TOP THIS!

Before writing this book, Porcaro on the Four Tops' *Tonight!* was not on my radar, but what a joy when I discovered it! It is a true treasure. The 1981 Casablanca release actually contained a few hits, including "When She Was My Girl," and between Levi Stubbs' voice and Jeff's playing, the album bowled me over!

Producer **DAVID WOLFERT** says he believes it was pianist/arranger/producer Bill Meyers who suggested Wolfert hire Porcaro for the record. "He was amazing, especially on 'When She Was My Girl,'" Wolfert asserts, adding that he recalls Jeff very happy while cutting the "Motown/Philly" type beat. "We had top and bottom mics on the snare, and one of the mics crapped out in the middle of the take and we didn't know it until way later, but the feel was so perfect on that take, that we just said, 'Screw it!' and that's the hit. It was pretty big; actually a No.1 R&B hit. It certainly revived (the Four Tops') career because they were not really working, and they got a good three or four years out of that album. We did it at Cherokee with Al Schmitt. I remember it like it was yesterday. They were great sessions, and the Four Tops were great guys. Everybody grew up on the Four Tops so just to be in the same room with them was amazing—and no one could believe Levi was still singing that good. Every song on there was great."

Wolfert adds that everyone—even Schmitt, who had recorded practically every famous person—was excited to be in the studio with the group. "I saw Al forty years later, and he mentioned that session because of what a thrill it was to hear Levi sing into a microphone. Everyone was excited." Drum tech Paul Jamieson, who worked that session for Jeff, concurs: "Jeff was absolutely *blown away* by Levi Stubbs, one of the *greatest* voices to come from Detroit."

Wolfert is pretty sure he met Jeffrey on that same 1976 Helen Reddy session on which Jeff met producer Joe Wissert. I discovered during the writing of this book that the connection to Wissert, and therefore ultimately Boz Scaggs, was made through contractor Frank DeCaro, but we will get to that shortly. Reddy's album *Music, Music* was recorded at Sound Labs, where Wolfert says he was one of the arrangers. He doesn't remember anything about the session except admiring Jeff's Mercedes. Wolfert says DeCaro probably introduced him to Jeffrey, singing DeCaro's praises as an amazing resource.

Wolfert was immediately struck by Porcaro's abundant enthusiasm. "I don't remember, but I'm sure my arrangement was less than fantastic and I'm sure the songs weren't that great and I'm sure there were places he would rather have been, but he was just so great on the sessions," he says. "Through the years I worked with all the great L.A. drummers and each one has brought something different to the sessions. They're all amazing, none of them bad, but they all brought a different vibe, and Jeff's was always energetic."

BILL MEYERS

It was indeed composer/pianist **BILL MEYERS** who suggested Wolfert hire Jeff for the Four Tops project. "David Wolfert did a good job producing the album and treated us very well. I arranged and played on a number of songs. The Four Tops were some of the nicest people I've ever worked with," Meyers recalls, adding that it was amazing to hear Jeff and Levi Stubbs in his headphones, but then again, the entire tracking crew was phenomenal. "Everything felt great with Jeff—but don't forget the entire section had musicians of extremely high quality. We all needed to vibe the track the right way to make the magic happen. Levi took us all back to Motown at its height with his voice. It was wonderful."

Meyers had met Jeff that same year, when his buddy David Foster couldn't go on the road with Boz Scaggs after recording *Middle*

Man with Scaggs. Meyers went on tour in Foster's place, which was his first encounter with the drummer he ended up calling a god. "I was absolutely blown away by his playing," Meyers exclaims. "I had never played with anybody who sounded like that or felt that good from that point on or ever. It felt so good, so in time. The fills were so instructional—how much to play and how loud to play."

Meyers says one of the seminal musical events in his life occurred at a San Francisco concert where Scaggs was returning to his home area. "He had Mike Landau and Steve Lukather on guitars. Boz was so excited to be triumphantly coming home to play, and we started with the song 'Middle Man,' which was mid-tempo," Meyers recalls. "I would have thought we would have started with a shuffle or something uptempo, but he started with that because he wanted to get it out there. So Boz waves off Lukather to play the riff, and they've been having a little bit too much fun, and he starts it off way too fast. I look at Jeff, he looks at me and I know it's way too fast and the next part that comes in is the piano part behind that riff. I had to cement it. What could I do? Jeff is pissed off; I know it by the way he hits the cymbal in the fill going into the first verse. But here's the brilliant part about it: When Jeff plays, he commands everyone in the band; he's so strong. There's a long first verse and a B section before you get to the hook again, about 24 measures. We're playing it and we get back to that same fill that was so sped up before. As we're playing it, I realize that we're at the correct, slower tempo. It was astounding that Jeff could do that and I didn't feel it. He slowed it down one increment at a time, every measure, to the point that not even we musicians could feel that he was bringing that ridiculously fast tempo down to its original tempo. I remember coming off saying to Lukather, 'That is the most amazing thing I have ever experienced! That was amazing.' Lukather said, 'We're fucked up all the time; he just brings us back all the time. He's used to it.' It just shows you how strong Jeff was and what he said behind the drums went. You could feel the power."

While they were on tour Meyers brought out his backgammon set on the bus, and Jeff came over and said, "Here, take a hit of this." Meyers couldn't say no to Jeff, so he got himself through one more game of backgammon and staggered into the hotel. Mike Porcaro came to his rescue. "He was banging on the door, walked me around the room, washed my face," Meyers recounts, laughing. "His shit was the strongest shit I ever smoked. It further cemented my nickname, Snow White."

Years later, it happened again. Meyers found himself on a David Williams session with Jeff and they were listening back to the first take. "Someone from behind me hands something to me and immediately I knew I was in trouble," Meyers says. "It was the strongest shit I had ever smoked, and Jeff leans over with a huge smile on his face. Now I'm panicked and I can feel it growing, so I step outside and I'm trying to figure out what to do. I pass the kitchen and I see the coffee so I think, 'Coffee will help me wake up.' That was the wrong thing to do—I was a combination of hyper inside and pudding on the outside. So we sit down to do the take again and Jeff is smiling the whole time. We started to play, and suddenly the music sounded heavenly. It sounded better than anything I had ever heard in my life. I don't remember which song it was, but it was a beautiful pocket and a mid-tempo song, and it was the take they kept."

Meyers did many sessions with Jeffrey, including one for Engelbert Humperdink for the 1981 album *Don't You Love Me Anymore.*

He says they were all fairly boring ballads, and by the time they got to the final one, everyone wanted to go home. "We do this ballad, and everyone plays what they're supposed to play," Meyers recalls. "At the end of the take, somebody jumped the gun on the final chord and then somebody else came after him, so we didn't hit the last chord together. This was in the days when it was pretty hard to intercut. This just shows the power of Jeff; I'll never forget this: The producer says, 'Man, that was beautiful, but was the ending ok?' We all look at one another and all of a sudden Jeff says, 'Yeah, man, we tried something different. It was a cascade ending.' And that was the end of the session."

In 1981 Meyers put together a group with Vinnie Colaiuta, Neil Stubenhaus and Carlos Rios. "I had the good fortune of meeting a fellow named Guy Thomas, who was a terrific songwriter and had a great voice. We started writing songs," says Meyers. They ended up calling the band 213, Los Angeles' only telephone area code back then. They booked a studio to cut a demo, but at the last minute, Zappa called Vinnie, and Jeff agreed to take his place, free of charge. During the cutting of a ballad Meyers co-wrote with Thomas called "Woman," which he describes as a moody, smoky song, something Jeff said to him was revelatory. "I had rhythm section charts for everybody, including Jeff," Bill says. "Jeff looked at me and said, 'Hey, where are the lyrics?' I said, 'They're in the booth there with Guy. I got a drum chart there for you.' He said, 'Yeah, I know. I wanna see the lyrics.' I said, 'Oh, ok,' and went into the booth, got a photocopy of the lyrics, brought them to Jeff and said, 'Here. Why do you want them?' Jeff took a big hit out of a joint and held it for a minute, and then he said,' You don't fuckin' get it. It's all about the lyrics. It's all about the lyrics. Everything you play is all about the lyrics.' And it changed my life. Some of the best work I've done."

Meyers included Porcaro on his 1990 release *The Color of the Truth*, and he says the one time he saw Jeffrey flustered occurred during these sessions. They were cutting the track "I'm Still Standing," which Meyers had co-written with Jakko Jakszyk, who was working with Level 42. "There was a loop Jeff was playing with, so we told him not to swing it at all," recounts Meyers. "I could tell he liked the song, but he kept saying, 'I don't know if I got it.' He seemed a little nervous about it. Jakko said he liked the groove, so I said to Jeff, 'Come on, you're on it, man. Give me another one. I could have taken the last one, it's no big deal.' That's the only time I ever saw Jeff where he didn't feel like he nailed it."

FRANK DECARO SINGING PRAISES

In the early '70s, arranger Nick DeCaro gave his brother **FRANK DeCARO**, originally a session guitarist, the opportunity to contract musicians for recording sessions. Early on, he was hiring Earl Palmer, Hal Blaine and among the "younger guys," Jim Keltner. The Helen Reddy album *Music, Music* was one of the first big projects for which DeCaro hired Jeff (two tracks). "Joe Wissert was an underrated genius," DeCaro asserts. "I knew him from the Turtles (Wissert produced their album *Happy Together*). When I heard Jeff, I said, 'Wow.' I had already heard him on records like with Seals and Crofts; he was already working on hit records. He had such a solid sound. It was different to me; he reminded me of Count Basie's drummer Sonny Payne. When I told him that, he was really surprised. He never thought of himself as a jazz drummer. I always tried to pick players by what I heard sonically of what attracted me."

For the two Helen Reddy tracks, DeCaro asked Porcaro if there was someone he'd like to recommend, and Jeff immediately suggested David Hungate on bass and David Paich on piano. They added a young Dean Parks on guitar. "I liked Jeff a lot—so personable and so much good energy. I realized at that point I could put my faith and future in Jeff and that rhythm section," says DeCaro. As time went on, he began to get calls from France, Italy, Germany, Spain and Japan to procure that rhythm section for artists who would come to Los Angeles to record. (DeCaro recalls hiring Steve Lukather while Luke was studying for his high school finals.)

DeCaro remembers speaking with Boz Scaggs at the request of Joe Wissert. He says Scaggs had been working with jazz musicians and asked who DeCaro had in his arsenal. "I said, 'I've got Jeff Porcaro, David Hungate and David Foster.' He said, 'Great, I want to meet them.' He met them, he loved them, he hired them and boom," DeCaro recalls, although when Foster did not end up doing the album (and Foster doesn't recall why) as usual, when Jeff had the opportunity to bring Paich into a situation, he did so.

Frank says Jeff never disappointed him. "Jeff was always a gentleman. We sent him on a couple of dates with great producers where he never got to play at all, because sometimes on dates things go in different directions." DeCaro explains that they had sent him in on an album date with a non-specified recording schedule. "I think it happened during an Arif Mardin date. Arif Mardin dates were always sessions Jeff wanted to be on—he was always such a sensitive musician, producer and gentleman. But he wasn't playing. He said, 'Frank, I think the time has come where dates have changed. You can't get the one-size-fits-all musicians.' He was right. I used to get the one-size-fits-all musicians because you never knew what song they were going to pull up. He was saying, 'You've got to know what the songs are so you can have the right person for the right songs. You've got to cast it. The business is changing, and you've got to change with it.' Here was the finest musician on the globe doing nothing." This experience caused DeCaro to reevaluate his business practices.

DeCaro says Porcaro's integrity was unquestionable. While working with Al Jarreau on an album Jay Graydon was producing, Jarreau had requested a certain unnamed drummer from New York. DeCaro says he didn't know this drummer, but certainly knew of his great musicianship. "I didn't think that group of New York guys were worth any more money than anyone else. It cost more money to import them and then to house them and then rent cars in some cases, depending on the player. In this case, this player was very demanding," Frank says. "He not only wanted triple scale, which was the going rate for New York guys (out here it was double scale), but he wanted first class airfare for his girlfriend and him. And while I would rent cars for guys sometimes, which I often let the record companies handle, this time it got messy. The end result was I had to go to the president of Warner's to get the first class for him and his girl, and not only did he want a car, but he wanted a sports car. In the end, he got everything he wanted, except the sports car, but this episode hurt me. Jeff spoke up saying it was unfair to our players—the guys we needed on 99.9% of the dates, which were very successful records. I agreed with him—and not because Jeff said something, but because I also felt the same way. I ended up having a face-off with Jay Graydon on the matter, but ended up losing that contest, which I knew I would. Jeff would stand up morally as a good businessman and a fair and kind person."

DeCaro says all that became very evident on a later date with producer Bob Johnston, known for his work with Bob Dylan. DeCaro could not recall the session, but he remembers that he had secured the "cream" musicians, including Jeff, for Johnston. "We were running it down and getting takes and then getting into a groove, sounding like a take. Bob Johnston is all excited and says, 'Guys, that's it!' Everyone is anxious to hear a playback and they go into the booth, and it turns out there is no playback. The assistant was a girl; you didn't see too many females in those days doing that job," Frank explains. "You never saw them as engineers or producers and this girl was learning. She didn't know what to say. And Bob, being as flamboyant as he was, walked out into the room and said, 'This girl did it; she blew it. It wasn't recorded,' and he went on ranting. And Jeff said, 'No, no, no, wait a minute, man, that wasn't a very good take. I knew it wasn't because I blew it right from the start. Let's do another one. Come on, now. Let's just do another one.' When Jeff spoke, they all listened and they all sat down and boom, knocked it out, great take, and that was the last thing said on that topic. I'm sure it wasn't the last the girl heard about it, but it was a lesson all those players knew about; they all screw up. He covered for her like a chivalrous old soul."

No doubt about it, DeCaro adored Jeffrey: "Jeff was like his dad. He gave you everything he had as a player. He wasn't physically big, but he gave you a big heart, big beat and great time," Frank says. "I always looked forward to talking and working with Jeff. He could light up a room. And the groove he put down was unmistakable. When he was there, he was in control."

RANDY GOODRUM

Of all the tribute songs written about Jeffrey, "Ode to Jeff," (placed at the beginning of this book) written by **RANDY GOODRUM** and Larry Williams, is perhaps the most detailed and personal profile I've heard to date. And what is incredibly amazing is that it was written in March 2022, so on the day that Williams sent over some chords to Goodrum for a new song, it just so happened that Goodrum had been reminiscing about Porcaro.

Goodrum explains when he writes a song, even though he writes on piano, he programs the drums, and has had the opportunity to learn from the best. "I had the good fortune of being a studio musician back in the analog days in Nashville first, working with great drummers like Larrie Londin and Kenny Malone and then later in L.A. with Jeff and Vinnie and some in New York as well," Goodrum explains. "I got some of the idiosyncrasies that I will use, like a fill or a hi-hat thing a la Jeff, and Kenny Malone had a few little hi-hat things he did that nobody else did."

That particular day in March, Goodrum was thinking about Jeff while he was working on another song, he says because Jeff was "so original and one of those drummers that you could count on one hand, that when you saw him walk in you just knew it was sort of like the track was done." Goodrum says Jeff was amazing in so many ways. "There are loads of Jeff admirers and fans out in the world, Larry and me included," he says.

Goodrum had already had huge hits as a songwriter in the late '70s, with such songs as "You Needed Me" (Anne Murray) and "Bluer

Than Blue" (Michael Johnson), among others, before writing with Steve Lukather and meeting Porcaro. He says he got his record deal due to the hits, and when Polydor asked him to make his own record, they wanted him to cut it in New York. He was living in Nashville at the time, and he told them he knew plenty of good producers in Nashville, but Goodrum says he believes they were concerned it would end up being a country record. He met with a few people they suggested, but he really connected with Elliot Scheiner and loved his previous work.

Scheiner went to Goodrum's house in Nashville and listened to Randy's songs, and he recalls that Scheiner said, "I know just the man we need." Randy said, "I could do it with some guys here," but he added, "But that's okay, I'll defer to you on this." So, they put together a band for what became 1982's *Fool's Paradise* recorded at New York's Automated Sound, with Jeff on drums, Neil Jason on bass, Steve Khan on guitar and Goodrum on keyboards. "I met with these guys, and they were all great guys and every song on that record, except for maybe one, was a first take," Goodrum reveals. "I would just play a little bit of the vibe that I wanted and let them play. I didn't say anything like, 'Jeff I want a cross stick here or a fill here.' I learned early on if you're going to have some great, legendary musicians and you have this thing in your head that you want to hear, get to that second. Hear what they might do first, and then if it's not what you want, you can say, 'Well, I was thinking of it more like…' So I gave everybody the benefit of the doubt on that record. I'm sort of groove oriented; I like everything to feel good. I grew up in central Arkansas where a lot of the blues and R&B originated; it's in your blood."

Goodrum says it took a minute to connect personally with Jeff. "It wasn't that he was aloof; I just hadn't gotten him quite figured out yet," Randy admits. "But I remember having discussions with him about Bernard Purdie and the 12/8 thing he did, because I was a student of all that stuff, so I remember when the album was done and we had cut all the tracks and we started doing overdubs, one day he just came into the studio and sat down on the couch. I said, 'Hey, man, we're done with tracks. You're free to go.' He goes, 'Hey man, I'm into the hang.' He just wanted to hang out; he enjoyed it. And I thought, 'That's his thing.' He didn't have to. And we joked around and had a good time."

Sometime later, having written with so many people from L.A., Goodrum finally moved there. He and Steve Lukather wrote "I'll Be Over You" for Toto's 1986 album *Fahrenheit.* He says there is no intro to the song, but this was not done purposely. "I had done a demo with Luke and on the intro of the demo, it is two bars of drum groove. When Jeff cut the drum track, which they cut first, Jeff played to the demo and they overdubbed to that," Goodrum exposes the interesting accident. "So he used that opening two bars of my demo as his count-in. To him and to the band, I suppose, that simply was a count-in, whereas, when Luke and I were doing it, we were trying to set a groove: 'Wouldn't it be cool to have two bars out front?'"

Goodrum and Lukather also wrote "These Chains" for 1988's *The Seventh One*. "I loved the way Jeff played the Bernard Purdie 12/8 thing on 'These Chains,'" says Goodrum. "As a matter of fact, one of my songs on *Fool's Paradise*, 'One More Fool,' had that. I programmed the track on my Linn 9000 for 'These Chains' and I remember going to the Complex, and they had already started cutting tracks for the record. I had the demo, and Luke said, 'Play it for these guys,' so I went into the control room. I was sitting at the console and Jeff walked up near the left big speaker and was leaning against the wall. I started playing the intro, which had a drum pickup just like he did on 'These Chains.' He looked at me after about three bars and just nodded his head and smiled and gave me the finger and I said, 'Yes!' That was the best compliment I ever got. That was one of the happiest moments in my musical life."

After Toto cut "Anna," another Goodrum/Lukather composition on *The Seventh One,* Luke contacted Randy and said that Jeff wanted him to come to the studio. "I went over there, and I was afraid. I thought, 'Uh oh, I'm going to have to change a lyric or something,' but Jeff wanted me to hear the mix," Goodrum remembers. "He said, 'Check this out,' because I had done this real quirky percussion loop to write the song to, and Lenny Castro and Jeff sort of duplicated it. They did it better, of course. He just smiled. Jeff had this uncontrollable smile."

It was previously erroneously reported in Jeff's discography that Jeff played on Goodrum's entire 1992 release, *An Exhibition.* Randy programmed the drums on most of the album (and did a great job, which is why Jeff gave him the finger after hearing the demo on "These Chains." Goodrum learned how to program drums so well from being around Jeff!). Jeff only played on two tracks: "Touch" and "Flight 136," both of which are outstanding, of course.

Regarding "Flight 136," Goodrum recalls when he told Porcaro that he wanted him to play "kind of a jazz feel," Jeff quickly quipped back, "Hey, I'm not a jazzer." "I said, 'You play jazz.' He was real self-conscious about it. I said, 'Don't worry about it. You don't have to overtly go nuts; just keep a pocket with it. Just think low-key, because it's really just a low-key song.' And he did," Goodrum recalls. "And I said, 'When you get to that 6/8 or 12/8 part, just be yourself.'" On "Touch," Jeff is playing brushes. "I love brushes and I love what Jeff did on 'Touch,'" Randy asserts. "My God, what a pocket."

Goodrum remarks that there was "a lot of regular guy" in Jeff, probably because of the family in which he was raised, Goodrum speculates. "I think there's a lot of power if you can draw from the various parts of him and not just the cool part," Goodrum says. "I tell young writers, 'Embrace your ordinariness. Learn all the nuance of your ordinary. You will find an awful lot of vocabulary and emotional content that you're running away from now because you think it's not cool.' I saw Jeff one time at a Cirque du Soleil show and in the parking lot later I said, 'Man that was a great drummer, wasn't it?' And he said, 'Yeah, he was great.' I saw his kid and everything and I thought, 'There's some Ozzie and Harriet in this guy.' I like that. I mainly saw him in work environments."

ELLIOT SCHEINER

ELLIOT SCHEINER produced and engineered Goodrum's *Fool's Paradise.* Scheiner says after hearing Goodrum's songs, when it came to hiring a drummer, there was no reason to use anybody but Jeff. Scheiner loved the way he played. "His backbeat was always dead on," Scheiner declares. "Everything was perfect the way he played. And when he put in a fill, it was an appropriate fill."

Scheiner also knew he was always cool to be around. "I knew he wouldn't give me or anybody else any grief, and he'd be playing with guys that he hadn't played with much, like Will Lee and Steve Khan,"

Scheiner explains. "And that's what happened. He did what he did, and everybody was happy."

Scheiner recalls meeting Porcaro on the recording of "Gaucho." He says his first impression of Jeff as a person was that he was very friendly and very warm. He really didn't know much about his playing because Jeff was still fairly new on his radar. "When he played, I realized how good he was," Scheiner says. "In the past with most drummers, you would say, 'The snare is a little loose, could you either put a wallet on it or pad it up?' And the same thing with the bass drum: 'Do you mind if I stick a blanket in the kick?' When we started, I put a blanket in the kick and I said, 'Jeff can I hear that?' He hit the drum and it sounded perfect. After the first take I said, 'When you hit the drum

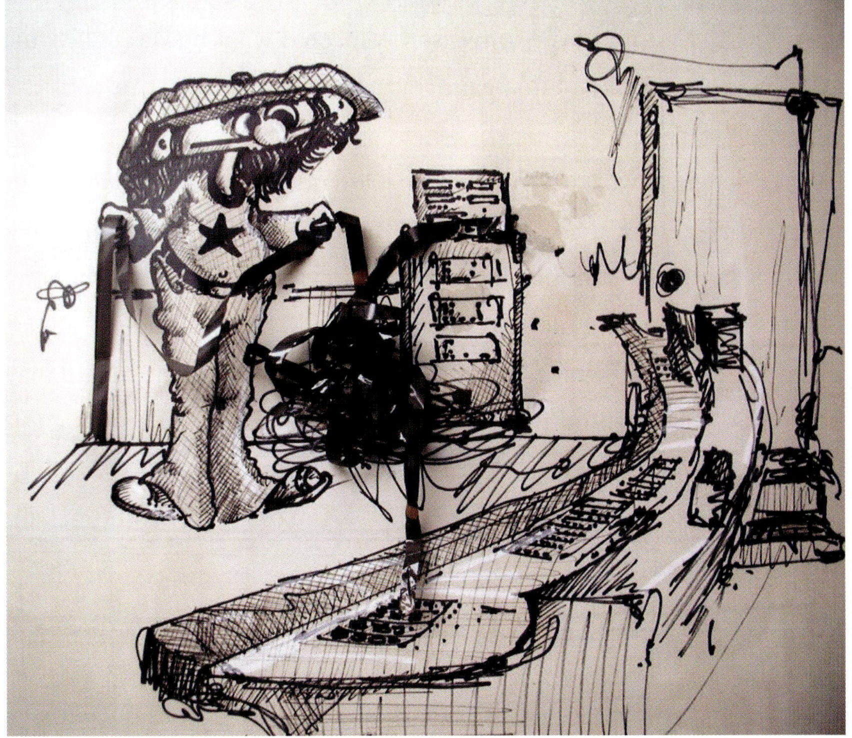

Jeff's rendering of Roger Nichols in the studio. (Courtesy of the Roger Nichols Estate)

initially, it was perfect, but when you started to play you weren't hitting it as hard as you were during sound check.' And he said, 'That's the way I feel it.' Ok. I'm with that because I would never want to change or inconvenience a drummer. In the end, I ended up dealing with it and putting it through a compressor, which I don't normally do. I liked the way Jeff played, so I was willing to work with anything he gave me. I learned early on that you can't invade a way a person plays. They play a certain way. When I place a mic, I always ask, 'Are you bothered with this here?' You don't want to interfere with what they are doing. It's only going to hamper what they come back with.

"I remember hearing the Kyle Lehning story. You couldn't tell Jeff how to play something," Elliot says of a story that Lehning revealed in *It's About Time*. "Jeff would never get me in a room and say, 'Hey, I don't like the sound of the toms,' so I respected what he was telling me and I never, ever asked him again."

Scheiner worked with Jeff on Donald Fagen's *The Nightfly* but reveals that all the tracks Jeff played except one was Wendell, Roger Nichols' sampler/drum machine. Even "Green Flower Street," the song Fagen says is his ultimate Porcaro song, was Wendell. "We did all the drum tracks at the Village, Studio B, and guys would come in and play on a song, and it would never be what (Fagen) wanted. They (Nichols and Fagen) would keep the drum tracks and turn them into samples," Scheiner confides. "'The Goodbye Look' is the only live drum track on the entire record."

JULIAN MARSHALL

After working with a singer-songwriter from the U.S. named Deborah Berg, Englishman **JULIAN MARSHALL** attracted the attention of producer Gary Katz, who wanted to make an album with them in 1981 and got them signed to Warner Brothers. Marshall came to Los Angeles to record the project, which they named Eye to Eye, and Katz hired lots of the high-profile cats, including Jeffrey for six of the tracks. (Although "Hunger Pains" is listed in the discography, and if you listen to it you will hear it sounds different, and that is because it is Wendell.)

Marshall had loved Steely Dan and was very inspired by their artistic values, so Marshall was very aware of Katz and the musicians he had called to Village Studios. If his memory serves, they were there for about six days. "It was jumping in the deep end, particularly working with a very name producer who had produced one of the most inspiring bands I had ever heard in my life," Marshall admits. "It took a while for me to feel empowered to be confident. One of the things I absolutely remember about Jeff is his extraordinary generosity. He came into the studio, and it mattered not at all that we were artists he had never met before, didn't know, and that we were brand new and had just signed to Warners. It made no difference at all. The level of application and engagement he gave was absolutely extraordinary from the first moment. To say he gave 150% is a cliché, but it's true. He gave so much more than the expectation could have been of a top session guy coming in."

Then Marshall told me something I definitely had never heard before: "I remember very well him showing me some pattern—I think it was some fugue, a canon—where patterns overlap and develop alongside each other—some sophisticated thing he was developing. Jeffrey was working on some wonderfully complex thing like that with a drum pattern. I don't know if it was something just for the drums, or if it was going to be a piece, but he actually showed it to me on paper. It was just remarkable," Marshall recalls, adding that he also saw Jeff doodling in the studio.

Marshall says that Katz chose to create the basic tracks with vocals and keyboards as guide tracks with a click and then had the musicians come in one by one to play to that. "Jeffrey embraced that wholeheartedly and really thought about what parts were relevant for each song, not just the accepted kind of go-to ideas," Julian says. "He was thoroughly creative and inventive from the beginning."

Among Marshall's favorite tracks are "Nice Girls," and he notes "Jeffrey's compelling groove." "Jeff's drumming on 'Progress Ahead' is really phenomenal," Marshall points out. "It's a song I like, but now looking at it, I think it's somewhat undeveloped. If we were playing it today, we would develop it more. I think there's more to say. I really like 'Time Flys' too."

Marshall describes Porcaro as so musical, enthusiastic, and dynamic with cranked energy. "As you said so many times in your (first) book, it was never about technique, it was never about trying to do something, it was about trying to contribute something," Julian comments.

AMY HOLLAND AGREES

In 1981, **AMY HOLLAND**'s significant other and future husband Michael McDonald produced her second album, *On Your Every Word.* Previously, he had produced her first, self-titled album with the Top 30 hit "How Do I Survive" (the song received the 1981 Grammy Award for Best New Artist). For the second outing, McDonald called Jeffrey to play on three tracks: "Anytime You Want Me," "I'll Never Give Up" and "Rollin' By."

While Amy can't recall if she had met Porcaro before these sessions, she says she was totally aware that when McDonald included him on them, she was "in for a thrill; getting a good thing," as she put it. Like most of us 40 years later, Amy's memories are scattered, but some are very vivid. Before we spoke, she listened to the three songs Jeff

Leland Sklar, Jeff Porcaro and Richard Marx during the recording of the song "One Man," from Marx's 1982 album *Paid Vacation*. (Courtesy of Richard Marx)

played on (which I have encouraged people to do for these interviews), which conjured up some wonderful recollections.

"I remember watching Jeff," Holland says. "He was always so fascinating to watch. He just had this otherworldly place he went to when he played, and that was so interesting to watch for me. When he hit a certain groove, like on that song 'Rollin' By'…" Amy tries to put it into words. "When I listened to that again, I specifically remembered watching him play that because he kind of got this little pirate grin kind of thing. It was really interesting to see this place he would go to—wherever it was—in his head. That was really fun to remember about him."

Amy co-wrote "I'll Never Give Up," so it was a thrill for her to have Jeff on that cut. It is a slow, moody, slightly jazzy and ethereal song, and when she listens back to it now, she says her thoughts are, "Just that he made the song come alive from what we wrote. It was interesting to hear his take on it. When we were writing it, we didn't have a drummer playing it, so it was wonderful to hear drums on a song that sensitive; it was amazing to hear how able he was to feel the vibe. He played it in such a tender way that it just really spoke to me. It was like, 'Oh, yeah, that's how it's supposed to be played.'"

Holland says Porcaro's being was indelible. She remembers watching the video for Toto's "I'll Be Over You," in which McDonald participated, since he sang on the song. It jumped out at her how charismatic Jeffrey was. "He always stood out to me that way; that he had this thing about him. A lot of drummers didn't catch my eye that much, but he did. He had just a real presence about him; not just the talent, but a presence and that stuck with me."

PINO PALLADINO

Bassist **PINO PALLADINO** met Jeff Porcaro recording David Gilmour's *About Face* in Paris in 1983 (released in 1984). Although he would go on to play with such luminaries as John Mayer, Jeff Beck, The Who, Elton John and Eric Clapton, it was still an early time in Palladino's career. He says he was approached out of the blue by Gilmour when the guitarist was rehearsing with a local band in South London. He couldn't believe it when he was asked to play on Gilmour's album. When the manager mentioned that Steve Winwood was going to be on the album, it "almost made me shit a brick."

The manager proceeded to tell him about the musicians who would be on the sessions with him and then said, "I don't know if you've heard of this guy, but he's an American from L.A.; he's a session guy called Jeff Porcaro." "I was more than aware of Jeff," says Palladino. "I knew him from various things; I was a fusion fan back in the day and a big Toto fan. And I was completely blown away that I was going to get to play with Jeff Porcaro." Palladino had no idea that this man was about to have a huge impact on his life.

They met the night Jeff flew into Paris. They were all staying in an old, beautiful turn-of-the-century apartment building. "We didn't say much that first night, but we got to the studio the next day and started cutting David's first track for the record," Palladino recounts. "I was understandably nervous. Bob Ezrin was producing, and David Gilmour, Jeff Porcaro, and all these legends were in the room—and there's little me from Cardiff (Wales) just a couple of months earlier, and I couldn't believe what was going on. Yeah, I was nervous as hell. And Bob Ezrin wasn't the easiest guy. He'll tell you straight what's going on. Once I got to understand that, I gave it as good as I got, but at the beginning…

"Jeff could see I was a little nervous and he called me over after the first run-through and said, 'Hey man, you sound great, bro.' I was like, 'What? You've got to be joking!'" Pino continues. "He had a piece of hash and rolled up a dollar bill and said, 'You wanna hit this, man?' And I said, 'Yeah.' And we just started laughing and from that day on, that just cemented our friendship. It was a real fun time in the studio with David, and I learned how to deal with Bob Ezrin as soon as I figured out the dynamic of the situation. Being validated by someone like Jeff Porcaro back in those days, to me, was very important and made me believe in myself. Of course, when you're a young musician like that, you think, 'Oh my God, this guy has played with Leland Sklar and Chuck Rainey and reams of incredible bass players. It's that 'I'm not worthy' kind of thing, so that validation is very important. And I learned this from Jeff: that when I'm in a position as the elder statesman, so to speak, and there are young guys, I try to put them at ease. He did that for me, and it really made an impression."

They stayed in France for two months, working at Pathe-Marconi Studio in Boulogne-Billancourt. Palladino says Gilmour took them out to generous dinners every night and "there was some partying going on, too." "I remember one day Jeff and I were walking down the street. We had gone shopping together, I guess, and there was a guy down the street, and I guess he recognized Jeff, because he started waving at us," Pino recalls. "We walked over. His name was George Acogni, from Senegal, West Africa. He wanted to say how much of a fan he was of Jeff's, and we became friendly with George. Whilst in Paris, George invited us to a couple of clubs to see some musicians and maybe join in, and that's where I met Manu Katché. Jeff had never met him before either. We had a lot of fun in Paris. Many years later I worked with Manu and told him that story and he said, 'Oh my God, that was you who was with Jeff Porcaro?' I said, 'Yeah, that was me, the nobody guy.'"

Upon leaving Paris, Porcaro extended an open invitation to Pino: "If you're ever in L.A., give me a call," he told the bass player.

In 1982, Pino had started to work with a fledgling artist named Paul Young, becoming a big part of his sound with his fretless bass right out of the gate with Young's first offering "Wherever I Lay My Hat." Palladino ended up working on several of Young's albums, sometimes traveling to Los Angeles to record. On his first trip there, he took Porcaro up on his offer. Jeff sent drum tech Paul Jamieson (Jamo) to pick Pino up and take him to his house on Hesby Street. "Jeff was so warm. He really extended a hand of friendship to me," Palladino says. "He had said, 'Once you get to L.A., call me up and if you need a little smoke, I'll get you hooked up.' That was Jeff, right? I was at his house twice. The first time I was there, I was just over chilling with Jeff. The second time, the band (Toto) was there working in Jeff's studio, and I met all of them, and Niko Bolas."

In the late '80s, the two played together on Don Henley's "New York Minute" from *The End of the Innocence.* Jeff's only on that one track, but Pino says sometimes Jeff came by the studio (A&M) when he wasn't tracking.

Then they worked together on Jeff's last album, Paul Young's *The Crossing.* Palladino recalls: "I flew over with Paul to do the album.

There were a lot of legendary musicians on that album—and they were some heavy musicians to be playing with. Once again, Jeff did that thing he did. He always just played the right thing, the right beat for the song. He just knew; he had an innate instinct of what to play for the song and it was one or two takes." On breaks, they hung out behind Ocean Way Recording Studios, Studio 2. To this day when he works there, he thinks about all the time they spent outside together. "I remember him saying he wanted to chill a little bit," Palladino recalls. "I said, 'What do you have coming up, man?' He said, 'I just want to spend some time at home with the family and ease up on things and just have a life,' and I thought, 'That's just so cool.'"

When Pino thinks back about Jeff, he really does believe it was he who gave him the confidence to be who he became as a musician.

ONE DRUMMER TO ANOTHER

BOBBY COLOMBY recalls that he met Porcaro at United Western Studios in about 1973 when he was producing a song for Blood, Sweat and Tears, the group which he had helped form in 1967. While waiting for co-producer Roy Halee and the band to show up, he was alone, playing the drum set out in the studio. "I was having a good time," Colomby recalls, and then says with a laugh, "I could still play then. (Note: As Colomby became a producer and industry exec, he did less and less actual drumming.) All of a sudden, a guy appears with his glasses and his arms folded. I'm playing and I look up and say, 'Oh, sorry. How ya doing? Who are you?' He says, 'I'm Jeff Porcaro.' I said, 'How you doing, Jeff? I'm Bobby Colomby.' And he says, 'Oh, I know!' That was my first encounter with the guy. I had no idea who he was. He was extremely nice."

In 1981, Pages asked Colomby to add to the self-titled album they had recorded with Jay Graydon. Colomby had been the A&R guy to originally sign Pages to Epic Records, produce their initial records and sign them to Capitol when he went over to that label. He had them write a couple of new songs to record—"You Need a Hero" and "Come on Home"—and then Colomby took them into the studio and they recorded them, beginning to end, in two days. "I had heard stuff that Jeff did, and I was just looking for someone who could get it," Colomby explains. "The thing about everything I've heard that Jeff does, when you're doing studio work, it's very different from live playing. I don't think I would have made a very good studio drummer. When you're a studio drummer, what you're supposed to do, starting with your sound, is you must understand exactly what it's going to take to support the music that is going to be played. 'Hey, look at me' has nothing to do with it. Playing for the song is exactly what he did. He would sync it."

"HOW'S THAT FOR A POCKET!"

... says Bobby Colomby about his favorite thing he did with Jeff. It was for a Rodney Crowell song on his 1992 album *Life is Messy*. "It was a song that was finished and well done, but I had worked on all the material before he went in the studio," Colomby recalls. "He had a million songs, and he was playing them for me, and I would do things like, 'Can I have just the melody and the vocal? Can I give it to someone?' knowing that there was a better way to support the melody than what he had been playing on guitar. There was one song, 'It's Not for Me to Judge,' where Rodney said, 'I can see you're not thrilled with it.' And I said, 'I told you when I heard it, it should be Bob Dylan playing with the Rolling Stones.' So I went into the studio and took the track that he had, and I had Jeff come in and play a new drum track. I added a great guitar player, Steuart Smith, and I said, 'Think Keith Richards.'" When Colomby sent Crowell the finished product, the artist's response was, "I love you forever."

Colomby says he compares a great drummer to a great basketball player. He loves watching basketball and used to play the game himself. "When someone drives to the hoop and he's doing an underhand layup at the rim, there are hands swishing around, flying around, trying to block him and all that stuff. When Michael Jordan does it, everything for him is slow motion, so when he sees a hand come in on his left side, he doesn't jerk to his right, he just moves enough to get past the hand, because it's slow motion to him. That's what makes that kind of athleticism. Drums, to some degree, have some kind of athletic component. Like Michael Jordan, everything for Jeff is in slow motion," Colomby asserts. "That's why every beat is identically spaced between the other beat, before and after. It's unbelievable. He is able to play like a metronome because it's slow (for him). He's a great studio drummer. When he sees on the paper a rest for four bars, and then he'll see a fill for two bars, most drummers look at a rest differently than when they're playing. A studio drummer just sees it as he's not playing at that moment, but he's still engaged. And when he knows a fill is about to come, he doesn't get nervous—'Here it comes, here it comes.' There's no difference to a studio drummer between filling and space; it's the same. But Jeff took it to another level because of his innate musicality."

David Paich and Jeff Porcaro at Sunset Sound Recorders, Hollywood, California, during the recording sessions for 1982 Grammy winner *Toto IV*. (Courtesy of Barney Hurley)

THE ENTIRE "AFRICA" STORY

(Note: *It's About Time* included a discussion of some of the making of "Africa," but here I am including a much more detailed account. I wrote a "classic track" article for *Mix* magazine about the song in 2005, and what follows is that article, with some slight additions/alterations. Since the time the article was published, both Al Schmitt and Greg Ladanyi have passed away. For those who are audiophiles, there is a lot of technical info, and for those who are not, well, you can skip all that—but here is the *Mix* article, and it is as in-depth as it gets.)

DAVID PAICH told me he wrote "Africa" on his living room piano. "Over many years, I had been taken by the UNICEF ads with the pictures of Africa and the starving children. I had always wanted to do something to connect with that and bring more attention to the continent. I wanted to go there, too, so I sort of invented a song that put me in Africa. I was hearing the melody in my head, and I sat down and played the music in about ten minutes. Then the chorus came out. I sang the chorus out as you hear it. It was like God channeling it. I thought, 'I'm talented, but I'm not *that* talented. Something just happened here!'"

Paich worked on the lyrics for six months and brought the skeleton to Jeff with the idea of having percussion being an integral part of the composition. "Jeff got out African sticks with bottle caps that his dad and Emil Richards (both percussionists) used on National Geographic films. He brought in a marimba and a wooden xylophone kind of thing—this was pre-synthesizer; we didn't have samples back then. You're hearing bass marimba, that other instrument, and you're hearing probably one of the first loops that was ever done."

"I was about eleven when the New York World's Fair took place and I went to the African pavilion with my family," Jeff told me in a 1988 interview for *Modern Drummer* magazine. "I saw the real thing; I don't know what tribe, but there were these drummers playing, and my mind was blown. The thing that blew my mind was that everybody was playing one part. As a little kid in Connecticut, I would see these Puerto Rican and Cuban cats jamming in the park. It was the first time I witnessed somebody playing one beat and not straying from it, like a religious experience, where it gets loud and everyone goes into a trance. I have always dug those kinds of orchestras, whether it be a band or all drummers, where a bunch of guys are saying one thing. So when we were doing 'Africa,' I set up a bass drum, snare drum and a hi-hat, and (percussionist) Lenny Castro set up right in front of me with a conga.

We looked at each other and just started playing the basic groove: the bass drum on 1, on the 'and' of 2 and 3. The backbeat is on 3, so it's a half-time feel, and it's 16th notes on the hi-hat. Lenny started playing a conga pattern. We played for five minutes on tape—no click, no nothing. We just played. I was singing the bass line for 'Africa' in my mind, so we had a relative tempo.

"Lenny and I went into the booth and listened back to the five minutes of that same boring pattern," Porcaro said. "We picked out the best two bars that we thought were grooving and marked those two bars on tape. We made another mark four bars before those two bars, and went back out. I had a cowbell; Lenny had a shaker. They gave us two new tracks and gave us the cue when they saw the first mark go by, and Lenny and I started playing to get into the groove, so by the time that fifth bar came (which was the first bar of the two bars we marked as the cool bars we liked), we were locked, and we overdubbed shaker and cowbell. So there was bass drum, snare drum, hi-hat, two congas, a cowbell and a shaker. We went back in, cut the tape and made a one-bar tape loop that went 'round and 'round and 'round.

"We took that tape, transferred it onto another 24-track for six minutes, and David Paich and I went out in the studio. The song started, and I was sitting there with a complete drum set and Paich was playing. When he got to the fill before the chorus, I started playing the chorus, and when the verse or the intro came back, I stopped playing. Then we had piano and drums on tape. Then we had to do bongos, jingle sticks and big shakers doing quarter notes, maybe stacking two tracks of sleigh bells, two tracks of big jingle sticks and two tracks of tambourines all down to one track. I was trying to get the sounds I would hear Milt Holland or Emil Richards have, or the sounds I would hear in a National Geographic special, or the ones I heard at the New York World's Fair."

AL SCHMITT recalled being at Sunset Sound working on the track; he remembers Porcaro's original process going to a 2-track machine. "After choosing the looped bars, we put a music stand out and had the tape go around the music stand and back into the tape machine."

Then everything else was overdubbed. Paich recorded the opening sound on a Yamaha CS80, "then David Hungate put his bass on, Steve (Lukather) put a guitar on, I put some more piano on," says Paich. "We did the track, and I was still working on the lyrics. Everyone tried to sing the song; there were a lot of lyrics to fit into a small amount of space. Bobby (Kimball) tried to sing it and he couldn't phrase it right. Steve Lukather tried, but I ended up doing it by default. I'm an Elton John fan, and he fits a lot of words into his songs. When we get to the chorus, it's Bobby, Steve and Timothy B. Schmit singing. The legendary Jim Horn came in and played recorders in the second verse.

"We recorded 24-track with lots of slaves," Paich continues. "We learned that approach from Paul Simon, who I think was the first to do it. As soon as he did the rhythm track, he would put the master away so it wouldn't get worn down, and you'd make another 24-track tape for vocals, one of guitars, et cetera, and we made a lot of those. By then, I had my first little 24-track studio (dubbed Hogg Manor) at my house, which was a Trident Fleximix console, two JBL 4311 speakers, and two Ampex MM-1200s, and we messed around doing overdubs there. We were recording 30 IPS, non-Dolby, if you can imagine! There was a Yamaha instrument called a GS1, a prototype for the DX7, which at that time was the new little digital synthesizer, so the kalimba sound you hear is that. And we used a CS80, which is very unique.

"On the vocals, I think we had a U47, probably through an LA-2A limiter. Whenever you hear my lead vocals, they're tripled. Each line has three vocals on it. I got that from listening to a lot of Beach Boys and Beatles records. I like that layered sound."

"Then and still today, I'm an SM57 kind of guy," says **STEVE LUKATHER**. "I'm a big Shure fan when it comes to guitar amps."

"On the guitar, we used a close mic on the amp and then we had a mic about fifteen feet back for room ambience," Schmitt added.

"It was a time when we wanted to experiment a lot," Lukather recalls. "We lived in the studio. It was before any of us were married and had kids, so we rented a Winnebago and had it in the parking lot at Sunset Sound, so we didn't have to go home. We would record all day and all night. If anyone wanted to sleep, they could go into the Winnebago."

GREG LADANYI then came in to mix the album. "I think we used three 24-track machines for 'Africa' and 'Rosanna,' which was something a little bit ahead of its time," he said. "We were at the Sound Factory, and we had to mix 'Africa' in sections because the console wasn't big enough—it didn't have enough faders for the amount of tracks that were on the record. We had to mix sections, and I had to edit the 2-track together to complete the mixes: the verses got mixed, the chorus would go by, and then once the verses were mixed, we mixed the choruses and cut the choruses into the verses. The guys in the room were involved in moving faders because we had no automation on the console then. I would be mixing, and I'd have Lukather on one side of the console and Paich or Porcaro on the other side of the console, and we would do the rides all live. We kept doing the mixes over and over until we got the rides the way we wanted to hear them.

"We used the Eventide Harmonizers for chorusing and harmonizing, a lot of analog effects like tape delay and ¼-inch slap. There was (a) Publison (compressor/limiter), and the Sound Factory had the great EMT 140 plates, so all the reverb pretty much came from that. So much of the stuff has come and gone now.

"One other cool thing about the record is something we need to go back to: The lack of compression used on the final process for the record to be pressed was not an issue like it is today, so the great dynamics of Toto as a band were really felt and heard by the listener. Today, almost every record you hear is so compressed. A musician's ability to play with their feel is all about their dynamic range, and when that gets taken out of the mix, the end user has no relationship with the musician or artist and how they feel things. (*Toto IV*) had all that. It was a great record, and it's still the record that I hear on the radio when I travel the world, even in places like South Korea or South America."

MAROTTA'S MEMORIES

Around 1977, before drummer **RICK MAROTTA** moved to the West Coast, he met Porcaro for the first time while he was doing a session in a Los Angeles studio. Marotta remembers that Porcaro, who was working at the same studio that day, sought him out. "I had heard some stuff about Jeff—what a great guy he was, what a great drummer he was," says Marotta. "The thing I remember that was most relevant was that his first thought in response to me was, 'Hey man, you're in town, if you need anything, or you would like me to recommend you for any work or anything, I'd be happy to do that.' I didn't say anything. I was really swamped with work. That's why I was in L.A. and then I was going to go back to New York, but his first thought was to help. But then he had this funny conversation with himself: 'What am I talking about? You're Rick Marotta!' And he reached into his pocket and grabbed a handful of change and shoved the change in his mouth as a joke, like, 'What an idiot, I'm going to eat my own change.' And we both just burst out laughing and that was my first meeting with him.

"He also told me that he had to talk about 'Peg.' He gave me one of the biggest compliments I have ever gotten from anybody," Rick continues. "He said when he heard the record, he made a loop of 'Peg' on a cassette and got in his car and just drove and drove and listened to it over and over and over again."

Marotta comments that "Room 335," a Porcaro played track from Larry Carlton's 1978 self-titled album, is as perfect as it could be played. "When I toured with Larry, we were joking that I had to learn my part all over again because Jeff had played it on the album," Marotta says with a laugh.

Rick says he and Jeff became good friends. He says all the Porcaros opened their hearts to him when he moved to Los Angeles. "They were like family when I first came out here. Jeff would always call and check in with me," recalls Marotta, who made the move around 1983. "One day I got a call from Jeff, and he says, 'Listen, I'm working on this Donald Fagen album, but it's just not happening. I'm not the guy, and I told Donald, 'Marotta is the guy.' And they're recording at Jeff's house on Hesby. The next thing you know, I'm there playing on the sessions that he's supposed to be playing on, and he's there, just hanging with us drinking a cup of coffee, coming in and out of the studio. I mean, that's the kind of guy he was. Who is going to give up a Donald Fagen solo album that is recording at their house? Who does that?"

Marotta remembers Jeff relaying the famous story of Boz Scaggs' generosity, the details of which I had never heard: "Jeff was in the apartment he was renting, and it was pouring rain outside, just pouring. There was a knock at the door. He goes to the door and there, wrapped in a raincoat, is Boz, out of thin air. Jeff said, 'Hey man, what are you doing? You want to come in?' Boz says, 'No, no, I just came to give you something.' From under his raincoat, standing in the downpour, he pulls out this gold or platinum record, hands it to Jeff and says, 'I wanted to give this to you personally.' Jeff says, 'Thanks man, that's cool. That's really great. You sure you don't want to come in?' 'No, no, I really gotta go.' Then Boz reached into his jacket and pulled out an envelope, handed it to him and said, 'Thanks for everything man, this is for you.' It was a check I think for $30,000. Jeff told me it was the down payment for his house. Then I loved Boz!"

GREGG BISSONETTE'S RECOLLECTIONS

The first time **GREGG BISSONETTE** ever saw Porcaro play live was while Jeff was playing with Toto at the Royal Oaks Music Theater in Royal Oaks, Michigan, a suburb of Detroit. Gregg was home during a school break from North Texas State. In May 1982,

Gregg moved to Los Angeles, and he distinctly remembers the moment he heard the opening of "Rosanna" on his car radio.

"I went, 'What in the world is this?'" says Gregg. "I had to pull my car off the freeway and just listen. A few nights later I went to this club in Encino called the Flying Jib to hear Vinnie Colaiuta play, and all these guys in the Dave Boruff Band—Vinnie on drums, Michael Fisher on percussion, Neil Stubenhaus on bass, Barnaby Finch on piano, Pat Kelley on guitar and Dave Boruff on saxophone—started jamming on 'Rosanna.' They were going, 'How about that new Toto single, 'Rosanna?' And Vinnie was going, 'Jeff, Jeff!'"

Gregg Bissonette, Jeff and son Christopher. (Photo courtesy of Jay Rubin)

Bissonette got a gig playing with his bassist buddy Bob Birch at the Smokehouse in Burbank, where they played "Rosanna" every night. Gregg says he began to get the knack of it, so that by the time he played the Jerry Lewis Telethon in the fall of '82 —his first big job in L.A.—with Joe Guercio conducting and Joe Porcaro on percussion behind Gregg, he had the guts to say, "Hey Mr. Porcaro, what do you think of this?" and he began to play "Rosanna." Gregg laughs at the memory. "He started smiling and nodding his head like, 'Yeah, every drummer in the world is trying to play "Rosanna" like Jeff.' In his great, classy way, he said, 'Pretty close.' Nobody could ever play that like Jeff." Later in the fall of 1982, Gregg landed the gig with Maynard Ferguson. (Gregg's brother Matt had already been playing bass in the band for a year.) He stayed until spring of 1983, when he came back to Los Angeles to focus on this recording and other touring opportunities.

One evening after finishing a performance of *Little Shop of Horrors* at a Westwood playhouse with his friend Bob Birch, they were walking out of the theater and Gregg noticed someone walking in front of them. "I said to Bob, 'That looks like Jeff Porcaro.' I had never met him. I said it kind of loud. He said, 'That's not Jeff Porcaro.' I said, 'I think it *is* Jeff Porcaro.' Jeff turned around and my heart stopped beating. He was so nice," Gregg says. "He stopped and I said, 'Jeff, I'm a drummer and I'm your biggest fan. It's so great to meet you,' and my friend Bob sings, 'Meet you all the way,' (the line from "Rosanna."). Jeff just laughed that guttural laugh and then said, 'Who do you play with?' And I said, 'I just got off the road with the Maynard Ferguson Big Band.' He lit up and said, 'Yo, Maynard. Alright, alright.' And then he introduced me to Susan, and that was my first meeting with Jeff. He could not have been cooler."

Gregg's second meeting with Porcaro was when he went to see him play with Los Lobotomys at the Baked Potato. "He does this incredible fill on 'Lobotomy Stew' and my friends Chris Brady and Mark Morales, who were my drum students at the time, were listening to that fill and trying to remember it, so we went to the back of the club and were hanging out there, playing it on our legs. I said, 'Hey, here comes Jeff. I'm going to count it off: 3, 4…' and we went into it. He got this big smile on his face and puts his hands up in the air and his exact words were, 'Oh man, you guys are stealing all my best stuff.' We all just cracked up," Bissonette recalls with a laugh.

Once, Gregg went to see Jeff play at the Baked Potato, and he recalls how impassioned Porcaro became during one break in the song. "He was playing with David Garfield, Steve Lukather, John Pena and Brandon Fields. Jeff stands up and he's so full of passion and without even thinking about it, he wants to hit something, so he turns to his left and without looking, goes bam on the wall maybe six inches apart, and he hit this Yamaha poster of Tom Brechtlein, putting his sticks into Tom's eyeballs without even knowing it," Gregg remembers. "I'd look at that poster for years; they only recently took it down."

Bissonette continued to go to see Jeff with Los Lobotomys at the Baked Potato, and even started subbing for him at those gigs. Sometimes when he'd go see Jeff play, Jeff would call Gregg up to sit in, telling him how much his hands hurt. Sometimes Jeff even needed help to pry his fingers open. "They were shut so tight because of his health issues with his arteries and everything," Gregg says. "I'd play with Los Lobotomys a bunch, and then I got the gig with David Lee Roth.

The first year in the David Lee Roth Band (1986), the album had just come out and some of the guys in Van Halen—I think Alex and Eddie, Michael Anthony, Billy Sheehan and Steve Vai and I—went over to a theater in Pasadena where Toto was playing, and it was amazing. Then we heard they were having a little get together at a bar across the street. I was hanging with Jeff, and he looked over at Alex Van Halen, pointed at him and said, 'That's the guy, that's the godfather of big rock.' Jeff had so much respect for other players."

The next time Gregg saw Jeff was after Jeff had moved to Hidden Hills, which Gregg says he called "Hidden Bills." "I lived in Woodland Hills and went to Builders Emporium nearby. I pulled into the parking lot in my black Porsche and I see Jeff walking out, carrying a couple of furnace air filters," Gregg recalls. "He sees me and comes over. I have my window rolled down and he looks in and lets out the loudest guttural laugh because in between my legs I have a bowl of pasta, which I'm eating with a plastic fork as I'm driving. He yells out, 'Yo Biss,' and he's pointing to the Mostaccioli and he's laughing that infectious laugh he had."

In 1988 there was a benefit at Hollywood's Guitar Center for drummer Mark Craney (Gino Vannelli, Jethro Tull) who had just had a kidney replacement due to diabetes. Porcaro was there with his four-year-old son Christopher. "I said, 'Jeff, you gotta get up on stage and play,'" Gregg recalls. "And he said, 'I'm just here to watch and hang.' He just wanted to be there to be supportive."

Recalling a funny anecdote, Bissonette says around Christmastime 1988 at Topanga Mall, as Bissonette was coming down the escalator, he saw Jeff with a bag in his hands.

Jeff to Bissonette: "Yo Biss, any idea where I can get one of those things that you can recharge that cleans up stuff on a counter?"

Bissonette to Jeff: "You mean a Dustbuster?"

Jeff to Bissonette: "Yeah, yo Biss, the Dustbuster! Where can I get one of those?"

"I think I pointed to Sears or something," Bissonette recalls. "And we're sitting there talking about this new thing that just came out called the Dustbuster."

The last time Gregg saw Jeff play was at a Remo party at NAMM. "Jeff came out and played one song in 7: 'Jake to the Bone.' He walked off stage and the whole audience was going, 'What just happened?'" Bissonette says.

After Jeff passed away and Toto hired Simon Phillips, Simon needed to take some medical leave in the fall of '95. Gregg got the call to sub 36 shows in Europe, and he says he and Mike spoke often about how Mike and Jeff were so connected on drums and bass. Mike told him particularly on the breakdown B section of "Rosanna" with the finger snaps, that's "where we'd take it to church."

Over Gregg's shoulder, on the screen behind him, was a huge photo of Jeff. "It was so heavy," Gregg says. "It was such an honor to be there. No one could play like Jeff—no one could play like Simon either; *Tambu* with him was out, and I did my best to play like he did on that album, but I really tried to do my best Jeff Porcaro imitation.

There was a fill that Jeff did in the video *Toto Live in Paris* (DVD) on "Africa," instead of the one that was on the album, that I learned. I thought, 'I'm going to do that because when you played those gigs in France, especially Paris, those audiences knew their music. Lukather would call them superfans. When I would do that fill, the audience would go wild."

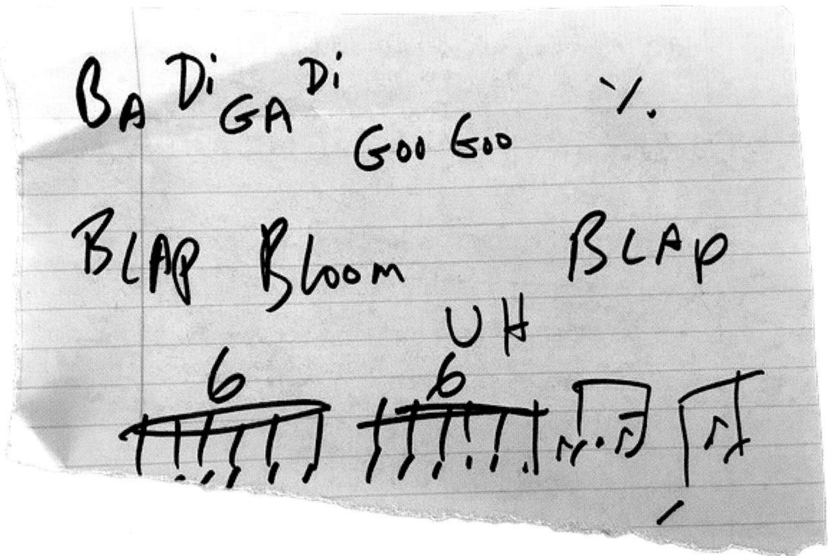

Gregg Bissonette's note showing Jeff's live fill on "Africa." (Courtesy of Gregg Bissonette)

Toto's Planet Earth Tour, 1990. (Photo by Knieps Oliver. All rights reserved.)

Chapter Four

The Nineties

"THE SUN AND THE MOON"

And this Go West track *is* the sun and the moon as it is as close to perfection as you will ever hear! It was recorded sometime between 1989 and 1991, released in '92 and produced by **RON FAIR**. Luckily. And I say luckily because the backstory is one of those kismet kinds of events that only the universe can understand.

I shall condense: In 1985, Fair was a young A&R rep for Chrysalis Records. He would go on to produce number one hits for artists including Mary J. Blige, Fergie, Black Eyed Peas, Christina Aguilera, huge soundtracks, and would head record labels, but at the time, he was just making a name for himself. At this moment, he was stuck in England because the project he was supposed to produce fell apart and his return ticket was far too expensive to change. His boss at Chrysalis in L.A. told him he had to wait it out, so Fair called the only person he knew in England to pass some time. As they were chatting, this friend asked if she could play Ron some music. Fatefully, she let him hear Go West. Chrysalis U.K. had passed on the group three times, but the U.S. had never heard them. She played him "We Close Our Eyes" and "Call Me," and Ron fell in love with them. He played them over the phone for his boss in the U.S, who told him to sign the group while he was there. Fair took the demos, upgraded them, had them mixed and used the same audio—never re-recording a single note—and they both hit #1 in the U.K.

Fast-forward a few years, which included a series of rollercoaster events for the band, and Fair became the producer for the third album, *Indian Summer*, which he wanted to sound a little more rock/soul and less synth-oriented. "Jeff was the holy grail. It was either him or

Steve Gadd," Fair says. "Jeff was legendary. Go West was a musician's musicians band, with the best in sound and best lead singer, so the musicality of Porcaro fit the ethos of Go West. It was a shuffle, which is funny, because reading the first book, it talks about Jeff's shuffle phobia—while he was the best at it."

The session was at Music Grinder Studios, and it was an opportunity to hire Porcaro for the first time. Fair remembers it well: "He was not interested in knowing who I was or maybe he knew who I was and didn't let on," Fair considers. "He was very insular to himself in the booth. The whole thing was about an hour and a half; very short. I had a chart, which I had written out. He went in the booth and played it and that was the first take. After we listened to it, not because I didn't like the first take, but because I like to edit between takes and have options, I said, 'Let's lay down one more and get a few more things, maybe this bar 41, the "and" of 4,' or whatever I said. And he said, 'No dude, no, that's it, you got it.' I didn't have the friendship or camaraderie with him to be on his page, and I said, 'What do you mean? You only ran the song once through.' And he said, 'Yeah, that's it. That's my thing. You got my thing,' and he walked out."

When Jeff left, Fair says he was less concerned about the interaction as the practicality of "did he have what he needed?" As a producer, he always wanted more than one take and he was worried that somewhere he would need to comp something. "I don't know that I ever had done a first take and said, 'Ok, that's it,' and not do take two," Fair confesses. "I might do take two and use take one, but I don't know that I would stop and not do take two or ever have."

But Fair had what he had, and yes, it was perfect.

"When I listen back to it now, with the clarity of the rearview mirror these many years later, he was right," Fair admits. "Of course, he was right because it's inspired and perfect in all the right places. It didn't need to be any more or less than it is, and it's very profound. It goes through a pretty big arc of small to big, and it's cinematic. Listening back to it and with the mythology of this beautiful man behind it, of course it's like a little miracle in my pocket."

MEANWHILE…

Jeff worked on 10cc's *Meanwhile,* which was recorded between 1990-1991. The record company wanted the band to work with an American producer, which led them to Gary Katz, who brought in Porcaro. They worked together at Bearsville Studios in Woodstock, New York. "We tried various things to actually break big in the States," explains guitarist **GRAHAM GOULDMAN**. "Although we had a couple of big hits, we never broke as a live act or as an album act. When Gary's name was mentioned, it was perfect because obviously we were big Steely Dan fans."

They loved all the players Katz recommended, even though it was a departure for the group to work with outside musicians. At that point, the band was led by Gouldman and Eric Stewart, so they made the unilateral decision, which Gouldman says was probably a mistake. "We lost some kind of an identity. It was quite an unhappy time. There was friction between myself and Eric," Gouldman admits. "It wasn't a happy experience, although as far as Jeff was concerned, he was an absolute delight, and I'm glad that despite all the hassles, which had absolutely nothing to do with him whatsoever, it was an honor to work with him and play with him."

Working with Porcaro and Freddie Washington was the best part of making that album, Gouldman explains. "Jeff was a legend. It was not just the fact that he was an absolutely wonderful drummer, but he was also a very generous kind of guy. He would—and quietly—make a suggestion or observation. He was very nice about it. He got involved in a way, and very gently, with the music," he says. "He came up with some ideas and suggestions like percussion overdubs. He was more involved really than someone who was 'just a session drummer.' I would like to think he integrated into being part of the band rather than just a hired hand. That was one of his main attributes."

As they played the songs, Jeff "got it" immediately. "He instinctively knew what was needed. Everything he did was tasteful. To play with him was like being sucked into his time. He was a charming man," says Gouldman.

THE TIME JEFF (UNWITTINGLY) SAVED A CAREER

Engineer **MARC DeSISTO** recorded two takes of what will remain an un-named project with Jeff on drums. He decided that the second take was the keeper, although both takes were great. DeSisto was running late to his next appointment, so he asked the assistant engineer to make a slave of the master. "(The assistant) happened to put the master on the erase tape, so he erased the master," DeSisto confides. "He didn't erase the whole thing, because he realized he had screwed up. I got a phone call from the kid telling me what he did and that he left his keys at the front door at the studio and left. It was for a major producer and a huge corporation. I went in the room and I'm thinking, 'I'm fucked.' So I look at what there is. Two takes. He had erased the drums, the bass and the scratch guitar, and it suddenly hits me: 'Oh, I did two takes with Jeff Porcaro on this!' And God love him, the first take felt good, and I was able to keep the second half of the partially erased take. I edited together the first half of the first take and the remainder of the second, and no one ever knew, because when I put the two takes together it was 'master good.' Jeff was so good that the first take and the second take were identical. I was able to save the song, my life and my career!"

Thanks to a suggestion from Niko Bolas, DeSisto kindly put some confusion to rest about the title track of Warren Zevon's 1991 album *Mr. Bad Example* with regard to whether it was just Jim Keltner on drums or both Jeff and Jim. When I spoke to producer Waddy Wachtel for *It's About Time*, he said it was just Jim, and Jim could not recall playing along with Jeff—yet **JORGE CALDERÓN** swore it was double drums. To reiterate the story, Jeffrey was the drummer on the album, but when they got to the track "Things to Do in Denver When You're Dead," Jeff told Zevon and Waddy that Keltner was the right drummer for that track. Wachtel told me they respected Jeff's opinion so much that they called Keltner. Jim came in, played on that track and stayed and played double drums on the title song. DeSisto even recalls the two of them warming up together and getting samples from them.

After the conversation with Marc, I got back with Keltner and we spent about 45 minutes one day talking about it, dissecting the song and looking at a photo that Jorge Calderón (who played bass on the track) sent over as evidence of the double drumming. The photo showed Jeff standing in front of Jim at the drums; it was indeed Jim's kit, which meant there were two sets of drums in the studio. After listening

Jeff with Jim Keltner during Warren Zevon's *Mr. Bad Example* recording sessions, 1991. (Courtesy of Jorge Calderón)

Warren Zevon *Mr. Bad Example* sessions, 1991. L to R: Jorge Calderón, Warren Zevon, Waddy Wachtel, Charley Drayton (behind Waddy), Jim Keltner and Jeff. Note: Charley Drayton did not play on the track, he was just hanging out in the studio. (Photo courtesy of Jorge Calderón)

to the track carefully, Jim said he could clearly hear two backbeats. In addition to helping prove that Jeff and Jim played together, Calderón has some vivid memories of the day. "There was a pretty heavy sense of a mutual admiration between those two, Jeff being the young one, of course, but it was the same going the other way from Jim also," he recalls. "The chemistry was instant; they found their place in the song's groove, and we just did it.

"I had played with Jim a lot through the years with Ry Cooder and the band, but I had only played on one song with Jeff," Jorge continues. "The song was 'Quite Ugly One Morning' on that same album, and it had a strong Zeppelin-esque bounce. It was all pretty easy and natural for me to play on 'Mr. Bad.' I had written the song with Warren and the choice of having Jim and Jeff on it was just perfect for us."

DeSisto recalls meeting Jeff when he was assisting producer Jimmy Iovine at A&M and Porcaro was doing sessions for Iovine. "There was a Judson Spence record that he did, and Don Henley's *The End of the Innocence.* I remember recording 'New York Minute.' I recall that Jeff was one of the first drummers who was replacing drum machines. Most records were made with drum machines and that was it, but some people made the song with a drum machine but would have Jeff overdub later," DeSisto says. "I thought, 'This guy is just a craftsman; he was the finishing guy, but when he played, it was like he was there from the beginning.' No one else could ever do that. When you would punch in, he was exact, which could be tricky, and then punching out, but with Jeff it was flawless."

DeSisto says Porcaro also taught him about tuning drums back when he was an assistant engineer: "I was always around during the set up. He'd have a drum guy come and they'd set up the drums. Then Jeff would come and put the final tuning on it," DeSisto remembers. "I said, 'Jeff, how do you do that? What is the key to that? How do you get your toms so unique sounding?' He showed me how he tuned cross, from one stick across to the other side, this sort of pattern, and when it was right, he'd tune the lug down just a little bit. And the snare, the same way. It was fun being around him because even though I was a nobody kid assistant, he was kind as hell to me."

C.J. VANSTON'S HERO

C.J. VANSTON describes Jeff as the "king of all session players ever, no matter what instrument. That's the guy!"

Probably around 1990, a couple of years after keyboardist C.J. Vanston first moved to Los Angeles, he was fortunate to connect with engineer/producer Greg Ladanyi. Vanston was working on the soundtrack for Dolly Parton's *Straight Talk* with Ladanyi during the day while Ladanyi was working with Toto at night and playing them tracks from the Dolly sessions he had done earlier in the day. The Toto guys liked what they were hearing and asked who was on keyboards. Ladanyi told them it was this guy named C.J. Vanston.

"I had done a song on Luke's first solo album, so I got to know Luke from that and then David Paich and Steve Porcaro wanted to come over," Vanston recalls. "They had heard me do a certain sound I did on the keyboards, and they wanted me to play on 'The Other Side' on *Kingdom of Desire.* So Paich and Steve came over to the studio where Greg and I were set up doing Dolly Parton. I did a couple of overdubs for them, which blew me away because they were such heroes of mine—they're such great keyboard players, what did they need me for? This was all getting back to Jeff; he was hearing all this stuff: 'C.J., C.J., C.J.'"

But while Jeff and Vanston had met briefly during a Toto playback that Ladanyi was producing, they still hadn't worked together—until C.J. got called to play on David Crosby's 1993 release *Thousand Roads* at East West Studios. "I walk in and see this drum kit. The producer was Don Was. I said, 'Whose kit is that?' He said, 'Jeff Porcaro's.' And I thought, 'Oh boy! I finally get to play with Jeff. This is going to be awesome.' I'm sitting there playing piano, warming up when the door kicks open, and Jeff is standing there smoking a cigarette. He looks over and says, 'C.J. fucking Vanston! Let's see what all the fuss is about.' I said, 'Come on man, don't put that kind of pressure on me.' I'm always actually up for pressure, but what a way for him to walk in. But what he didn't know, I was such a scholar of Toto that I had picked my place as a keyboard player as right in between David Paich and Steve Porcaro. David did all the super jazz, great blues, New Orleans, B3 piano and all that stuff, while Steve Porcaro was the mad scientist with the modular synths and everything. Of course, I'm generalizing, but I wanted to be the guy right in the middle of those two, and that's kind of where I schooled myself."

The drums were set up beside Vanston. Jeff was facing him without gobos. They started the take. "There's no separation at all; we either get the take or we don't," Vanston says. "There's a piano intro all by itself, and Don says, 'I want it to be right in time, no click,' and then Jeff came in and man, we just locked—we locked in like it was ridiculous. He's doing the big jazz face while he's playing, and he's looking at me, and we're just into it, playing the shit out of this track. We get done with the track and it was just a great pass, a first pass. He spins around on his drum stool and lights up a cigarette. I'm waiting. Then he gets up and walks right by me and out the door. I thought, 'What? How? No! We just had this incredible… how is this possible?' I sat there crestfallen. All of a sudden the door kicks back open and Jeff comes back in going, 'Ahhhhhh, ha haaaaa!' He comes running over, grabs me and says, 'You motherfucker! You're a monster. I knew I was going to love playing with you.' He gave me this big hug, put his arm around me and said, 'Let's go listen to what we did.' We walk into the control room, and Jeff went around to the back of the console. Coincidentally, I also always went around the backside of the console, looking in the back at the rest of the band. I always liked standing there and checking things out. Jeff saw me do this and said, 'What are you doing?' I said, 'This is where I like to listen.' And he said, 'This is where *I* like to listen.'"

Jeff had this Casio watch that had a calculator. As the intro went by, he took it off his wrist and hit the button every four bars. "I go, 'What are you doing, man?' He says, 'Checking you out, man.' I go, 'Whaaat?' He says, 'Yeah, I'm just checking your time.' And I said, 'How am I doing?' And he said, 'Dude, this is the best anyone has ever timed out. You're within a tenth of a second,' is what I think he said. 'Your time is dead on.'"

While Crosby put on a scratch vocal, Jeff suggested he and Vanston go outside and smoke a joint, where they exchanged some stories. The only thing C.J. really recalls is that they both ended up talking about how they shared an interest in the Civil War. "He was mostly asking me questions like, 'Where did you come from? Where did you learn how to play like that?' I thought, 'Man, our future is going to be so great.' We were musical brothers and we had so much music ahead of us."

They went back in and ran down a couple more takes. Vanston never saw him again.

MANY LESSONS

Drummer **RON WIKSO** sought lessons from Joe Porcaro soon after he arrived in Los Angeles. As he got to know Jeff years later, he learned that Jeff was a product of his own lessons: great parental upbringing. It was around 1983 when Ron went to the Porcaro family's Valleyheart Drive home in Sherman Oaks for drum instruction with Joe. As Wikso recalls it, Joe asked him to play various beats for about 45 minutes and at the end of it, he told Ron his best advice was for him to "get out and play;" that he didn't think there was a lot he could do for him. "I was dumbfounded," Wikso says. "On the one hand it was a compliment, but on the other hand I was 23 years old, and I'm thinking, 'I'm sure there's a lot you can teach me.' He was super nice and very encouraging and just said, 'You just need experience. Just get out there and do stuff.' I was both thrilled and disappointed at the same time because I wanted to study with him, but thrilled because he thought I had a shot."

Fast-forward to his big first shot: a major tour with Cher that began in 1989. In October 1990, they performed in London for about five shows at Wembley Stadium. Jeff happened to be in London as well, recording Dire Straits' *On Every Street* and staying in the same hotel as Wikso. Cher's bass player, Hugh McDonald, who knew Jeff from session work, introduced the two of them one night in the hotel bar after Wikso's gig and Jeffrey's session. "Of course, I'm sitting there drooling, going, 'Oh my God, it's Jeff Porcaro,' and he was *the* nicest person ever on the planet," Wikso recounts. "He was so very encouraging to me, which is the reason I connect it to my story with Joe. I don't drink much, but any time I'd have a beer now and then, he'd never let me pay for anything, no matter how much I would insist. I would say, 'God, I have to reciprocate.' He'd say, 'No, no, no. You're up and coming, man.' I ended up hanging out with him for four or five nights. And one night we met at the bar—Jeff, Hugh and I—and I said, 'I'm kinda hungry. Are you guys hungry at all?' Neither one of them was, but they said they'd go with me, so we jumped in a cab and went to the Hard Rock Café, and of course Jeff paid for the cab. Then the bill came, and Jeff paid for my meal. He didn't even eat. I was going, 'Dude…!' He paid for the cab back and of course he knew I was a struggling guy trying to get my grounding in the business. He was just so, so aware and sympathetic of that."

Since Wikso and Jeff both played with Cher as an early break in their careers, the two drummers talked about the gig, and also discussed records and sessions. In fact, Wikso remembers asking him about a story a guitarist friend told him that he witnessed on a session where Jeff was replacing drums on some songs for a well-known '80s rock band. "My friend told me he played the track, he came in to listen and everybody said, 'Yeah it sounds good, there's just this one spot in the bridge that sounds maybe not quite there,' so Jeff says, 'Ok, no problem,' and he goes back out and does another take and they say the same thing, 'It sounds great, there's just this one spot in the bridge.' So very diplomatically Jeff says, 'Can I hear just the drums and the click? I just want to see where I'm at—if I need to push it or pull or whatever.'

They separate the drums and the click and of course it's perfect, and they go, 'Oh…I guess it's us.' He didn't have to call anybody out; he just very diplomatically took care of it. It was just an illustration of him handling a delicate situation," Wikso recounts. "He didn't want to gloat. It was a diplomatic technique to use instead of pointing fingers, and it was a great lesson (from Jeff). I've used that on sessions ever since then, where I'll say, 'Let me just hear myself,' and I've insisted on using a click. It's a cool thing I learned from him, and it has served me well."

DEFINITELY A TREAT

Trick or Treat by **PAUL BRADY** was another Gary Katz production with Jeffrey at the drums. The 1991 release remains one of Brady's most popular albums to date. If you haven't had the opportunity, do take a listen!

Before the recording, Brady had never met Porcaro. "It was a thrill to do," says Brady. "I was being offered the chance to play with some of my idols. I had always been a Steely Dan fan, and I loved the stuff that Toto had done. The chance to work with Jeff, David Paich, Michael Landau, Freddie Washington and Jimmy Johnson was just an amazing opportunity for me. I took to it like a duck to water. I spent about five seconds being intimidated by the prospect and eventually I went, 'Well, Gary likes the songs, he thinks they're good for the boys to play, so I'll put my best foot forward and go over there without any fear.' And that's what happened. When I got there no one had ever heard of me. I think the guys were pleasantly surprised that they could get off on the songs. That gave me a lot of confidence. When I would sing the track, I could see on their faces that they were enjoying what I was doing. They picked up on the emotional core of the song and were able to convey it, all of them."

Arriving from Ireland, Brady met Jeff and the rest of the musicians on the first day of sessions at A&M Recording Studios in Los Angeles in 1989. "We were in the big room, and the day we arrived, Jim Keltner was working in the other studio. He and Jeff were chewing the fat for a while, so I got to meet Keltner, too!" Brady recalls.

The process was a bit of an eye-opener for him. These were the early days of digital computer sequencing, and Brady says he had worked up his songs on a rather primitive computer. "I had demo drum parts on my sequencing recordings that Jeffrey found a little bit difficult to deal with at first," Brady confides. "I'm not surprised, because it was a little bit all over the place. Some of the songs were in 12/8 time, and the computer parts didn't swing like they should; all the sixteenths, all the twelves, all the hi-hat beats were kind of stiff. He was trying to overdub to that, and naturally he was struggling with it. But we got through it, and we eventually found a way to incorporate some of my sequences, but let him play drums live. Once I got that into my head and figured that out, we had no problems and we really enjoyed playing together."

Paul says having come from being a solo performer, he has a strong sense of his rhythmic core. "Any band I had been in prior to that, I kind of drove the track with my guitar playing, and the drummer followed me. It took me a while to let go of being the rhythm in the track and just trust that what Jeff was doing was right for the track—which was ridiculous, I mean, this was Jeff Porcaro," he says with a laugh. "But I had had a whole life of being the center of the track and had always fought with drummers in the past. So many drummers would learn the song and play, and then wouldn't listen to anything else on stage. I always wanted to work with a drummer who listened and followed me, so that took a little while to settle with Jeff, but as soon as I relaxed into it, it was just a wonderful feeling of security to know he was right there on the money, even before me."

All that to say, it took a minute for the two to get used to how the other worked and to trust the situation, but it paid off in the sessions—and later: When Jeff was called in for Bonnie Raitt's "Luck of the Draw," written by Brady (and discussed earlier, in the Don Was interview), he knew how to handle Brady's oddly-written drum parts. Brady wasn't present when the drums were recorded for "Luck of the Draw." He came in later to overdub his part, and in fact until the day I told him it was Jeffrey on drums, he just assumed it was Raitt's drummer Ricky Fataar. Upon that revelation, he said: "No one talked to me about it. I guess I just assumed Ricky played on the whole record and never looked at the album credits. Jeff had a problem or two dealing with my drum programs on *Trick or Treat,* so it's not out of the question he'd figured out where my head was at by the time he heard my 'Luck' demo! I love how the Bonnie track turned out."

Brady says Jeff's sound was all-enveloping when he was working with him. His drums were tuned well and once they got into a groove, he was able to "sync up with my inner click track," says Paul. "We fell into sync very quickly. I knew when he was going to come down on a beat. There are times at the end of a verse where you want to pull back a little bit, sort of create a feeling that you are going around another corner into another musical area, and he picked up all that sort of stuff instinctively with me; he breathed the track just in the same way as me. That was an absolute thrill, and very few drummers I ever found were able to do that."

Distilling the process, Katz explained that Brady would play the song and then present the chord chart. "We worked from there like almost everything I did, including Walter and Donald, except (with Steely Dan) we didn't have demos, so Donald would sit at the piano, and we would have chord charts. Brady would sit with his guitar and play it for them, and we had chord charts. And the guys were the guys; they would add the fairy dust. Jeffrey never once played to the chart, not on my dates. I'm sure there were dates where he did, but not on mine. The only chart I saw a drummer use was Gadd on the song 'Aja,'" says Katz. "Other than that, Jeff would come in, Rainey and whomever, and they'd play and come in and listen to it and we would talk about what we liked and what we didn't like. Then they'd go back out and do it as we spoke."

Brady mentions the album's opening track "Soul Child" as particularly memorable. "I suppose that was the song that showed off my American Steely Dan, Toto roots more than anything on the record. In a way, I was trying to make that kind of music myself," Paul explains. "That was one of the first ones we cut and that was one of the first ones that turned out really, really good." He also points to "Blue World" as a favorite, which he still loves. "That was a very personal track for me; a kind of confessional track," he admits.

After Los Angeles, they finished up at Bearsville in Woodstock, where mostly it was about the recording, but Brady says they did share some meals, some wine, a joint or two, some laughter and yes, "a lot of fun."

PORCARO AND PAISTE

As Artist Relations Manager for the Paiste cymbal company from 1987 to 2006, **RICHARD MANGICARO**, whom Porcaro called "Mang," enjoyed a close relationship with Jeff. They even shared a few things outside of cymbals, such as a love of painting; since Mangicaro's father was a classic, award-winning artist and Jeffrey loved to draw and paint, they often conversed about that. "We shared that a lot. We talked a lot about illustration and sonic illustration," Mangicaro recalls.

Rich Mangicaro and Jeff. (Courtesy of Rich Mangicaro)

They also spoke a lot about their families and from where they came, since both their families originated from the same region of Calabria, Italy. "My dad was born one hour away from the Porcaro's family," Rich explains, adding that both their last names were originally different in Italy. Jeff's family was Porcara and Rich's family was Mangiarucca. "We also discussed that, and Jeff used to say, 'You're very family to our family,'" Mangicaro recalls.

Rich thinks he may have had his first major encounter with Porcaro at a Toto rehearsal. "He and the band embraced me and I ended up going to a lot of rehearsals," says Mangicaro. "One of them was really special. Jeff and I were working on a new setup for a tour. He was using a combination of 2002s and 602s, and we had some new cymbals we were working on at the time. They were an extension of the Signature series called Sound Formula. A couple of things happened during this time: one a rehearsal at the Power Plant, and the other was the Bruce Springsteen *Human Touch* session."

Mangicaro got to the Toto rehearsal and was the first one there—except for Jeff, who was always at a job before everyone else. "Jeff was behind the kit, and he and I were talking about how he was bummed out at some of the sounds he was getting from some of the other companies. We were talking about how the quality was going down. But he was really excited about these new cymbals, and we were trying out a couple of new crashes at this rehearsal. The guys came in and they were running down a couple of intros, and then they got to the song 'Home of the Brave' off *The Seventh One*," Mangicaro recalls, saying it was incredible to watch Jeff during the working out of the drum part of the intricate and complicated breakdown section. "Not very often does someone get to say they heard Jeff fucking up! He was so frustrated trying to get that down, and I was thinking, 'Holy shit, I can't believe I'm seeing this!' They finally got it down and it was killing; it was so perfect. It wasn't just him—everyone was trying to figure out that tricky break. I felt like such a lucky guy getting to see that."

Jeff was very involved in choosing his sounds, Rich says, and Jeff was instrumental in helping them come up with the Signature line. During Paiste's development of the series, Mangicaro was the liaison between the Switzerland factory and the artists, traveling throughout the U.S. to demo the cymbals to the artists. "Jeff's feedback was so valuable," Rich reveals. "We were showing them to him, as well as Keltner, Steve Jordan, Sheila, Stewart Copeland and Billy Higgins. They would give us their feedback, and I had to translate their words into some sort of descriptive language to the factory in Switzerland so they could turn it into a sound."

Rich says Jeff was very good at describing a sound he was looking for: "For example, he would try a ride in the new series and say, 'It's too washy,' or 'I'd like a little more definition' or 'I really like this cymbal because I can really hear the tip, and in the tip you can really hear the wood of the stick. I like that definition, and we don't want the wash to overtake the definition of the cymbal, so you still hear the definition.' For example, on the Signature crashes, he loved the Full Crashes (16" and 18"). It was the combination of the higher range of frequency with the fullness of that cymbal and the way it sustained and then decayed after he struck it. He loved that, and he gave us some pointers on it like, 'Hey, it would be really great if it had a little more sustain and kept that fullness, but not too gongy.' He didn't like gongy cymbals."

When Jeff was working on Springsteen's *Human Touch* at A&M Studios, he wanted to try a new set of hi-hats. "I went over there early and met him in the drum booth, and we were trying out a bunch of different things. We ended up settling on this one pair of Sound Formula 14" hi-hats," Rich recalls. "He said, 'I'm going to use these, Mang.' Then we went out onto the patio and he rolled this huge joint. I took one hit and he smoked most of it. He told me I couldn't go in because it was a closed session, and I said, 'That's okay.' I gave him a big hug and got in my car, and sitting at the wheel I was thinking, 'Where am I going?' I had to go to my next appointment and I was stoned. I thought, 'How's he going to do that session?' I called him the next day and said, 'How did it go?' And he said, 'Fine man, first take.' That great track, 'Human Touch,' in one take, after that joint!"

Mangicaro nearly always visited with Jeff up in the San Fernando Valley, as Paiste's offices were located approximately sixty miles away. He says Jeff stopped there on the way to Disneyland with his family a couple of times, though. One sweet memory Rich has is the time he went to Jeff's home in Hidden Hills to bring him a set of cymbals and Jeff directed him to knock on a side door, which led into a bedroom. "I walk in, and Jeff says, 'Hey Mang, grab that paint brush.' He was on a ladder, painting this room," Rich recalls with a laugh. "'Wanna help?' I ended up helping him paint this room. It's just one of those moments where you're going, 'I'm painting a fucking bedroom with Jeff Porcaro.'" Mangicaro says they didn't talk about music that day. They conversed mostly about family and kids.

Another precious memory took place in Porcaro's Hidden Hills house. Jeff called Rich to tell him they were planning his father's surprise 60th birthday party at his home. "He said, 'We're going to get David Garfield and his band, we're going to have a jazz quartet out by the pool, and we're going to have a bocce court. You've gotta come.' I was close to Joe, so of course I went. It was so fantastic," Rich remembers. "The family was there, the food was fantastic, David Garfield's band was killin' it, and we were all playing bocce. At one point Jeff came over and said, 'Hey man, do you want to hear a little bit of the record?' I said, 'Sure.' It was the unreleased *The Seventh One*. We went into this room that was his studio where his Grammy Awards were on the mantel with his hi-fidelity system, and we just sat there and smoked some pot and listened to the record, just me and him. He was so proud of it. He was going, 'Check this out. Remember that shit we were working on? Listen to this.'"

Another highlight was during a Paiste photo shoot at the Hollywood Hills home of drummer/photographer Jack White and actress Katey Sagal, who were married at the time. It was the summer of 1992, and it would be the last time that Jeff, his father Joe, Emil Richards and Jim Keltner would ever be all together. Mangicaro describes it as a "silly day." "First of all, Jim was (Jeff's) best friend, Emil was his godfather, and then there was his dad. They were all just so ball-breaking the whole time," Rich says with a laugh. "They were teasing each other about what they were wearing, and they were laughing and cracking each other up the whole time, so it was just hard to get the shot. Jack is really great and really fast at catching stuff. We were eating, drinking coffee and laughing. Basically, Emil was just telling gross jokes. That day was just so special because it was so loving. It was just the four of them plus Jack and me, and we talked about it years after Jeff died."

Jeff performing at the Los Angeles Memorial Coliseum, 1979. (Courtesy of Barney Hurley)

CHAPTER FIVE

The Art of Double Drumming (and More)

Jeffrey obviously enjoyed double drumming. He did his share of it. It didn't always work out. His brother Steve reminded me about something that Luke mentioned to me in *It's About Time*, a fairly well-kept secret: After Steve Porcaro had left the band, Luke brought Tommy Lee in to record double drums with Jeff. "It was a disaster," says Steve. "Luke put it all together because they were buddies."

But Steve confirms that Jeff enjoyed playing with another drummer, and that Rural Still Life was modeled after Mad Dogs and Englishmen, with two drummers. "Rural Still Life had two drummers with Kelly Shanahan," says Steve. "Kelly's father, Dick Shanahan, was a show drummer. Kelly was the one who used to blow everyone's mind; he took all the solos because Jeff didn't like to take solos. The whole double drum thing started because Kelly and Jeff modeled themselves after the whole Keltner and Gordon thing. Jeff was always good at it." (Actually, it wasn't just Kelly Shanahan, it was his younger brother Danny, who was Jeff's age, as well. We will get to that in a moment.)

The first big session Jeff did, Steve reminds us, was the Jack Daugherty session at A&M, playing double drums with his idol, Jim Keltner. Steve was there that day for the recording, and says he even remembers seeing Jeff play the Daugherty material live afterwards, double drumming with Jim Gordon. "I remember there were some rehearsals and live gigs with Jim Gordon. I only remember Jim Keltner doing the recording in the studio on the Jack Daugherty stuff," says Steve. "I never heard Jeff play the way he played with Jim on that Jack Daugherty stuff." (Keltner doesn't remember it being extraordinary material that made for an extraordinary performance, but that session was Jeff and Jim's first meeting. Before they recorded was Keltner's notable story of setting up and hearing some "inside out" playing behind him and turning around to find a young Jeff. Jim noted that Jeff had chops for days but was mature enough to know when not to use them.)

Jeff had already left North Hollywood High for Grant High, but the Shanahans were still close with him. Danny Shanahan says Kelly and he went out to see Jeff play for the first time in tenth grade for a school dance. It was a Blood, Sweat and Tears type band, playing that material and old Sam & Dave stuff. "They had horn players, including Scotty Page, and trumpet player Frank Szabo, as well as David Paich and really good singers," Danny recalls. "Kelly and I were watching him, going, 'This kid has some chops!' He was just kicking that band. It was amazing."

Midway through eleventh grade, sometime in the middle of the school year of 1971, Jeffrey told Danny that the band, now named Rural Still Life, was changing its direction. He wanted Danny to come aboard as a second drummer to create a Mad Dogs and Englishmen vibe. "I was like, 'Are you kidding? You want me to play with you?' And he said, 'Yeah. I'll show you the parts. We'll work it all out,'" Danny recalls. "We studied what Keltner and Gordon did. We had about three sessions where we played together, and we had about six or seven patterns. It was like half time against cut time; the same thing they did. He would look at me and say, 'two,' and we'd play the two pattern because it fit the song, or 'five,' or 'six.' He'd call out the pattern and we'd do it, and we locked in really good. I was following him, but we both had parts that countered each other, so it was like counterparts. We'd play the basic feel together and then it might go to something where he would play on the ride cymbal, and I'd stay on the hi-hat, or I'd play backbeats and he would do cut time. It was just a really neat pattern of things we'd do. The band had about three rehearsals. We played all the Mad Dogs and Englishmen songs and then all of the old R&B, Sam & Dave and Blood, Sweat and Tears stuff. On the material that wasn't Mad Dogs and Englishmen, we'd just play the same thing. Of course, he'd do all the fills and I'd keep straight time through it. Occasionally, we would trade fills. And we got all these background singers and two lead singers. It was like, 'I can't believe I'm doing this.' Jeff gave me all the confidence: 'You can do this; it will be great.' We played a bunch of proms and dances, and it was a blast. Later, it got more into Kelly and Jeff. In fact, Jeff couldn't make it to one of the Rural Still Life gigs and Kelly and I played double drums; we did that all the time at home."

JIM HODDER AND JEFF

From what Jeff "Skunk" Baxter observed in the Steely Dan situation, he says that Porcaro and Hodder determined their subtle differences immediately and "figured out right away how to be bigger than the sum of the parts. They worked together so well. They were able to read each other while some people are not able to read one another."

Skunk says playing double drums can be difficult for some because the drummer sees himself as the purveyor of the rhythm/pocket. "But because Jeff was so open to ideas, he adapted right away to playing with Jimmy," Skunk asserts. "Jimmy's style was, in a way, professorial. If you listen to the first Steely Dan albums, in my opinion he was approaching it from a professorial point of view. Jeff brought a different kind of energy."

Baxter says they spent the time working it out together, song by song: "They worked like two artists who had respect for each other and enjoyed the joy of freewheeling. Yes, you had a set of rules, but they went past the constraints."

JEFF AND TONY

The night before Les Dudek was to cut the last song on his album *Say No More*, Dudek and producer Bruce Botnick went to a concert featuring the Tony Williams Lifetime and Chick Corea's Return to Forever. Dudek has said it was at the Santa Monica Civic Auditorium, but research doesn't verify the two groups together during that time period at that venue. However, Corea's group did play there on April 8,1977 and obviously the following story did take place, as there is recorded evidence on Dudek's second album, released that same year.

According to Dudek, during the concert, Botnick asked him if he would want any of the musicians in the bands on his session the next day, and Dudek says he remembers laughing and saying, "Yeah, I'll take David Sanchez on keyboards and Tony Williams, and I have Pops Popwell from the Jazz Crusaders, but you have to take me home right now because I have to write a whole new song." He had a song written already for the next day's session, but now given the caliber of players he was going to have, he decided he needed to have a much better song for them to play. "So I went home and wrote 'Zorro Rides Again.' Zorro was my bird, my blue and gold macaw," Dudek explains. "At 7:30 in the morning I thought, 'I have to have Porcaro on this,' so I called up Jeff and I said, 'I'm doing this track today and I really want to do a double drummer thing like I did with the Allman Brothers when we did 'Ramblin' Man' and all that.' And Jeff was still getting loogies out of his throat. He said, 'Who's the other drummer?' I said, 'Tony Williams.' There was this big pause and he said, 'Let me cancel all my sessions today. When's the downbeat?'"

Jeff was obviously so excited that he called his brother Steve and asked him if he wanted to attend the historical session. "As much as Jeff and I could be at each other's throats when we were in close quarters, like living at home together, or being in a band together, he was always the coolest about letting me come to gigs," says brother Steve. "I remember he even let me bring friends when he was rehearsing with Steely Dan. I got to go to a shitload of those rehearsals."

As I see it, it wasn't just that Jeff let his brother come. I believe Jeff wanted to share the excitement with him. True to form, the thought of playing with Tony Williams was so exciting he wanted to share it with his brother. Steve wouldn't have missed it for the world. Tony Williams was legendary in the Porcaro household. "He was my dad's hero," says Steve. "When we were growing up and hearing the very first Beatles' album, my dad's rock star was Tony Williams. I mean, he had other people who influenced him, but Tony Williams was the shit."

Steve remembers meeting a cigar-smoking Tony in the parking lot that day. "We were very excited to meet him," says Steve, who was very comfortable being there also because he knew Dudek from working with him on *Silk Degrees.* They recorded the track at Capitol, studio A. "It had one of the best reverbs in the city," Dudek says. "They used the elevator shafts for reverb." Recalling the recording, Steve says,

"Jeff was really good at the double drum thing. A lot of drummers weren't good at double drums. Jeff was always great. That whole Jim Gordon, Jim Keltner thing was a big part of Jeff when Jeff's whole thing was forming. Jeff was always good at it. I always knew how sensitive he was while playing with another drummer."

Bruce Botnick recorded the session so one set of drums is on the left side and one set of drums is on the right in the stereo mix, says Dudek. "We ran that song down maybe three times," Les recalls. "We might have gotten it down on the third take. I wrote it like a controlled jam, so I didn't want to really get too anal with it. It was like, 'Here are the sections, here's what we're going to do, let's run it down so we know what the sections are and then let's just cut this thing. Let's not waste any time; let's have fun with it.' And that's what we did."

Percussionist **LENNY CASTRO** recalls when Jeffrey was telling him about the experience of playing with Williams, his statement was: "What the hell was I doing there? Why was I playing double drums with, of all people, Tony Williams?"

"SATURDAY NIGHT LIVE" AND BEYOND

September 1976 was monumental! Bassist **WILL LEE** and drummer **CHRIS PARKER** met Jeffrey playing for Boz Scaggs' performance on "Saturday Night Live." Parker got to play double drums with him. "He was great at double drums!" says Lee. "Elliott Randall was on guitar, and Jay Winding and Steve Porcaro were on keys. Not a bad little band! After that I started getting calls from Jeff and Lukather to move out to L.A. and do Toto. I was honored, of course, but I didn't want to leave a career in New York City that was

Boz Scaggs *Silk Degrees* Tour, California, 1976. (Courtesy of Andrew Leeds)

Boz Scaggs *Silk Degrees* Tour, California, 1976. (Courtesy of Andrew Leeds)

Boz Scaggs *Silk Degrees* Tour, California, 1976. (Courtesy of Andrew Leeds)

building fast."

Parker says he and Porcaro were instant friends. "I knew who he was, his reputation, who Joe was, although I hadn't met either one of them," says Parker. "Jeff was already legendary for having played with Sonny & Cher at seventeen; he was the California wunderkind. The meeting was fabulous. He was really sweet, generous, funny and hip, and he had all the great studio stories."

When pressed, Parker recalls that Jeff told him a story about Sol Gubin. He couldn't remember if Jeff had been present or had only heard the story, but recounting the story, he says Sol Gubin was playing for an actress who had an epileptic seizure while she was coming down a flight of stairs. "Sol Gubin thought it was part of the act and caught every jerk and move—snare rolls, cowbells, timpani rolls, cymbal crashes—and she ended up in a crumpled pose at the bottom of the stairs. Nobody realized until a couple seconds later that it wasn't part of the act. I heard that story from Jeff first, and then I worked with Tom Scott, and he said, 'Oh yeah, that's a famous story,'" Parker recalls. "Jeff had other stories about Glen Campbell in the studio and the Wrecking Crew, what geniuses they were and names I hadn't heard before like Larry Bunker, and I knew about John Guerin and Harvey Mason. I hadn't really heard about Vinnie, and I didn't meet him until he came and played 'Saturday Night Live' with Frank Zappa. By that time I think I was in the ('S.N.L.') band."

At the Boz Scaggs "S.N.L." dress rehearsal, Parker says it was very easy. "It was pretty organic," he recalls. "I said, 'Jeff, you just do what you do, and I'll just fill in around you.' And he said, 'No, no, you just do what you do.' He was very gracious and generous." They played

"Lowdown" and "What Can I Say," both of which were already hits.

Jeff was soon going to be leaving Boz to go off with Toto. He promised he'd go out for the first month of the Scaggs tour with Parker playing drums with him, and then Chris would eventually take over the drum chair by himself. They didn't go on the road right away, but Parker says when they did "it was incredibly great."

At rehearsals in Los Angeles, the first thing they did was rent extra 22" bass drums from Studio Instrument Rentals without the front heads so they could make each of their bass drums twice as long. They did this by putting two headless bass drums end-to-end, and then they hung a mic in between the two bass drums. "So instead of being one 14" x 22", it was like 28" x 22"," Parker explains. "This was before samples and triggering, so this was an amazing sound, and it just lit up our faces every time we hit the bass drum. It was ridiculous. We tuned them to the same pitch, padded them the same way and hung the mic between the two openings. I looked at his setup and made mine very similar to his: the angles of the toms, a sizzle cymbal for a crash (which I still do to this day). The pitches were similar, and we went out and duplicated that rehearsal setup for every gig, and it was the first month of the tour, ostensibly for me to get the feel and the grooves the way Jeff did and I just soaked it up. I loved it—all those tunes, all those hits: 'What Can I Say,' 'Lowdown,' 'Lido.' We were playing the *Silk Degrees* album. Duplicating Jeff's fills exactly with those bass drums and our tom-toms was so much fun. His grooves were so amazing; the shuffles and the straight stuff and the funk stuff. He was always crediting Purdie for the half-time shuffle—and he played it better than Purdie!

"In between, on the soundchecks and stuff, we would go off

on tangents, some funk thing like some Earth, Wind & Fire groove. We had very similar interests. I would tell him about a record I always loved, like Count Basie's 'Jumpin' at the Woodside' with Jo Jones, and he would tell me about something that Shelly Manne played on. Obviously, there was no YouTube or internet. He had cassettes and it was, 'Check this out,' and he'd hand me the headphones. The (Sony) Walkman (had come out). I believe we all had a Walkman, which was amazing because you could have cassettes of rehearsals and stuff."

One thing Jeff didn't have was a gadget that Sony only released in Japan, which Chris had acquired there while touring with Stuff. "It was the size of an LP, like 12" x 12", and it had a cassette machine in it, but it also had a rhythm ace built into it. It also had a quarter-inch input so you could plug your guitar, bass or keyboard in. So you could listen to the radio, play along and record it with a cassette, and sync the rhythm ace to it, and any number of possibilities," says Parker. "You could listen to the radio on the headphones and play the rhythm ace. I had described it to Jeff at 'SNL,' and he said, 'I want one, I want one,' so when I went to Japan right before we went on tour, I brought one back for him. At the time, it was like 420 yen to the dollar, so they were like giving it away. I got him one in time for the rehearsals at S.I.R., so we were fooling around with that. It was a primitive rhythm ace, but it had a cha-cha, a waltz and a swing beat. As primitive as they were, the rhythm aces could be funky if you turned them up fast and then subdivided. You could get some weird hybrid groove like part bossa nova and part cha-cha. He loved it. He kept saying, 'It's so cool, it's so cool,' and we had a ball with it."

Flying around on Elvis' old plane, Chris recalls a great 30 days. He and Jeff had a lot in common besides the drums: Chris had four younger brothers, of which three were drummers, and of course Jeff came from the most musical of families. The two drummers hung out every day on the tour. Parker says he and Lenny Castro were big jokers. "I had these tee shirts that had been gifts in Japan that were from a brand called Kitty, with an image of a cat. It was a big thing in Japan, although it meant nothing to me, but people kept giving me these tee shirts. So a lot of my sound check wardrobe was these tee shirts, and they started calling me 'Kitty.' I remember going to the crew meal and they said, 'We got your lunch for you; it's over here. We got you covered,' and they left a bowl of cat food for me," Parker recalls, laughing. "They were always joking. Nothing was mean-spirited; we were just like high school or junior high school kids. Lots of good times and a lot of good talks about music—Jeff would talk about the L.A. music scene and I would tell him about the New York music scene, and we had session stories; we'd compare notes and dish the dirt: 'this singer, or that contractor, or some conductor.' The overall vibe was so wonderful and so hip. It was a great hang. I was so sad when the month ended."

Playing-wise, Parker says, "You couldn't talk about any drummer or feel that he couldn't improve on. And he'd say, 'What about this?' He'd suggest things and it would be brilliant. Probably the impression that hit the deepest was the conviction he had while playing. He never played anything that he wasn't totally convicted about. He had total confidence in what he was playing. He was never tentative, he was never anything but 100% present and 100% believing this is where 1 is, and this is where 2 goes, and this is the feel, and this is how we're going to subdivide. And the seriousness of how he played the music was in such contrast to his personality, which was fun-loving and gregarious. He was gracious, welcoming, embracing and inclusive. I cherish all the memories of walking around backstage and getting ready to go on with the same kind of adrenalin pumping and his positive vibe and his positive energy and amazing performance. It's a treasured memory."

DREAM OF A CHILD

RICK SHLOSSER recalls playing with Jeff on Burton Cummings' *Dream of a Child* in 1978. Shlosser recalls that Cummings would arrive at the studio with mason jars full of marijuana and as everyone walked through the door, he'd hand them each a jar.

He says he knew going into the session that it was going to be a double drum date with Jeff, and he was really looking forward to it. He knew Jeff from various interactions after moving to Los Angeles from Northern California, including one time when Jeff told him that he had listened to Andy Pratt's *Records are Like Life*, one of Shlosser's first recordings. "He said he used to put on his headphones and play to it. He said he loved it, loved the record, loved my playing, and then he had heard I had been in an accident and lost an arm," Rick says. "Of all the weird things, right? And I said, 'No, no, got 'em, they're here.' He said, 'I was always really bummed about that for a while.'"

Shlosser says he doesn't recall really discussing anything before playing together; they just sat down and played. "I didn't want it to sound like a herd of elephants. With two drummers it can easily get overcomplicated. I think when it comes to double drums, we both have that approach where we realize there's another guy that is going to do something, so just try to keep the groove going and maybe play off something that he's going to do—but it's never about me, listen to me, I want my part to stand out. It's a reciprocal agreement to just make it work. Egos shouldn't be involved. It was that easy with Jeff, without saying a word. We just listened to one another," Shlosser explains. Sitting beside Jeff, playing felt completely natural. "Playing with Jeff was…," Rick pauses. "Just knowing Jeff was wonderful. He was a very giving, generous man." Shlosser recalls how supportive Jeff was. "He'd listen to a fill I did and say, 'Oh God, I love that fill!' It wasn't anything earth-shattering or anything, but he was always that kind of guy, supportive of everyone."

Not quite double drumming, but double drummer duty for Shlosser came when he received a call from Boz Scaggs. Boz was on tour in 1976, and Jeff was having trouble with his hands cramping. Shlosser had been on the road with Scaggs previously, so Boz was confident that Rick knew the old material and could get up to speed on the new songs quickly. They flew Shlosser to Phoenix, where he learned the new *Silk Degrees* material, rehearsed, and played the show that night. In the next city, Jeff seemed fine, and they started the show. "I was on the sidelines and in the middle of the show, after a song, Jeff looked at me and said, 'Come here, come here,' and I jumped on and did the next couple of songs, and then he was able to continue," recalls Shlosser.

JEFF AND ALLAN

Few people realize that Jeffrey and **ALLAN SCHWARTZBERG** played a couple of tracks together. "Just a Thought" and "When You Got the Music (Part 3)" were cut by the two drummers together, and the songs appear on 1977's *Elliott Randall's New York.* It's not a coupling often on people's radar because Schwartzberg is known for being an East Coast drummer and Porcaro was predominately a West Coast musician, but Randall had Jeff come to New York to play on his solo record, and there the two drummers met for the first time.

As previously mentioned, Randall had met Jeff on a TV show while they were both performing for different acts. Then in 1976, Randall was hired to play the momentous "Saturday Night Live" show that had Jeff double drumming with Chris Parker. It was Randall's first time playing the show, then in its second year, before becoming a consultant for "S.N.L." "I always love double drums, especially because I'm a drummer," Randall says. "There's something about playing in an egoless fashion that makes it magical, and one of the things about Jeff is that he left his ego at the door. Always, when it came to musical interactions, it was 'what can I do to make it really great,' and that was it," he says, adding that Parker also is a completely egoless drummer.

The following year, Randall cut his solo album, and he remembers doing the two tunes in one evening and overhearing the two drummers in conversation. "They're sitting there, and Allan is saying, 'Why don't you play the fills?' And Jeff's going, 'No, you play the fills,'" Randall recalls. "And it was one of those arguments about who was going to do less to let the other do more, which was a wonderful moment. It really, really was. And that is what makes a musician really superior in my mind, when they say, 'It isn't about me; it's about the ensemble. What is going to make this thing shine?'"

Schwartzberg is hazy on some of the details, but he does remember it was a great session and says, "It was a good feel all the way around." Allan knew of Porcaro and also had heard about him through Randall. "I went into the session thinking, 'I'm just wide open. Let's see what happens here.' I had a great lesson in playing double drums with Tony Bongiovi, the master engineer at Media," Schwartzberg explains.

"I learned that two drummers can't play the same thing. It's like two things in the universe can't occupy the same space. If you're going to sit down at a set of drums and play the same part as the other guy is playing, you're just going to cancel each other out. It's like you don't even want to hear one flam, but an entire track of nothing but flams?

"I remember Jeff and I were playing one song and I took a shot—because it could have evoked a response like, 'That's what you're playing? That's your contribution?'—but what I did was I put, like, buzz rolls in between what Jeff was playing, as if I was playing a little (New Orleans) Second Line style. Jeff was playing his ass off and it was great to hear. I remember saying to him, 'Man, you sound great, just beautiful—and the sound of the drums. I've played on that kit, and you just make them sound like different drums.' And then he said to me, 'Yeah, but what about what you were playing? I loved that. It just enhanced everything. It brightened up everything.' You don't know how something is going to be accepted. I did a Brecker Brothers record with Terry Bozzio playing drums, and that didn't go well at all."

On the other tune, Allan played the "decorations" while Jeff took the reins. He says they didn't discuss their parts; what came out was totally organic. "Jeff was a beautiful player, and he was the guest," says Schwartzberg. "He was the guy that Elliott brought in from Los Angeles, so I felt like he was drummer number one and I was drummer number two, so I let him play more notes than I did. I could have played more, but I chose not to."

Regarding the cutting of Randall's album, bassist Will Lee says: "We had a great time, laughing and playing. Elliott is a sweetheart, and the vibe was all about grooving and being positive, looking to get a good sound on the instruments and making sure Elliott was happy. It wasn't a bunch of dark, serious cats competing to be the best—far from it. We were partying the whole time. As a drummer, Jeff was more like a producer/arranger from behind the kit. He had a rare and uncanny ability to objectively look over a session from above while supplying the groove from below, shaping a song and uniting all the players. His level of hipness and humor was rare. His feel is, of course, legendary. A normal player would be happy to master any one of those attributes, but Jeff was able to juggle them all at once! The recorded music is all the proof you need. Listen to any Jeff track and you'll hear taste, groove, dynamics and sure-footedness at work, from his earliest to his later recordings and performances. We miss him dearly."

JEFF AND GERRY

Gerry Brown recalls being at Studio 55 during the recording of the Brothers Johnson's 1981 album *Winners*. Gerry was scheduled to record that evening. Jeff was in the midst of cutting tracks, so Gerry came early to hang and check it out. There were two kits set up: the one Jeff was recording on, and the one Gerry would be playing later. During some downtime, Louis Johnson called Gerry to the other kit and said, "While they're getting stuff together, let's just play, double drums."

Gerry says he was a little nervous at first, but it wasn't long before he was right into the music, playing for about thirty to forty-five minutes, about three or four different grooves and slightly different tempos with Jeff, the guy he calls the "King of Groove." "One would play a four-bar fill and then we'd come back, both playing groove," Brown recalls. "Jeff was the leader of that. It was like it was he and

Louis and I just playing around in that groove, but he was leading it. I let him take charge. They would play a groove, then Jeff would give a cue and then we'd break and then Louis would play like a four-bar solo, then we'd come back in. I'd have my little four bars—keep it in the pocket, keep it in the pocket, then come back in. I will always have that memory."

"YOU BETTER HANG UP"

Neither Don Henley nor Danny Kortchmar can recall whose idea it was to have double drums on Henley's "You Better Hang Up" on his first solo album *I Can't Sit Still* (1982). Henley says it was either Danny's idea or Jeff's. Either way, it was a good one. Kortchmar, who was producing (along with Greg Ladanyi and Henley), says everyone loved the idea.

Henley says it came together naturally for both of them. "There may have been a brief discussion (about parts they would play) before we began recording, but it was mostly just an organic thing," says Henley. "Spontaneous." Kortchmar concurs that it wasn't worked out too much. "Double drums either works or it doesn't," Danny says. "For instance, Ringo and Keltner: it just works. Jeff and Don sounded great together."

FROM MENTORING TO DOUBLING

Jody Cortez says his dream came true when he got to play double drums with Jeff in 1989 at the Hollywood Guitar Center for a big gala event that Scotty Page was heading up. The nucleus of the musicians were from Page's band Hang Dynasty, with Page on sax, Kal David, Mike Finnigan and Bob Glaub, along with Lukather, Lenny Castro, Fred Tackett and as Cortez put it, "every horn player in town."

SCOTTY PAGE says the Guitar Center event was called the "First Dance," and confirms it was an expanded version of Hang Dynasty. "There were probably thirty guys on stage, including the Tower of Power horns and Supertramp," says Page. "The whole idea of that was an experiment around a project I was calling Visual Sound, where I created these zooming microphones and MIDI-based tripod system ideas, where the cameras would zoom in and bring up the sound. I had mics everywhere, so imagine if I'm in the back of the room, it sounds different if I'm standing right in front of Jeff. The whole idea was to give people an audio-visual experience. Now you're starting to see more and more of that—where they are mixing the audio to match the visual."

Page recalls that he built a stage in the store for the seven-camera shoot, and that David Gilmour was there that night as Jeff's guest. "Jeff was playing on the Pink Floyd stuff that day in the studio," Page recalls. "Jeff had to leave the session promptly to make my gig because it was a seven-camera gig, so he said to David, 'Hey you wanna come?' so Gilmour came that night! I got called a couple of days later to put solos on the Floyd record, and that's how my whole journey with Pink Floyd happened." (Note: Page was prominently featured with Pink Floyd during the tour supporting *A Momentary Lapse of Reason* and its associated live albums and videos.)

Scotty was a fan of double drums. He had done a lot of the annual holiday parties for the popular radio personalities Mark &

Brian, which Jeff and Keltner did a time or two (Keltner talks about it in *It's About Time*). He even recalls the Rural Still Life Shanahan double-drum days. So for this event, he booked Jeffrey and Jody. "Jeff was such a groovemeister. He always said, 'Don't play a fill until you can't stand it,'" says Page, referring to Porcaro's restraint and style. "With another drummer he just played simply. He understood what not to play."

Cortez describes the music at the Guitar Center gala as "explosive blues rock" and "Cajun second line grooves and shuffles." "It was insane," says Cortez. "The pulse on stage, the energy field was lit up. Jeff was a genius; there was so much restraint—both when he spoke and when he played. He fricken played with his magic trick bag wide open."

LIKE RIDING ON A CLOUD

That's how **VINNIE COLAIUTA** describes how it felt playing with Jeff on the Los Lobotomys version of Miles Davis' "All Blues." The eponymous record was recorded live on April 29, 1989 at the Complex in West Los Angeles in front of an invited audience. While he doesn't recall for sure whether they rehearsed ahead of time, he doesn't think so. "Usually in this kind of situation, there is a pre-game huddle, but a lot of times you just know, 'Oh, we're going to do fours now.' That's just how it rolls," Vinnie notes. "You're just up there and it's, 'Ok, we're trading fours; I see what's happening.' You see what's happening, and you're ready for it."

The original recording of the track was 15:17; the longest on the record, including a couple of drum solos. Vinnie says Porcaro was extremely generous in his approach. "What was extraordinary about playing with Jeff was you hear what he does and the dimension of it when you hear him play as a drummer or any musician of any import," Colaiuta states. "You can hear what he does and understand where he puts the time feel and appreciate that 'x' factor, but what happens when you are actually playing with him is you go, 'Oh, now I get it! Now I see what everyone raves about, because I've experienced it.' And once you've experienced it, you realize it's really kind of difficult to quantify it in a way that really creates that feeling in other people just by describing it. When we were playing, it was literally like riding on a cloud. It was an amazing experience. He played everything so effortlessly. He was so supportive and giving. Here's a guy who is so confident, but his confidence was never disruptive or prevented him from yielding and just cradling somebody. That combination of characteristics, when you know when it's being that nurturing, and when you know when to be that confident and assertive and how to balance them, is no small feat. That's just one of the things you experience when you play with that guy. I can't think of anybody else like that off the top of my head. I mean, there are people like Herbie Hancock or (conductor) Gustavo Dudamel who are in that category of musical and personal evolution and maturity. You have to be really evolved and sometimes you have to just experience it."

Vinnie continues to talk about the evolved musical intuition of someone like Dudamel conducting the L.A. Philharmonic with a give and take, allowing someone like Colaiuta to sometimes set the time and other times having him yield to the conductor. He says Jeff had that same kind of intuitive development, but he could only really know that by playing with him. He can still remember sitting and looking over and seeing Jeff playing beside him and thinking, "'Wow, I'm playing with Jeff Porcaro! This is crazy!' It's like being so close to a car that you start feeling the vibration in your body," he says. "You can feel it."

A GROOVE FEST

All the rest of the tracks on the *Los Lobotomys* record, except "Dismemberment" (on which Jeff played percussion while Lenny Castro and Carlos Vega played drums—Castro and David Garfield wrote it), were double-drummed by Jeffrey and Carlos Vega. Since obviously Carlos is sadly not here to comment on playing with Jeff, I spoke with Lenny about playing with the two of them together. "Jeff was very polite when it came to playing with other drummers," says Castro. "He was always worried about overplaying or getting in the other guy's way. He wanted things to lock. He didn't want it to be a mish-mash of 'this is what I can do' and 'this is what I can do'—an ego competition. Jeff had seen too many car crashes as far as double drums. He wanted to be a little more pensive and considerate. He hated awards and he hated when people asked him who his favorite drummers were. It irked him so much."

When he heard Porcaro and Vega play together, Castro thought, "This should have happened a long time ago! Both of them were from the 'Mutual Admiration Society.' Carlos adored Jeff for his attitude and for what he did as a musician, and Jeff had a hard time playing in front of Carlos. He had the utmost respect for him," Castro reveals. "They both enjoyed each other's playing very much and to be able to play together in the right circumstance—that kind of loose situation—was perfect."

Castro says it's hard to put into words what it felt like to actually play with the two of them. "I click with almost every drummer I work with, but those two especially. Carlos was my best friend, and I was very close to Jeff. To be sitting in between the two of them playing together, listening to the conversation they were making..." Lenny pauses. "I'm not even worried about what I'm doing. I'm sitting there enjoying the conversation going on between the two of them. It's magical. Jeff would do some little thing, and then Carlos would work off of that, and it was just this wonderful, wonderful conversation going on back and forth. I was just lucky enough to be sitting in the middle of it and trying to keep up with them. It was a beautiful thing to be present for that, to watch and listen and feel that appreciation between them; it was so strong. It was an amazing thing to see, and I'm so glad I got to experience that one time in my life."

Castro says the project, put together by David Garfield, was just a bunch of friends getting together to have some fun. "All our friends came down, and we ordered a whole bunch of sushi and drank. How often does that get to happen?" says Castro. "There was no other motivation except to create great music with your buddies. We weren't looking to make a hit record or anything. It would have been nice to get attention, but it was just fun," says Lenny. Castro actually came up with the name of the band. One day he was hung over and had an early rehearsal. The night before, he had been on a rave, saying, "What's with all this 'los' this and 'los' that? I want to put together a band of lobotomized musicians and call them Los Lobotomys—guys who have had to play all kinds of weird shit sessions, to play some crazy-ass music that we love."

And that was it.

Left: Toto's Jeff Porcaro and Bobby Kimball, Los Angeles, 1982, Michael Ochs publicity shoot. (Courtesy of the Bobby Kimball Estate) Right: Jeff during the filming of the video for "Goodbye Elenore" from *Turn Back*. (Courtesy of Barney Hurley)

Still from the promo video for Toto's 1979 single "St. George and the Dragon," from their *Hydra* album. (Courtesy of Barney Hurley)

NERVES AND AWE

That's what **RUSS KUNKEL** felt playing live beside Jeff at a show to benefit the renovations of the Santa Barbara County Bowl at the request of Sam Scranton, who led the Foundation at the Bowl. The band included Steve Lukather and David Paich, among others, including, he believes, David Crosby and Kenny Loggins—an all-star jam.

Kunkel and Jeff had met in a studio somewhere, Kunkel recalls, possibly at Studio 55, where Toto was recording while Kunkel was cutting Stevie Nicks' *Bella Donna*. He does remember the first time he ever became aware of Porcaro's groove, and that was when he heard Boz Scaggs' "Lowdown" on his car radio. "I had to pull over and listen to the whole thing," Kunkel admits. "I said, 'Okay, who's playing drums on this?' And I did my research and I thought, 'Okay, hello! There's a new cowboy in town!' Then I looked back and saw that he had recorded *Katy Lied* and everything—but I was in my own world doing my own tours and recording. I'm sure when I met him it was a love fest of, 'Oh man you did...' 'Yeah, but oh man, you did…'"

By the time the Santa Barbara event took place, they knew each other, but Russ admits they sort of ran in different musical circles. "All I can say is before we ever played a note, the trepidation that I felt was a tip of the hat to Jeff's greatness. We rehearsed for two days in L.A.," recalls Kunkel. "The main thing I remember was that I was in such awe of Jeff and so nervous playing next to him, just because of what a monster and icon he was. I looked up to him, even though he was younger than I. His prowess as a drummer—I'm sure you won't speak to any other drummer who doesn't feel the same way."

Despite the anxiety, Jeffrey relaxed Russ quickly and made the experience fun. "As soon as we started playing, he made me feel completely at ease, and the music just took us away. The grooves were very deep," Kunkel recalls. "When really good drummers play double drums, they tend to make space for the other person, and it works out really great. That's certainly how I look at it—and I've done it with Keltner, Joe Vitale and even Ringo. It was a really wonderful experience."

As Russ recalls, he and Jeff both played some selections singularly and some together. He says he doesn't remember that they discussed a plan for the songs they played together. "I think someone would count it off and we'd just start playing. I would be looking at Jeff and he would be looking at me with nothing but smiles and nodding our heads," says Kunkel. "There was a lot of simpatico up there."

JEFF AND READING

The photo on the cover of this book is reportedly from Barbra Streisand's *Superman* sessions, and all that music in front of Jeffrey got me thinking about how he always put himself down as a reader. I went back to page 37 of *It's About Time*, where I referenced our conversation about how he sometimes cut class at Grant High to go across to Valley Junior College and sight-read with their big band. Big band music is not easy, and we've already established that he wrote some intricate marching band cadences. He told me he could hold his own with the big band: "When you're dealing with eighth notes and reading figures that you would do just hand-to-hand on a practice pad, it's pretty much the same as reading a chart. The figures are there; you know what they are and it's just applying the fact that you're playing time and then you want to kick a figure or play a figure. I'm really not an incredible, incredible reader, but I can read well enough to do what I've done so far," he had told me for a *Modern Drummer* interview. "But you just get to know it. It's like reading words. You'll see two bars playing a groove, and eight bars ahead on the paper you see this figure coming up, and you don't even have to read it. All of a sudden, the figures look like a word; you know what it says just by the way it looks."

Steve Porcaro pretty well describes it the same way and indicates that Jeff didn't always give himself credit for being a good reader, because he was comparing himself to Vinnie Colaiuta and the guys who played with Zappa. "But in 99.9% of the sessions he did, Jeff could read just fine," Steve says. "It's just like for keyboard players or guitar players: You walk in to certain sessions and see something written out, and especially like piano music when blues licks are written out, it looks like the hardest Chopin etude in the world. It's so daunting. But then when you hear it, you go, 'Oh, it's *that*,' and you play it. Some (composers or arrangers) might write out some super complicated drum fill or whatever, and when you first look at it you go, 'Holy shit!' But then you realize what it is, and it's no problem. (This also happens when) something is syncopated and they're tying notes over; you're going to see twice as many noteheads as are actually sounded when they try to spell it out in notation, and they don't want to have just notes with dots. A lot of times guys will want to show where all the beats are, so they'll just tie notes together and it can look very complicated, but often it isn't at all."

Steve says Jeff would go over the tune and mark his charts, which would become a road map for him. "He got really good at it, and there was never any problem," says Steve. A "road map," which is the type of chart they encountered most often, doesn't have every note written out on it. "This is the bridge, this is the chorus, this is the verse, there's going to be a fill here," explains Steve. "After the bridge are we going straight to the B section, or is it going straight to a chorus? Is there a little intro for two bars before it jumps to the coda, the last chorus? Maybe there's a very specific figure written out that would be marked if we were doing a James Newton Howard & Friends thing, but usually Jeff would just have it in his head. He would learn it and know it, and he was very good at retaining that kind of stuff. Regarding fills, Jeff didn't write them out, and people didn't write them out for him, either. They wanted to see what he came up with, which was always great—that's why they were hiring him."

JEFF AND THE CLICK

Steve and I also talked about a part of the recording process about which Jeff had very strong feelings: playing to a click, which he disliked enough on tracking dates, but *really* did not like when he had to overdub drums on a track. "The bar for all these guys was Steely Dan, and Steely Dan was notorious for throwing out entire tracks if the drummer rushed a little bit going into any section of the song at all," says Steve. "Plenty of Toto songs got thrown out—some of the most potentially commercial songs we ever did—because it was rushing going into the chorus. I was always messing with sequencers and all this stuff, and if it was a Toto thing, Jeff would have nothing to do with it. There were exceptions—the way we did 'Africa' and the song 'Fahrenheit'—but overall, Jeff wouldn't fucking play to a click. He was proud of Toto—he looked up to Jim Gordon and Jim Keltner, and Jeff was all about having that perfect time from a very early age. But later on, especially the last couple of years of Jeff's life, he was walking into certain sessions and there was no discussion: He was going to play to a click. Guys wanted to be able to sync up to a drum machine or sequence after the fact, or it was a film thing."

Steve delineated between everybody in the room cutting to the click and the other scenario of the track already having been done to a click, to which Jeff had to overdub. "Let's say there was a click track and a percussionist laid down a part on top of the click. You or I would listen to it and the percussion would sound just fine playing to the click," Steve remarks. "Maybe it wasn't perfect, but it was fine. Now when another player came in, say it was a bass player, they would start locking into the percussion player and maybe the percussionist had strayed a little from the click, maybe on two beats of one measure. Now, all of a sudden, everybody you're adding is locking into one thing or another, and there's no single point of reference. When that was the case, it drove Jeff fucking nuts to overdub drums on top of that. When you're Jeff, he has a microscope on every fucking beat of every bar of the song and for beats three and four, the bass player who was all of sudden locking into the percussionist because that felt good, but neither one of them were on with the click—it would drive Jeff nuts! Jeff could sense that stuff because he was so sensitive to those things. I wouldn't even notice it. And at the end of the day, Jeff did what the job was, which was to kind of play right in the middle of it all and be the glue through it all, but it was difficult for him."

When people cut to a click, a lot of the sessions his brother ended up having to deal with were like that. "When they had to cut with a click on a tracking date, Jeff would—I almost want to use the word 'punish'—everybody. Lukather's hearing is impaired not because of his Marshall amplifiers, but because of the how loud Jeff would make everybody listen to the cowbell of the drum machine if they were playing to that, because it was like, 'You want to play with a drum machine? Then you're going to fucking play with a drum machine and not wander off and lock in over here with this guy or that guy,'" reveals Steve. "'You're going to play to the fucking drum machine. We're all going to play to the drum machine!' And if you strayed one iota from it, Jeff would make everybody turn up the fucking cowbell in their headphones. That's where Luke lost his hearing—from the fucking cowbell. It really kind of made the tracking session no fun, and it took the joy away from Jeff I think when there was a click he had to play to, because if it was going to be to a drum machine thing, he was going to be nailing it to that drum machine. It was going to be nailed, the way he did with 'Africa' or the way we did with 'Dirty Laundry.' I had played on the initial track of 'Dirty Laundry' and I was completely clocked perfectly; I was being gated by the drum machine, so my Farfisa part that everyone cut to was perfect, but on a lot of sessions and maybe even huge hit records, there would be (these minor time discrepancies with the click that) would infuriate him."

Recalling the way Seals and Crofts worked, Steve says Jimmy Seals actually constructed the click to change during parts to speed up and slow down. "And look at all those Steely Dan records from the '70s," he continues. "There's nothing like them, and all that insane stuff you heard go on, and everything having to be perfect and how they threw out whole tracking dates just because it felt a little funny in a couple of bars. They had the money and that kind of budget to do that. You've got to look back at that stuff, and there's nothing like those records!"

Toto 1979 publicity shot. (Courtesy of Barney Hurley)

Chapter Six

JEFF'S OWN WESTERN WALL

Don Was remembers the old Western Recorders, which became Ocean Way, then Cello, then East/West. When it was still Western, Was says, Jeff was there so much "he knew the holes in the wood paneling. He would hide joints all over," says Was. "There were roaches everywhere."

JOHN SEBASTIAN SAYS NO TO "PEA SOUP."

Jeff recorded John Sebastian's entire 1976 release *Welcome Back.* The album included the Sebastian-penned theme for the hit show "Welcome Back Kotter," which went to number one on the Billboard Top 100.

But Sebastian's biggest recollection comes from when he presented the other planned single, "Hideaway," to Jeff. "His face fell," Sebastian recalls. "'Oh, it's a disco thing. No, man, I wouldn't know how to do such a thing on purpose,' he said. I said, 'No, Jeff; straight eighths, yeah, but no pea-soup hi-hat!' He thought about it for a minute and then launched the next take with a fill that felt like falling down a set of stairs. It became a moderate hit in Germany!"

FLYING OVER KANSAS

In 1978, Greg Phifer was three years into his promotion gig for Columbia Records when Toto released its debut album. As the Denver rep, his territory was Colorado, Utah and Idaho, and his job was to garner as much radio airplay as possible for his artists—which was really the only vehicle for a band to sell records back then. (There was no internet or social media.) He not only loved Toto's music, but he was a closet drummer, so it was definitely a band he enjoyed promoting, and he'd spend whatever time he could with the band's drummer.

"Back in those days, local record company reps such as myself were given the task of befriending all the disc jockeys and program and music directors of all the radio stations that played current music," Phifer explains. "That meant using your charm, music acumen and promotional creativity to induce your stations to play and 'add' your artist's music on their respective playlists. Without radio airplay back then, you could not sell your artist's records. Period. Outside of concert appearances—which wouldn't happen without significant airplay exposure in the first place—there were no other vehicles (outside of press releases to your local newspapers) to let the public know your

Greg Phifer and Jeff, 1978. (Courtesy of Greg Phifer)

artist even existed. So when Columbia signed Toto back in 1978 and had established both an in-store album date and a radio single release date for 'Hold The Line,' my job was to create, at the local level, some sort of buzz or fanfare to coincide with these release dates."

That's when Phifer came up with his unconventional yet effective "Toto Lifts Its Leg Over Kansas" promotion. "I rented a turbo prop plane and rigged it up with a cassette player and two very large speakers," Greg recalls. "I got the entire band to fly up to Denver and loaded them up in the plane along with all the radio, retail and press folks that would fit in it, plus a plethora of booze and maybe some other non-legal mood enhancers. For the next hour or so we flew eastward to Kansas and listened to Toto's debut album collectively for the first time. Then we flew back to Denver in our altered states of euphoria. It was, by everyone's account, a roaring success. Immediate 'out-of-the-box' airplay created record sales right away, and the rest is history. I always enjoyed all of Toto's music and live concerts through the years, and being a garage band drummer back in the day, it was such a thrill for me to be able to hang with Jeff whenever I could go backstage and talk with/bug him about this riff or that fill. What a wonderful musician and human being."

SENTIMENTAL JOURNEY

In 1978, Jeff played all ten tracks on Country Joe McDonald's *Rock and Roll Music from the Planet Earth*. McDonald recalls that one of the songs struck a tender nerve with Porcaro. He says after playing on the song "Bring Back the Sixties Man," Jeff said to him, "I started crying during the take because I remembered when we all went with our father to see the Woodstock film, because we were too young to go alone."

"FM (NO STATIC AT ALL)"

According to Gary Katz, "FM" (1978) was everyone's introduction to legendary engineer/producer Al Schmitt. Donald Fagen had just written the title song for the film of the same name, and Katz's phone rang in the middle of the night.

"He said, 'Ya, know, let's go cut this track now.' It's not like we were ever that whacky or anything," Katz teases. "He had a problem sleeping sometimes, and he'd call and say, 'Let's do this track now. Call Jeffrey.' It was usually 1:00 or 2:00 in the morning. So I called Jeffrey and he said, 'I don't have my drums; they're up at Studio 55. I'm working with Richard (Perry).' Richard and I came into the business together—our mothers gave us each $4000 to go into the music business. He came to L.A. before I did; Richard and I have known each other for years. So I called Richard in the middle of the night and said, 'Would you ask one of your guys to go open the door for me? I need to go cut a track and Jeffrey's drums are there.' At around 3:30 in the morning we rolled up to Studio 55 and Jeffrey was there with a smile. An hour later we had a (drum) track for 'FM.' (The rest of the band was recorded later.) Donald says, 'Since it's for a movie, maybe we should put strings on here; it will sound more movie-like,' so we hired (arranger/conductor) Johnny Mandel. Through that, someone said, 'If you're going to do that, you have to do it at Capitol, and you have to work with this guy Al Schmitt.' So Al engineered the string date for 'FM.' When it came to the mix, we said, 'Let's mix with Al Schmitt; he's great.'"

Katz goes on to tell the famous story about how when he and Donald arrived at Armin Steiner's studio to work with Schmitt on the mixing, they didn't hear any music. When they walked up the incline to the console, there was Schmitt, with his head nearly down on the console, looking at the meters, mixing the song to the meters—*without sound.* When the story, which Gary and Donald spread after the fact, was told at Schmitt's memorial service, it was relayed as if it were fabricated, but Katz says, "It was not fictitious."

LARRY KLEIN

As a musician, Grammy-winning Larry Klein has worn the hat of session bassist and producer, and while his interactions with Jeffrey were limited, he wanted to share his thoughts: "There were people who worked more with Jeff, but I worked enough with him to know that he was the perfect drummer in many ways. It's no surprise to me that so many people felt the same way, because he had the perfect balance of elasticity, precision, superb intuition and creative imagination that anybody would want on a session or in any musical circumstance," says Klein, known for his work with Joni Mitchell, Herbie Hancock, Shawn Colvin and a plethora of creative projects. "I was lucky enough to work with Jeff and take advantage of sitting next to that and interacting with that kind of intuitive ability that he had."

When Klein found himself needing a last-minute drummer for a benefit gig with Joni Mitchell, he turned to Jeff. "He just stepped in and was absolutely superb, as usual," says Klein. "He was a lovely person as well as the perfect player for almost any situation: gracious, the perfect balance of humility and taking initiative when it was needed. It's very rare that you come across musicians who are so adaptable."

Although Larry can't recall specific sessions on which he played with Porcaro, he asserts: "I just remember every time I played with him, it was a pleasure and the absolute easiest and most wonderful kind of musical experience. He always had a smile and a certain kind of humility to find in a guy who was so amazing in any kind of situation."

MUTUAL ADMIRATION SOCIETY

Jeffrey always told me how much it meant to him to work with Barbra Streisand. While I was unable to reach her to speak for the book, I did connect briefly with her longtime A&R man and executive producer Jay Landers, who agreed that Jeff was the "gold standard in the industry" and told me: "Barbra has a hand in every decision that goes into making her records. Clearly, she admired Jeff, since she hired him for three consecutive platinum albums: *Superman, Songbird* and *Wet.* I think any studio musician would tell you that one of the sincerest forms of flattery is when they're repeatedly hired by the same producer or artist. That's the ultimate confirmation you've done your job well!"

MYSTERY SOLVED

Sometimes you could swear the stories you heard about Jeff were folklore. You heard them told by so many people, but never by anyone who was there, and no one could really tell you the *who, what* and *when*, so you—I mean *me*, the reporter—never wanted to repeat certain stories, because who knew if they were really true? Then there are some, like the gig bag story, that had so many different versions, that it was always worrisome to commit to one (which is why I talked to so many people about it).

There is one oft-told tale about Jeff getting up and leaving a session abruptly and saying, "I have to make a phone call," and not returning until the next day. When someone asked him, "What happened?" he replied, "I just got off the phone."

For years I'd heard that happened on a Streisand session, and I just couldn't square that with everything I knew about Jeffrey and how he felt about working with Streisand. During the work on this book, Neil Stubenhaus told me that the story was in fact true, but it happened on a 1977 Lisa Dal Bello record, which was produced by David Foster. Immediately I emailed Foster for confirmation—and *voila!* —Finally, a witness! Mystery solved. Foster confirmed it happened and told me it was indeed on the Dal Bello project.

ELTON AND A LITTLE MORE

Guitarist **RICHIE ZITO** (Joe Cocker, Cher, Eddie Money) remembers sharing the studio with Porcaro on Elton John's 1982 album *Jump Up*. He recalls first going to Paris for a month of sessions with a different drummer. For whatever reason, he says, they weren't able to get anything, so they left Paris and went to George Martin's AIR Studios Montserrat in the Caribbean to continue to work. This time they called Jeff, which Zito says, "ignited the fire." They completed the album in four weeks. Zito says he thinks they re-cut almost everything, perhaps keeping a few tracks. "Aside from being a very talented guy, Jeff was electric," says Zito. "He just lit a fire that we were desperately in need of. One of the tracks, 'Empty Garden,' was particularly special because it was a tribute to John Lennon. He had died within the year. I can picture Jeff on the drums, and I remember Jeff's drum fills in my head."

One of Zito's vivid memories is Jeff walking into the control room one day with a tape of a song Toto had recorded for their new album. He cranked it up on the huge studio monitors; it was "Rosanna." "He was obviously proud of it," says Zito.

Richie and Jeff would have meals together, barbecues on the beach and lots of "great fun." "They were special times," he says. "It was always special with Jeff. He had the best smile. There were times I got to see him overdub without a click track, and I think one of the songs was on that record. It might have been on a track they kept from Paris, maybe the one Pete Townsend played on ("Ball and Chain"). I have a feeling that's the case."

Zito had met Jeff during Neil Sedaka's Troubadour comeback show, which Jeff played. It wasn't too long after Zito first landed in L.A., and he recalls being very stoked as he looked around the stage and saw some heavy hitters, like Jeff, Danny Kortchmar and David Foster (even though they were all early in their careers). "We had to play something like twenty songs, and Jeff came in, sat down and played for an hour and a half without any music," Zito recalls.

JUST A LITTLE SHARED MOMENT

In about 1986, 21-year-old drummer/percussionist Kevin Winard was recording for Bobbie Vinton. The engineer was Tom Perry, who had recently engineered Boz Scaggs' *Silk Degrees.* Perry gave Winard the ultimate compliment, telling him he reminded him of a young Jeff Porcaro. Naturally, it stopped Kevin in his tracks; he stuttered and stammered out a "thank you." Perry and Winard struck up a friendship and stayed in touch. A few months later, Perry invited

Winard to a demo session happening right then at Ocean Way with Jeff on drums, Mike Porcaro on bass and Dan Huff on guitar. Winard hopped in his car and headed to the studio.

"I race over there, and I guess they already had done one tune, and I see Jeff on the stairway," Winard remembers. "He's got his boots on, his ripped jeans, you know, the washed-out jeans, and he's smoking a cigarette. He's by himself, just hanging out, sitting on the steps. He goes, 'How you doing?' in that deep voice. 'I'm Jeff.' I go, 'Yeah, I know who you are. My name is Kevin Winard. I play drums, too.' He goes, 'Oh, you're the drummer Tom said I should be looking out for and worried about.' I said, 'Okay, this is hilarious, but thanks.' He was very sweet."

They went back into the studio and Dan Huff was overdubbing a guitar solo—"just shredding it," Winard recalls. "Just killing it. It was a 'Lido Shuffle' kind of groove he was playing to." Then they recorded a pop ballad, which Winard says they ran through twice, no click. He remembers how cool Jeff looked when he played. "They were going in to listen to the take, and I asked Jeff if Steely Dan was going to do another album, and he said, 'I don't know,' because they hadn't recorded anything in about six years. They played back the take; he had done that kind of sixteenth-note-triplet thing where he ends with the bass drum and hits the cymbal. It was a classic ballad Jeff fill. He was leaning back in the control room, listening back, and the fill was just ever so slightly on top. I mean, just a hair—we're talking milliseconds. I mean, the entire take was amazing—I can't play two notes that would feel as good as Jeff. I'm watching him while he's listening, and he mouths the words 'fuck me.' He looks over at me, and I squint and put my fingers together like you do when you're saying, 'Just a teeny little bit.' He smiled because he looked over to see if I noticed. The way he looked at me was so endearing."

REFLECTING ON HIS MORALS

Don Was says the only time he ever saw Jeff unhappy at the studio was during a break at Western while overdubbing to an old classic Temptations record. "I saw him in the hallway on a break, and he was not happy," Was recalls. "He said, 'Ah, it's weird going back and playing on someone else's stuff,' and I thought the implication was that it was because it was people who weren't alive anymore that he didn't like doing it. And about a week later, I needed him to play on a posthumous Roy Orbison record where we took these demos of Roy and made records out of them. I was afraid to call him because I saw that he didn't like playing on that Motown record. I thought it upset him because the people had passed. I called and said, 'Look, I know you don't like doing this, but I can't think of anyone else who can play and do the thing that's necessary.' And he said, 'No, I'm happy to do it.' It turned out he had been upset that the original drummer who played on the Temptations record was still alive, and they didn't call him. That was his sense of moral ethics. 'Why am I playing on this when the guy who played the original part is still here?' He was physically upset about it.

"Think about that. How many musicians would give a shit about that?"

JEFF PORCARO DISCOGRAPHY

Provided by the website: Jeff Porcaro Session Tracks. Maintained by Mary Oxborrow. View the full discography with future updates at http://www.frontiernet.net/~cybraria/

10cc / *Meanwhile* (Polydor, 1992) 10 + 3 tracks Only drummer listed. Note: Three songs from the *Meanwhile* sessions which didn't make it onto the album were released as B-sides of singles: "Man with a Mission" (B-side of "Women in Love") and "Don't" and "Lost in Love" (both B-sides of "Welcome to Paradise").

A

Ai To Lu Na No Motoni [TV soundtrack] (Alfa [Japan], 1992) No track information

Airplay / *Airplay* (RCA, 1980) 7 tracks "Stranded," "Cryin' All Night," "Nothin' You Can Do About It," "Should We Carry On," "Bix," "She Waits for Me," "After the Love has Gone"

Alessi Brothers / *Alessi* (A&M, 1977) No track-specific credits; 1 of 4 drummers (also Frank Ravioli, Hal Blaine, John Guerin)

Alessi Brothers / *Long Time Friends* (Qwest, 1982) 1 track "Still in Love"

Allan, Laura / *Laura Allan* (Elektra, 1978) 4 tracks "Come as You Are," "Hole in my Bucket," "One Way Ticket," "Yes I Do"

Allen, Peter / *Bi-Coastal* (A&M, 1980) 3 tracks "Hit in the Heart," "Pass this Time," "When this Love Affair is Over"

Allman, Gregg — see *Black Rain* [film soundtrack]

Alpert, Herb / *Keep Your Eyes On Me* (A&M, 1987) 2 tracks "Cat Man Do," "Rocket to the Moon"

Alston, Gerald / *Open Invitation* (Motown, 1990) 4 tracks "I'll Go Crazy," "Never Give Up," "Tell Me This Night Won't End," "Still in Love"

America / *View From the Ground* (Capitol, 1982) No track-specific credits; 1 of 2 drummers (also Willie Leacox)

Anderson, Jon / *In the City of Angels* (Columbia, 1988) 3 tracks "If It Wasn't for Love," "Is it Me," "Top of the World (The Glass Bead Game)"

Anka, Paul / *The Music Man* (United Artists, 1977) 1 of 2 drummers (also Ed Greene)

Anka, Paul / *Walk A Fine Line* (CBS, 1983) 3 tracks "Darlin', Darlin'," "This is the First Time," "Golden Boy"

Anka, Paul / *Somebody Loves You* (Polydor [Germany], 1989) 6 tracks "Somebody Loves You," "You and I," "A Steel Guitar and a Glass of Wine," "Can We," "The Lady Was," "Never Gonna Lose You"

Anri / *Circuit of Rainbow* (For Life, 1989) 4 tracks "Shoo-be Doo-be My Boy," "Who Knows My Loneliness?," "P.S. Kotoba ni Naranai," "Sentimental o Suteta Hito"

Anri / *16th Summer Breeze* (1994) 1 track Disc 1, Track 14: "We Abandoned the Sentimental" (translation of Japanese)

Anri / *Opus 21* (For Life Records [Japan], 1995) 1 track Track 6: "A Thousand Words are Inexhaustible" (translation of Japanese)

Armand, Renée / *In Time* (Windsong, 1978) 4 tracks "Love on a Shoestring," "(We're) Dancin' in the Dark," "In Time," "The Bitter Taste of Wild Things"

Arthur [film soundtrack] (Warner Bros., 1981) 7 tracks "Arthur's Theme" (Christopher Cross), "It's Only Love" (Stephen Bishop), "Touch (Instrumental)," "It's Only Love (Instrumental)," "Money (Instrumental)," "Moving Pictures (Instrumental)," "Arthur's Theme (Instrumental)" (Burt Bacharach)

Asakura, Miki / *Su Te Ki* (King [Japan], 1988) 3 tracks "Find a New Way," "True Love," "Fall in Love"

Atkins, Chet / *Stay Tuned* (CBS, 1985) 2 tracks "Please Stay Tuned," "The Boot and the Stone"

Austin, Patti / *The Real Me* (Qwest, 1988) 2 tracks "Lazy Afternoon," "True Love"

Austin, Patti / *Love Is Gonna Getcha* (GRP, 1990) 1 track "The Girl Who Used to be Me" (Note: This track did not appear on the original album and was added as a bonus track in later pressings. It was originally recorded for the soundtrack of the movie *Shirley Valentine*.)

Austin, Patti — see also *Shirley Valentine* [film soundtrack]

Axton, Hoyt / *Fearless* (A&M, 1976) 2 tracks "Lay Lady Lay," "Beyond These Walls"

Axton, Hoyt / *Road Songs* (A&M, 1977) 1 track "Lay Lady Lay" (Previously appeared on *Fearless*, 1976)

B

B-52s / *Good Stuff* (A&M, 1992) 3 tracks "Hot Pants Explosion," "Breezin'," "Bad Influence"

Bachman, Randy / *Survivor* (Polydor, 1978) 8 tracks (entire album)

Bade, Lisa / *Suspicion* (A&M, 1982) 1 track "Suspicion"

Ballard, Russ / *At the Third Stroke* (Epic, 1978) 6 tracks "Dancer," "Helpless," "Cast the Spirit," "What Does it Take?," "I'm a Scorpio," "My Judgement Day"

Bateman, Justine & the Mystery — see *Satisfaction* [film soundtrack]

Batteau, David / *Happy in Hollywood* (A&M, 1976) 8 tracks "Happy in Hollywood," "Festival of Fools," "Oh, My Little Darling," "Orphee," "Walk in Love," "Spaceship Earth," "You Need Love," "The Gates in Your Heart"

Beck, Robin / *Human Instinct* (DSB, 1992) 4 tracks "Love Yourself," "Every Little Thing," "Bad on Love," "Changing with the Years"

Bee Gees / *Living Eyes* (RSO, 1981) 3 tracks "Living Eyes," "Soldiers," "Cryin' Every Day"

Bel-Air / *Turquoise Blue* (1991) 1 track "Salvia Flower"

Bell & James / *In Black and White* (A&M, 1981) 5 tracks "Love Call My Name," "You've Got the Power," "Gimme the Gun," "Runnin' for Your Life," "Don't Take the Money"

Benoit, David / *Shadows* (GRP, 1991) 5 tracks "Shadows," "Saudade," "Already There," "Castles," "Have You Forgotten"

Benoit, David / *Freedom At Midnight* (GRP, 1987) 5 tracks "Freedom at Midnight," "Along the Milky Way," "The Man with the Panama Hat," "Passion Walk"

Benson, George / *The George Benson Collection* (Warner Bros., 1981) 2 tracks "Turn Your Love Around" (Linn drum machine), "Love all the Hurt Away"

Benson, George / *In Your Eyes* (Warner Bros., 1983) 1 track "Lady Love Me (One More Time)"

Berger, Michel / *Dreams in Stone* (Atlantic, 1982) 6 tracks "JFK (Overture)," "American Island," "Walking through the Big Apple," "Apple Pie," "Rooftops," "Parade"

Berglund, Kristin / *Long Distance Love* (Talent Produksjon [Norway], 1979) No track-specific credits; 1 of 2 drummers (also Bruno Castellucci)

Berlin, Jeff / *Pump It* (Passport, 1986) 1 track "All the Greats"

Big Blue Wrecking Crew (Elektra, 1981) **" [single]** 2 tracks **"**We are the Champions," "New York, New York"

Bim / *Thistles* (Elektra, 1978) 7 tracks "Tender Lullaby," "Right After My Heart," "Waitin' for You, Mama," "Shell of a Life," "Broke Down," "Woh, Me," "Thistles"

Bishop & Gwinn / *This Is Our Night* (Infinity, 1979) 5 tracks "This is our Night," "Santa Monica Pier," "Livin' in Two Different Cities," "Ancient Egypt," "Delicate

Harmony"

Black Rain [film soundtrack] (Virgin, 1989) 1 track "I'll Be Holding On" (Gregg Allman)

Blades, Ruben / *Nothing but the Truth* (Elektra, 1988) 3 tracks "I Can't Say," "The Miranda Syndrome," "In Salvador"

Blakeley, Peter / *Harry's Cafe De Wheels* (Capitol, 1989) No track-specific credits; 1 of 5 drummers (also Jim Keltner, Russ Kunkel, John Robinson, Carlos Vega)

Blessing, The / *Prince of the Deep Water* (MCA, 1991) 3 tracks "Highway 5," "Let's Make Love," "Birdhouse"

Blunstone, Colin / *Never Even Thought* (Rocket, 1978) 9 tracks (entire album)

Bodine, Rita Jean / *Sitting on Top of My World* (20th century, 1974) 8 tracks "Pacified," "Sitting on Top of My World," "Wheels," "Frying Pan Song," "It Ain't Easy," "I was Mistaken," "Sweet Inspiration," "Knickerbocker Holiday"

Bolin, Tommy / *Teaser* (Atlantic, 1975) 4 tracks "The Grind," "Homeward Strut," "Dreamer," "Teaser"

Bolton, Michael / *Time, Love & Tenderness* (Columbia, 1991) 1 track "When a Man Loves a Woman"

Bolton, Michael / *Greatest Hits 1985-1995* (Columbia, 1995) 1 track "When a Man Loves a Woman" *(from Time, Love & Tenderness, 1991)*

Boylan, Terence / *Terence Boylan* (Elektra, 1977) 2 tracks "The War was Over," "Where are You Hiding?" (w/Boylan & Mickey McGee)

Brady, Paul / *Trick or Treat* (Fontana, 1991) Only drummer listed, but Brady listed for drum programming

Branigan, Laura / *Laura Branigan* (Atlantic, 1990) 1 track "Let Me In"

Brothers Johnson / *Winners* (A&M, 1981) 8 tracks "Dancin' Free," "Teaser," "Caught Up," "In the Way," "I Want You," "Do it for Love," "Hot Mama," "Daydreamer Dream"

Brothers Johnson / *Blast! The Latest and Greatest* (A&M, 1982) 1 track "I'm Giving You All My Love"

Browne, Jackson / *The Pretender* (Elektra, 1976) 4 tracks "The Only Child," "Daddy's Tune," "Sleep's Dark and Silent Gate," "The Pretender"

Browne, Severin / *New Improved* (Motown, 1974) No track-specific credits; 1 of 2 drummers (also Russ Kunkel)

Bugatti & Musker / *The Dukes* (Atlantic, 1982; re-issued Warner Bros. [Japan], 1999)

No track-specific credits; 1 of 2 drummers (also John Robinson)

C

Cadd, Brian / *Yesterdaydream* (Capitol, 1978) No track-specific credits; 1 of 4 drummers (also Alvin Taylor, Doug Lavery, Richie Hayward)

Caldwell, Bobby / *Carry On* (Elektra, 1976; Polydor, 1982) 4 tracks "Catwalk," "Jamaica," "Loving You," "Words"
Caldwell, Bobby / *August Moon* (Polydor, 1983) 4 tracks "Fraulein," "Cover Girl," "Class of '69," "Once You Give In" (Note: Drums and drum synthesizers)

California Dreaming (Music from the Original Motion Picture Soundtrack) (Casablanca, 1979) 1 of 4 drummers (also Rick Shlosser, William Leacox, Richie Hayward)

Camp, Steve / *One on One* (Sparrow, 1986) 9 tracks (entire album)

Carlos, Roberto / *Roberto Carlos* (1988) 4 tracks "Todo Mundo é Alguém," "Como as Ondas do Mar," "Se o Amor se Vai," "Papo de Esquina"

Carlos, Roberto / *Roberto Carlos* (1990) 1 track "Por Ela"

Carlton, Larry / *Larry Carlton* (Warner Bros., 1978) 8 tracks (entire album)

Carlton, Larry / *Sleepwalk* (Warner Bros., 1982) 5 tracks "Blues Bird," "Song for Katie," "Frenchman's Flat," "Upper Kern," "10:00 P.M."

Carlton, Larry / *Friends* (Warner Bros., 1983) 8 tracks (entire album)

Carlton, Larry / *Christmas at My House* (MCA, 1989) 3 tracks "Silent Night/ It Came Upon a Midnight Clear," "My Favorite Things/We Three Kings of Orient Are," "The Christmas Song"

Carmen, Eric / *Boats Against the Current* (Arista, 1977) 3 tracks "Boats Against the Current," "Love is All that Matters," "She Did It"

Carmen, Eric / *Change of Heart* (Arista, 1978) 3 tracks "Haven't We Come a Long Way," "End of the World," "Baby I Need Your Lovin'"

Carmen, Eric / *Eric Carmen* (Geffen, 1984) 1 track "She Remembered"

Carrack, Paul — see *Sing* [film soundtrack)

Carter, Raymone / *Raymone Carter* (Reprise, 1991) 1 track "I'll Always Be Around"

Carter, Valerie / *Just a Stone's Throw Away* (CBS, 1977) 8 tracks "Ooh Child," "Ringing Doorbells in the Rain," "Face of Appalachia," "So, So, Happy," "A Stone's

Throw Away," "Cowboy Angel," "City Lights," "Back to Blue Some More"

Carter, Valerie / ***Wild Child*** (Columbia, 1978) 10 tracks (entire album)

Cats, The / ***Hard to Be Friends*** (EMI, 1975) No track-specific credits; 1 of 2 drummers (also John Raines)

Cavaliere, Felix / ***Dreams in Motion*** (Karambolage, 1994) 3 tracks "Stay in Love," "Me for You," "Youngblood"

Cetera, Peter / ***Solitude/Solitaire*** (Warner Bros., 1986) Percussion only, no track-specific credits

Chamfort, Alain / ***Rock 'n' Rose*** (1977) No track-specific credits; 1 of 3 drummers (also Mike Baird, Ed Greene)

Champlin, Bill / ***Single*** (Epic, 1978) 5 tracks "What Good is Love," "We Both Tried," "Careless," "Elayne," "Keys to the Kingdom"

Champlin, Bill / ***Runaway*** (Elektra, 1981) 1 track "Without You"

Chanson / ***Chanson*** (Ariola, 1978) 6 tracks "Don't Hold Back," "I Can Tell," "I Love You More," "Why," "Did You Ever," "All the Time You Need"

Chanson / Together We Stand (1979) No track-specific credits; 1 of 2 drummers (also Harvey Mason)

Char / ***U.S.J.*** (Seesaw, 1981) 6 tracks "Give Me Some Time," "Street Information," "Cry Like a Baby," "Smokey," "You Can't Have Me," "Nice Changes"

Charles, Ray / ***My World*** (Warner Bros., 1993) 2 tracks "If I Could," "Still Crazy After All These Years"

Charts / ***L'Ocean Sans Fond*** (Klaxon [France], 1989) 1 track "Terre"

Charts / ***Notre Monde a Nous*** (Klaxon [France], 1993) 5 tracks "Comme un Magicien," "Insomnie," "Impazzire," "Aime-Moi Encore," "Terre"

Chater, Kerry / ***Part Time Love*** (Warner Bros., 1977) 10 tracks (entire album)

Cher / ***Bittersweet White Light*** (MCA, 1973) 9 tracks (entire album)

Cher / ***Stars*** (Warner Bros., 1975) No track-specific credits; 1 of 6 drummers (also Gary Mallaber, Hal Blaine, Harvey Mason, Jim Gordon, Jim Keltner)

Cher / ***I'd Rather Believe in You*** (Warner Bros., 1976) 10 tracks (entire album)

Cher / ***Prisoner*** (Casablanca, 1979) 1 track "Prisoner"

Cher / ***Take Me Home*** (Casablanca, 1979) 1 track "Git Down (Guitar Groupie)"

Cher / ***Love Hurts*** (Geffen, 1990) 7 tracks "Love Hurts," "Fires of Eden," "One Small Step," "Could've Been You," "When Love Calls Your Name," "Who You Gonna Believe," "The Shoop Shoop Song (It's in His Kiss)"

Chicago / *Chicago 17* (Full Moon/Warner Bros.) 1 track "Stay the Night"
Choir, Yves / *By Prescription Only* (New Musidisc, 1989) 6 tracks "Mad about Town," "After the Rain," "DB," "Bianca," "By Prescription Only," "Morocco Junction"

Clapton, Eric / *Behind the Sun* (Warner Bros., 1985) 2 tracks "See What Love Can Do," "Forever Man"

Clark, Gene / *This Byrd Has Flown* (1995) 1 track "All I Want"

Clark, Terry / *Welcome* (Myrrh, 1978) 4 tracks "Welcome," "Merry Go Round," "Red Cloud," "Living Loving Eyes"

Clarke, Stanley / *Modern Man* (Nemperor, 1978) 3 tracks "He Lives On," "Slow Dance," "Modern Man"

Clover / *Sound City Sessions* (101 Distribution, 2008) No track-specific credits; 1 of 2 drummers listed (also Michael Schreiner); previously unreleased sessions from 1975; "Child of the Streets," unknown others

Cocker, Joe / *I Can Stand a Little Rain* (A&M, 1983) 2 tracks "I Can Stand a Little Rain," "Don't Forget Me"

Cocker, Joe / *Civilized Man* (Capitol, 1984) 4 tracks "Civilized Man," "There Goes My Baby" (+ electric pencil guitar), "Come On In," "Tempted"

Cole, Jude / *A View from 3rd Street* (Reprise, 1990) 1 track "Compared to Nothing"

Cole, Jude / *Start the Car* (Reprise, 1992) 2 tracks "Open Road," "Tell the Truth"

Cole, Natalie / *Good to be Back* (EMI, 1989) 3 tracks "Miss You Like Crazy," "Gonna Make You Mine," "Starting Over Again"

Coltrane, Chi / *Road to Tomorrow* (TK, 1977) No track-specific credits; 1 of 3 drummers (also Jim Gordon, Michael Botts)

Conte, Luis / *Black Forest* (Denon, 1989) 3 tracks "Do the Shrimp," "Working in the Coal Mine," "Black Forest"

Coolidge, Rita / *Heartbreak Radio* (A&M, 1981) 1 track "Walk On In"

Crane, Stephen / *Kicks* (MCA, 1984) 2 tracks "Joanne," "Kicks"

Crawford, Randy / *Secret Combination* (Warner Bros., 1981) 10 tracks (entire album)

Crawford, Randy — see also *I Ought to Be in Pictures* [film soundtrack]

Crawford, Randy / *Windsong* (Warner Bros., 1982) 11 tracks (entire album)

Crawford, Randy / *Nightline* (Warner Bros. [UK], 1983) 2 tracks "Why," "Bottom Line"

Crosby, David / *Thousand Roads* (Atlantic, 1993) 2 tracks "Through your Hands," "Helpless Heart"

Crosby, Stills & Nash / *Daylight Again* (Atlantic, 1982) 1 track "Since I Met You"

Crosby, Stills & Nash / *Allies* (Atlantic, 1983) 2 tracks "War Games," "Raise a Voice" *(both tracks live)*

Cross, Christopher / *Rendezvous* (Polystar [Japan], 1991) 2 tracks "Rendezvous," "Is There Something"

Cross, Christopher — see also *Arthur* [film soundtrack]

Crowell, Rodney / *Life is Messy* (Columbia, 1992) 1 track "It's Not for Me to Judge"

Cummings, Burton / *My Own Way to Rock* (Portrait, 1977) 8 tracks 1 of 4 drummers (also Ollie E. Brown, Rick Shlosser, Lenny Castro) "Never Had a Lady Before," "Come On By" (with Ollie), "Try to Find Another Man," "Got to Find Another Way," "My Own Way to Rock," "Charlemagne" (with Ollie), "Framed" (with Lenny), "A Song for Him"

Cummings, Burton / *Dream of a Child* (Portrait, 1978; re-issued 2000) 3 tracks "Hold On, I'm Comin'," "Guns, Guns, Guns," "Roll with the Punches" (all with Rick Shlosser)

Cummings, Burton / *Plus Signs* (Capitol, 1990) 10 tracks (entire album)

Curiosity Killed the Cat / *Getahead* (Phonogram, 1989) 3 tracks "Cascade," "Trees Don't Grow on Money," "Who Are You"

D

Dal Bello, Lisa / *Lisa Dal Bello* (MCA, 1977) 9 tracks "Look at Me (Millions of People)," "(Don't Want to) Stand in Your Way," "My Mind's Made Up," "Snow White," "Touch Me," "Talk it Over (Even Though My Body's Cold)," "Stay with Me," "Day Dream," "Milk & Honey"

Danny & Joyce / *Ma La Lady* (Jasmine, 1975) No track-specific credits; 1 of 4 drummers (also David Kemper, David Paich, Jim Varley)

Daugherty, Jack / *Jack Daugherty and the Class of Nineteen Hundred and Seventy One* (A&M, 1971) 3 tracks (?) No track-specific credits; 1 of 4 drummers (also Jim Keltner, Hal Blaine, Paul Humphrey). It is probable Jeff is double-drumming with Jim Keltner on "Getting Up," "Feel so Good," and "Number Nine."

Deardorff & Joseph / *Deardorff & Joseph* (Arista, 1976) No specific track credits; 1 of 5 drummers (also David Kemper, David Paich, John Guerin, Ron Tutt)

Dee, Kiki / *Stay with Me* (Rocket, 1979) No track-specific credits; 1 of 2 drummers (also Jim Keltner)

Denander, Tommy / *Less Is More, Part One* (Local Dealer, 1995) 1 track "5492"

Denander, Tommy / *Limited Access* (Noble House, 1997) 2 tracks "5492," "Remember My Conscience"
"5492" appeared previously on *Less Is More, Part One* (1995)

DeVille, Willy / *Miracle* (A&M, 1987) 2 tracks "Could You Would You," "Miracle"

Dick Tracy [film soundtrack] — see Madonna / *I'm Breathless*

Dion, Celine / *Unison* (Epic, 1990) 1 track "Have a Heart"

Dire Straits / *On Every Street* (Warner Bros., 1991) 8 tracks "Fade to Black," "When it Comes to You," "On Every Street," "How Long," "My Parties," "Ticket to Heaven," "Iron Hand," "You and Your Friend."

Doheny, Ned / *Prone* (Columbia, 1979) 2 tracks "Guess Who's Looking for Love Again," "The Devil in You"

Donovan / *Lady of the Stars* (Allegiance, 1984) 1 track "I Love You Baby"

Doonesbury — see Thudpucker, Jimmy

Dore, Charlie / *Listen* (Chrysalis, 1981) 10 tracks (entire album)

Dr. John / *In a Sentimental Mood* (Warner Bros., 1989) 4 tracks "My Buddy," "In a Sentimental Mood," "Don't Let the Sun Catch You Cryin'," "More Than You Know"

Dudek, Les / *Les Dudek* (CBS, 1976) 8 tracks "City Magic," "Sad Clown," "Don't Stop Now," "Each Morning," "It Can Do," "Take the Time," "Cruisin' Groove," "What a Sacrifice"

Dudek, Les / *Say No More* (CBS, 1977) 7 tracks "Jailabamboozle," "Lady You're Nasty," "One to Beam Up," "Avatar," "Old Judge Jones," "What's it Gonna Be," "Zorro Rides Again" (with Tony Williams)

Dudek, Les / *Ghost Town Parade* (CBS, 1978) 2 tracks Both with Jim Keltner: "Bound to be a Change," "Friend of Mine"

Dudek, Les / *Deeper Shades of Blue* (Geosynchronous, 1994) 9 tracks (entire album)

Dudek, Les / *Freestyle* (E Flat Productions, 2003) 2 tracks "Hot Fun in Dixieland," "Wild Hearted Weekend"

Duncan, Bryan / *Anonymous Confessions Of A Lunatic Friend* (Myrrh, 1990) 11 tracks (entire album)

Dune [film soundtrack] (Polydor, 1984) Score composed by Toto; mostly performed by Vienna Symphony Orchestra; 1997 reissue includes previously unreleased tracks

E

Earth, Wind & Fire / *Touch The World* (Sony, 1987) 2 tracks "You and I," "Every Now and Then"

Edelman, Randy / *If Love Is Real* (Arista, 1977) 9 tracks (entire album)

Elias, Jonathan / *Requiem For The Americas* (Enigma, 1990) 1 track "Within the Lost World"

Elliman, Yvonne / *Yvonne* (RSO, 1979) 3 tracks "Love Pains," "Greenlight," "Rock Me Slowly"

Elliot, Brian / *Brian Elliot* (Warner Bros., 1978) No track-specific credits; 1 of 4 drummers (also Mike Baird, James Gadson, Gary Ferguson)

England Dan & John Ford Coley / *I Hear the Music* (A&M, 1977) No track-specific credits; 1 of 3 drummers (also Jim Gordon and Ronnie Tutt)

England Dan & John Ford Coley / *Dr. Heckle and Mr. Jive* (Big Tree, 1979) 2 tracks "Hollywood Heckle & Jive," "Broken Hearted Me"

Evans, Linda / *You Control Me* (Ariola, 1979) 6 tracks No track-specific credits; only drummer listed; 1 of 3 on percussion (also David Williams and James Jamerson, Jr)

Eye to Eye / *Eye to Eye* (Warner Bros., 1982) 6 tracks "Hunger Pains," "Life in Motion," "Nice Girls," "Progress Ahead," "Physical Attraction," "Time Flys"

F

Fagen, Donald / *The Nightfly* (Warner Bros., 1982) 5 tracks "I.G.Y.," "Green Flower Street," "Ruby Baby," "The Nightfly," "The Goodbye Look"

Farina, Sandy / *All Alone In the Night* (MCA, 1980) No track-specific credits; 1 of 3 drummers (also Ed Greene, Rick Shlosser)

Farrell, Joe / *Night Dancing* (1978) 1 track "Night Dancing"

Fields, Brandon / *Other Places* (Nova, 1990) 3 tracks "Undercover," "Gina," "Know How"

Fifth Dimension / *Earthbound* (ABC, 1975) 1 track "Moonlight Mile"

Finnigan, Mike / *Black and White* (CBS, 1978) 8 tracks "How Wrong Can You Be," "The Words," "Can't Keep a Secret" "I Could Never Leave You," "Sailfish," "Expressway to Your Heart," "Love Might Keep Us Forever," "Let Me Love You"

Flower / *Flower* (United Artists, 1977) No track-specific credits; 1 of 3 drummers (also David Wolfert, Ed Greene)

Flyer / *Send a Little Love My Way* (Infinity Records, 1979) 1 track "Send a Little Love My Way"

Fogelberg, Dan / *Windows and Walls* (Epic, 1984) 1 track "Gone Too Far"

Fools Gold / *Mr. Lucky* (CBS, 1977) 9 tracks (entire album) No track-specific credits; only drummer listed; also percussion

For the Boys [film soundtrack] (Atlantic, 1991) 1 track "Every Road Leads Back to You" (Bette Midler)

Ford, Dwayne / *Needless Freaking* (Epic, 1982) 4 tracks "Lovin' and Losin' You," "Stranger in Paradise," "The Hurricane," "Midnight Ride"

Ford, Robben / *Talk to Your Daughter* (Warner Bros., 1988) 1 track "I Got Over It"

Four Tops / *Tonight* (Casablanca, 1981) 9 tracks (entire album)

Fra Lippo Lippi / *Light And Shade* (Virgin, 1987) 3 tracks "Home," "Light and Shade," "Crazy Wisdom"

Frampton, Peter / *Breaking all the Rules* (A&M, 1981) 9 tracks (entire album)

Franke and the Knockouts / *Makin' the Point* (MCA, 1984) 1 track "Come Rain or Shine"

Franklin, Aretha / *Aretha* (Columbia, 1980) 4 tracks "What a Fool Believes," "Come to Me," "Can't Turn You Loose," "Love Me Forever"

Franklin, Aretha / *Love all the Hurt Away* (Arista, 1981) 10 tracks (entire album)

Franklin, Rodney / *In the Center* (Columbia, 1978) 5 tracks "Spanish Flight," "I Like the Music Make it Hot," "On the Path," "Sunrise," "Life Moves On"

Franklin, Rodney / *Rodney Franklin* (CBS, 1980) 3 tracks "Life Moves On," "I Like the Music Make it Hot," "On the Path" (Note: These tracks previous appeared on *In the Center* (1978))

Freneticas / *Caia Na Gandaia* (1978) 1 track "Dancin' Days"

Friendly Enemies / *Round One* (Prodigal, 1978) 1 track "Dark Eyes"

Fromholz, Steven / *A Rumour in My Time* (Capitol, 1976) 2 tracks "She's a Lady," "I'd Have to Be Crazy"

G

Gable, Bill / *There Were Signs* (BMG, 1989) 2 tracks "Go Ahead and Run" (hi-hat, surdo) "High Trapeze" (drums and percussion)

Gardestad, Ted / *Blue Virgin Isles* (Polar [Sweden], 1978) 1 of 2 drummers on 10 of 12 tracks (also Jim Keltner); 1 of several on percussion

Gatlin, Larry and the Gatlin Brothers / *Smile* (CBS, 1985) 7 tracks "One on One," "Say," "I Saved Your Place," "Can't Stay Away from Her Fire," "Get Me into This Love, Lord," "I'd Throw It All Away," "Indian Summer"

George, Lowell / *Thanks I'll Eat It Here* (Warner Bros., 1979) No track-specific credits; one of several drummers

Getz, Stan / *Apasionado* (A&M, 1990) 8 tracks (entire album)

Gianco, Ricky / *E' Rock 'n' Roll* (Fonit Cetra [Italy], 1990) 13 tracks (entire album)

Gilmour, David / *About Face* (CBS, 1984) 10 tracks (entire album)

Give My Regards to Broad Street [film soundtrack] (Capitol, 1984) 1 track "Silly Love Songs" (Paul McCartney), "Silly Love Songs (Reprise)" (Note: Jeff, along with Steve Lukather, also appeared in the film with the band that played this song.)

Glengarry Glen Ross [film soundtrack] (Elektra, 1992) 6 tracks "Main Title," "You Met My Wife," "The Plot," "In the Car," "Don't Sell to Doctors," "The Nyborgs"

Go West / *Indian Summer* (EMI, 1992) 2 tracks "Faithful" (cymbals kit), "The Sun and the Moon"

Gold, Andrew / *All This and Heaven Too* (Asylum, 1978) 3 tracks "Always for You," "Thank You for Being a Friend," "I'm On My Way"

Goodrum, Randy / *Fool's Paradise* (Polydor, 1982) 10 tracks (entire album)

Goodrum, Randy / *An Exhibition* (Polydor, 1992) 2 tracks "Flight 136," "Touch" (Note: Remainder of album programmed by Goodrum.)

Grand Canyon [film soundtrack] (RCA, 1992) No track-specific credits; on percussion only

Green, Kathe / *Kathe Green* (Prodigal, 1976) No track-specific credits; 1 of 2 drummers (also Kenny "Spider" Rice)

Greg Mathieson Project / *Baked Potato Super Live!* (CBS/Sony [Japan], 1982; re-issued Cool Sounds [Japan], 1989) all tracks "Bomp Me," "Thank You," "First Time Around," "Goe," "I Don't Know," "I'm Home," "The Spud Shuffle" (Note: A different version of "Bomp Me" appeared on the *Zapped* film soundtrack.)

Grimaldi-Zeiher / *Grimaldi/Zeiher* (1978) 3 tracks "La Star Des Couloirs," "Conversations," "Et Je Recommence"

Grimaldi-Zeiher / *Récidive* (RCA, 1980; re-issued Culture Press, 1998) 7 tracks "Sidonie," "Derniers Moments," "Cache-Toi," "Debout en Haut du Toit," "Récidive," "Mélo Dans la Tête," "La Califusa"

Grimaldi, Bernard / *Toute Ressemblance Avec Des Personnes Ayant* (Antenna [France], 1991) 4 tracks "La Star Des Couloirs," "Mélo Dans La Tête," "Sidonie," "Cité Des Anges"

Gross, Henry / *What's in a Name* (Capitol, 1981) 1 track "Why Go Falling in Love"

Guitar Workshop / *Guitar Workshop in L.A.* (JVC, 1988) 4 tracks "Take it All," "Donna," "Bawls," "Bull Funk"

Guitar Workshop / *Tribute to Otis Redding* (JVC, 1989) 2 tracks "I Can't Turn You Loose," "A Tribute to a King"

Gurvitz, Adrian / *Sweet Vendetta* (Jet, 1979) 4 tracks "The Wonder of it All," "The Way I Feel," "Free Ride," "One More Time"

H

Hall and Oates / *Beauty on a Back Street* (RCA, 1977) 8 tracks (entire album) Also on electronic drums

Hall, Lani / *Blush* (A&M, 1980) 1 track "Wish I Would've Stayed"

Hamlisch, Marvin / "Pachelbel Canon In D" (Planet, 1980) (B-side of 7" vinyl release of "Theme from *Ordinary People*")

Hamada, Mari / *In the Precious Age* (Victor, 1987) 2 tracks "999," "My Trial"

Hamilton, Dirk / *You Can Sing on the Left or Bark on the Right* (ABC, 1976) 9 tracks (entire album)

Hamilton, Dirk / *Alias I* (ABC, 1977) 1 track "In the Eyes of the Night"

Hammond, Albert / *Your World and My World* (CBS, 1980) 3 tracks "When I'm Gone," "Experience," "Take Me Sailing"

Hancock, Herbie / *Lite Me Up* (CBS, 1982) 1 track "Paradise"

Harris, Hugh / *Words for Our Years* (Capitol, 1990) 2 tracks "Love Kicks," "Rhythm of Life" (Note: Credit on first track reads Jeff "Drums is drums" Porcaro)

Hathaway, Lalah / *Lalah Hathaway* (Virgin, 1990) 1 track "Somethin'"

Hawkins, George Jr. / *Every Dog Has Its Day* (1996) 1 track "Every Dog" [sample]

Henderson, Finis / *Finis* (Motown, 1983) No track-specific credits; 1 of 3 drummers (also Carlos Vega, J.R. Robinson)

Henley, Don / *I Can't Stand Still* (Elektra, 1982) 4 tracks "You Better Hang Up" (with Don Henley), "Long Way Home," "Talking to the Moon," "Dirty Laundry"

Henley, Don / *The End of the Innocence* (Geffen, 1989) 1 track "New York

Minute"

Henley, Don / *Actual Miles: Henley's Greatest Hits* (Geffen, 1995) 2 tracks "Dirty Laundry," "New York Minute"

Hester, Benny / *Perfect* (Frontline, 1989) 10 tracks (entire album)

Hewett, Howard / *Howard Hewett* (Elektra, 1990) 1 track "If I Could Only Have That Day Back"

Hill, Warren / *Devotion* (RCA, 1993) 1 track "Another Goodbye"

Hodges, James & Smith / *What Have You Done for Love* (London, 1978) 1 of multiple drummers

Hodgson, Roger / *Hai-Hai* (A&M, 1987) 5 tracks "My Magazine," "London," "You Make Me Love You," "Who's Afraid?," "House on the Corner"

Holland, Amy / *On Your Every Word* (Capitol, 1983) 3 tracks "Anytime You Want Me," "I'll never give up," "Rollin' By"

Horn, Jim / *Work It Out* (Warner Bros., 1990) 2 tracks "My Reggae Love," "Rio Sunrise"

Howard, James Newton / *James Newton Howard & Friends* (Sheffield Lab, 1984) 8 tracks "Caesar," "Gone Buttlefishin'," "She," "L'Daddy," "Tandoori," "E-Minor Shuffle," "Slippin' Away II," "Amuseum"

Hudson Hawk [film soundtrack] (Varese Saraband, 1992) 1 track "Hudson Hawk Theme (Instrumental)"

Hughes, Bill / *Dream Master* (Epic, 1979) 4 tracks "Waiting for You to Fly," "Gypsy Lady," "Only Your Heart Can Say," "Dream Master"

Humperdink, Engelbert / *Don't You Love Me Anymore* (Columbia, 1981) 7 tracks "Don't You Love Me Anymore?," "Stay Away," "Say Goodnight," "Maybe This Time," "Baby Me Baby," "Heart Don't Fail Me Now," "Till I Get It Right"

Hungate, David / *Souvenir* (CBS, 1990; re-issued Clubhouse, 1994) 7 tracks "Lament," "Souvenir," "Dreamland," "Only a Heart Can Know," "Third Stone from the Sun," "A Perfect Love," "The Leap"

Hurley, Arthur & Gottlieb / *Sunlight Shinin'* (A&M) 1 of 3 drummers (also Jim Keltner, John Raines)

I

I Ought to Be in Pictures [film soundtrack] (Warner Bros., 1982) 1 track "One Hello"

Ian, Janis / *Restless Eyes* (Columbia, 1981) 1 track "Passion Play"

Iglesias, Julio / *Starry Night* (Columbia, 1990) No track-specific credits; 1 of 2 drummers (also Carlos Vega)

Iijima, Mari / *My Heart in Red* (Alfa Moon, 1989) 4 tracks "Still," "Send Love to Me," "Boyfriend," "Believe in Love"

Imperials / *Stand by the Power* (Day Spring, 1982) No track-specific credits; 1 of 2 drummers (also Carlos Vega)

Indigo / *Indigo* (Warner Bros., 1977) 10 tracks (entire album)

Ingram, James / *It's Real* (Warner Bros., 1989) 1 track "Love 1 Day at a Time"

J

Jackson, La Toya / *La Toya Jackson* (RCA, 1980) 1 track "Night Time Lover"

Jackson, Michael / *Thriller* (Epic, 1982) 4 tracks "The Girl is Mine," "Beat It," "Human Nature," "The Lady in My Life"

Jackson, Michael / *Dangerous* (Epic, 1991) 1 track "Heal the World"

Jackson, Michael / *Thriller: 25th Anniversary Edition* (Sony, 2008) 1 track "For All Time" (unreleased track from the original *Thriller* sessions)

Jacksons / *Victory* (Epic, 1984) 2 tracks "Torture," "Wait"

Jacksons / *2300 Jackson Street* (1989) 1 track "Midnight Rendezvous"

James, Etta / *Deep In the Night* (Warner Bros., 1978) 10 tracks (entire album)

Jans, Tom / *Eyes of an Only Child* (Columbia, 1975) No tracks specific credits; 1 of 3 drummers (also Jim Keltner, Harvey Mason)

Jans, Tom / *Champion* (Canyon, 1982) 2 tracks "Chambers of the Heart," "Visions"

Jarreau, Al / *Breakin' Away* (Warner Bros., 1981) 1 track "Breakin' Away"

Jarreau, Al / *Jarreau* (Warner Bros., 1983) 3 tracks "Mornin'," "Step by Step," "Black and Blues"

Jason, Lisa / *Envision* (2000) 1 of 4 drummers (also Carlos Vega, Joe Pet, John Morelli)

Jelly / *A True Story* (Asylum, 1977) 1 track "Susan"

John, Elton / *Jump Up* (Geffen, 1982) 10 tracks (entire album)

Jones, Rickie Lee / *Rickie Lee Jones* (Warner Bros., 1979) 1 of 3 drummers (also Steve Gadd, Andy Newmark)

Jones, Rickie Lee / *Magazine* (Warner Bros., 1984) 2 tracks "It Must Be Love," "Magazine"

Jordan, Marc / *Mannequin* (Warner Bros., 1978) 9 tracks "Marina del Ray," "Survival," "Jungle Choir," "Mystery Man," "Red Desert," "Street Life," "Dancing on the Boardwalk," "Only Fools," "Lost Because You Can't be Found"

Jordan, Marc / *Blue Desert* (Warner Bros., 1979) 3 tracks "I'm a Camera," "From Nowhere to This Town," "Release Yourself"

K

Kante, Mory / *Touma* (Mercury, 1990) 3 tracks "Kroughegne," "Mankene," "Faden"

Kapono, Henry / *Same World* (Browntown Records,1991) 4 tracks "Insy'a" (percussion), "All Because I Love You," "Papaya Blues," "The Hero"

Karizma / *Dreams Come True* (Vap, 1987) 1 track "Blues for Ronnie" (with Carlos Vega)

Katsuragi, Yuki / *L.A. Spirits* (Radio C, 1982) 9 tracks (entire album)

Kawai, Naoko / *Daydream Coast* (Columbia, 1984) 5 tracks "If You Want Me," "Second Nature," "Live Inside Your Love," "I Love It," "As Long as We're Dreaming"

Kawauchi, Junichi / *Juice* (Fun House, 1992) 9 tracks "Kimi no ude ni Dakaretai," "Save Our Love," "Virgin Smile no Kimi," "White Venus," "You're the Only One," "Rainy Weekend," "Studio-A no Yuujin," "Todokanu Omoi (Lovesick Blues)," "Murderess"

Kazu Matsui Project / *Time No Longer* (RVC, 1981) 4 tracks "Overture (Rainy Moon)," "Sunset and the Minstrel," "Voice from the Dark," "Bonfire (Centerdance)"

Keane Brothers / *Keane Brothers* (20th Century, 1977) No track-specific credits; 1 of 5 drummers (also Ed Greene, Harvey Mason, John Keane, Nigel Olsson)

Kennedy, Ray / *Ray Kennedy* (Columbia, 1980) No track-specific credits; 1 of 3 drummers (also Rick Shlosser, Mike Baird)

Kershaw, Nik / *The Works* (MCA, 1989) 1 track "Walkabout"

King, Marva / *Feels Right* (Planet, 1981) 2 tracks "Memories," "Feeling Wonderful Feelings"

Kipner, Steve / *Knock the Walls Down* (Elektra, 1980) 9 tracks "The Beginning," "Knock the Walls Down," "Lovemaker," "School of Broken Hearts," "War Games," "Love is Its Own Reward," "Cryin' Out for Love," "Guilty," "The Ending"

Kleinow, "Sneaky Pete" / *The Legend and the Legacy* (Shiloh, 1994) 2 tracks "Louisiana," "Silverbird"

Knighton, Reggie / *Reggie Knighton* (Columbia, 1977) No track-specific credits; 1 of 3 drummers (also Curly Smith, Richie Hayward)

Kraft, Robert / *Retro Active* (RCA, 1983) 4 tracks "Single, Solo," "Just Another Notch on the Bedpost," "Heartless," "On the West Side"

Kunkel, Leah / *I Run With Trouble* (CBS, 1980) 2 tracks "Let's Begin," "Never Gonna Lose My Dream of Love Again"

Kurozumi, Kengo / *Pillow Talk* (Sony, 1989) 3 tracks "Kanojyo wa Warukunai," "Pillow Talk," "You and Me"

L

L.A. Workshop with New Yorker / *Norwegian Wood II* (Denon, 1989) 5 tracks "Sgt. Pepper's Lonely Hearts Club Band," "Eleanor Rigby," "Norwegian Wood (This Bird has Flown)," "This Boy," "Roll Over Beethoven"

LaBelle, Patti / *Be Yourself* (MCA, 1989) 1 track "Need a Little Faith"

LaBounty, Bill / *This Night Won't Last Forever* (Warner Bros., 1978) 3 tracks "A Tear Can Tell," "Crazy," "I Hope You'll Be Very Unhappy Without Me"

LaBounty, Bill / *Bill LaBounty* (Warner Bros., 1982) 4 tracks "Dream On," "Comin' Back," "Look Who's Lonely Now," "Nobody's Fool"

LaBounty, Bill / *Time Starts Now: The Definitive Anthology 75/11* (Rhino France, 2011, box set, import) 8 tracks "She's So Popular" (previously unreleased track) and all tracks on the two albums listed above

Lake, Greg / *Greg Lake* (Chrysalis, 1981) No track-specific credits; 1 of 4 drummers (also Jode Leigh, Michael Giles, Ted McKenna)

Lasley, David / *Soldiers on the Moon* (Agenda, 1990) 9 tracks "It's Too Late," "Soldiers on the Moon," "Audrey," "You Bring Me Joy," "Give My Heart Back to Me," "Without the One You Love," "Roslyn," "Since I Fell for You," "God Bless the Child"

Liaison / *Liaison* (Frontline, 1989) 9 tracks "When the Kingdom Comes Down," "You are His Main Concern," "Go and Sin No More," "Man with a Mission," "The Way, the Truth, and Life," "Kick it Down," "The Light is On," "He Lives," "Give Me One Day at a Time"

Lofgren, Nils (& Grin) / *Night Fades Away* (MCA, 1981) 2 tracks "Sailor Boy," "Anytime at All"

Loggins, Kenny — see Various Artists / *In Harmony 2*

Los Lobotomys / *Los Lobotomys* (Maxus, 1992; originally Creatchy, 1989) 7 tracks "Oozer," "Purple Haze (truncated)," "Big Bone," "Jorainbo," "Lobotomy

Stew," "Little Wing," "All Blues"

Love and Money / *Strange Kind of Love* (Polygram, 1988) 11 tracks (entire album)

Lukather, Steve / *Lukather* (CBS, 1989) 2 tracks "Drive a Crooked Road," "Steppin' on Top of Your World"

Lynn, Cheryl / *Start Over* (Columbia, 1987) 1 track "Don't Run Away"

Lyons & Clark / *Prisms* (Shelter, 1976) 3 tracks "Keepin' the Heat Down," "Sweet Misery," "Open the Door"

M

MacGregor, Mary / *...In Your Eyes* (Ariola, 1978) 3 tracks "Memories," "Satisfied," "Hold Tight"

Madonna / *Like A Prayer* (Sire, 1989) 1 track "Cherish"

Madonna / *I'm Breathless* (Sire, 1990) 4 tracks (On cover: Music from and inspired by the film *Dick Tracy*) "He's a Man," "Hanky Panky," "Cry Baby," "Something to Remember"

Magnusson, Jacob / *Jack Magnet* (1981) 5 tracks "Meet Me After Midnight," "Movies," "From Now On," "Shell Shock," "Lifesaver"

Manchester, Melissa / *Hey Ricky* (Arista, 1982) 7 tracks "You Should Hear How She Talks About You," "Slowly," "Hey Ricky (You're a Low Down Heel)," "I'll Always Love You," "Race to the End," "Come in from the Rain," "Looking for the Perfect Ahh"

Mancini, Chris / *No Strings* (Atlantic, 1983) 2 tracks "(Here Comes That) Hurt Again," "Lovers in Love"

Mangione, Gap / *Suite Lady* (A&M, 1978) 5 tracks "Mellow Out!," "I Don't Know," "You Can't Cry for Help," "Sister Jo/Time of the Season," "King Snake"

Mangione, Gap / *Ardis* (Josh Music, 2002) 2 tracks "I Don't Know," "Time of the Season"

Manhattan Transfer / *Pastiche* (Atlantic, 1978) 2 tracks "Who, What, Where, When, Why," "Pieces of Dreams"

Manhattan Transfer / *Extensions* (Atlantic, 1979) 2 tracks "Birdland" (with Ralph Humphrey), "Twilight Tone" (also bongos & anvil)

Manhattan Transfer / *Bodies and Souls* (Atlantic, 1983) 2 tracks "This Independence," "American Pop"

Manhattan Transfer / *The Offbeat of Avenues* (Columbia, 1991) 1 track "Confide in Me"

Manilow, Barry / *Showstoppers* (1991) 1 of several on percussion

Marc Tanner Band / *No Escape* (Elektra, 1979) 2 tracks "Getaway," "Lost at Love"

Madrones, Benny / *Benny Madrones* (Curb, 1989) 5 tracks "I Never Really Loved You at All," "For a Little Ride," "How Could You Love Me," "Never Far Away," "Run to You"

Marlo, Clair / *Let It Go* (Sheffield Lab, 1989) 6 tracks "Til They Take My Heart Away," "Lonely Nights," "Let it Go," "All for the Feeling," "I Believe (When I Fall in Love it will be Forever)," "Where You Are"

Marx, Richard / *Rush Street* (Capitol, 1991) 4 tracks "Hand in Your Pocket," "Calling You," "Superstar," "Chains Around My Heart"

Marx, Richard / *Paid Vacation* (Capitol, 1994) 1 track "One Man"

Mason, Dave / *Mariposa De Oro* (CBS, 1978) 2 tracks "Will You Still Love Me Tomorrow," "Bird on the Wind"

Mathieson, Greg — see Greg Mathieson Project

Mathis, Johnny / *The Island* (recorded 1989; released Real Gone Music 2020) 10 tracks (entire album)

Matsuda, Hiroyuki / *Two of Us* (Tokuma, 1992) 3 tracks "Moving Night," "Stop Your Crying," "Surely Night Will Come" (translated from Japanese)

Matsui, Kazu — see Kazu Matsui Project

Mattogrosso, Ney / *Feitico* (1978) 1 track "Não Existe Pecado au sul do Equador"

Mayall, John / *Bottom Line* (DJM, 1979) 2 tracks "Celebration," "Come With Me"

McCartney, Paul — see *Give My Regards to Broad Street* [film soundtrack]

McCluskey, David / *A Long Time Coming* (GRT, 1978) 3 tracks "A Long Time Coming," "Let Me Be Alone," "One More Try"

McDonald, Country Joe / *Rock and Roll Music From the Planet Earth* (Fantasy, 1978) 10 tracks (entire album) (Note: With Chili Charles on one track)

McDonald, Country Joe / *Child's Play* (Rag Baby, 1983) 1 track "Power Plant Blues"

McDonald, Michael / *If That's What It Takes* (Warner Bros., 1982) 3 tracks "I Keep Forgettin'," "That's Why," "No Such Luck"

McDonald, Michael / *No Lookin' Back* (Warner Bros., 1985) 9 tracks (entire album)

McDonald, Michael / *Take It to Heart* (Reprise, 1990) 7 tracks "Love Can Break Your Heart," "Lonely Talk," "Searchin' for Understanding," "Homeboy," "No

Amount of Reason," "One Step Away" (programmed), "You Show Me"

Medeiros, Glenn / *Not Me* (MCA, 1988) 2 tracks "Someday Love," "Fallin'"

Meissner, Stan / *Dangerous Games* (Polygram [CA], 1984) 1 track "You Make It All So Easy"

Melanie / *Photograph* (Atlantic, 1979) No track-specific credits; 1 of 3 drummers (also Jim Gordon, John Guerin)

Melanie / *Seventh Wave* (Neighbourhood [UK], 1983) ? tracks No track-specific credits; 1 of 5 drummers (also Jim Gordon, Liberty DeVitto, John Guerin & Dennis Bryan)

Mendes, Sergio / *Brasil 86* (A&M, 1986) 5 tracks "Daylight," "Take This Love," "The River (O Rio)," "Flower of Bahia (Flor da Bahia)," "No Place to Hide"

Mendes, Sergio / *Arara* (A&M, 1989) 1 track "Some Morning"

Mendes, Sergio / *Brasileiro* (Elektra, 1992) 5 tracks "Indiado," "Lua Soberana," "Senhoras do Amazonas" (percussion), "Kalimba," "Barabare"

Messina, Jim / *Messina* (Warner Bros., 1981) 9 tracks (entire album)

Meyers, Bill / *The Color of the Truth* (Agenda, 1990) 4 tracks "I'm Still Standing," "Perfect Crime," "Just Say the Word," "Say What You Mean"

Midler, Bette — see *For the Boys* [film soundtrack]

Miguel, Luis / *Busca una Mujer* (WEA, 1989) 5 tracks "Esa Nina," "Separados," "Por Favor Senora," "Pupilas de Gato," "Soy un Perderdor"

Misato / *Flowerbed* (Epic, 1989) 1 track Track #7

Mitre, Fahed / *Toda La Verdad* (Sonosur, 1990) 4 tracks "Toda la Verdad," "Jennifer," "Si no Estas," "Un Juego"

Mizukoshi, Keiko / *I'm Fine* (Taurus, 1982) 10 tracks (entire album)

Moore, Patsy / *Regarding the Human Condition* (Warner Bros., 1993) 6 tracks "These Loving Eyes," "A City on a Hill," "Lies (That I Have Known)," "Shooting the Breeze," "With Regard," "The Pilgrim Song"

Moore, Sally / *Sally Moore* (Curb, 1990) 3 tracks "My Heart has a Mind of Its Own," "What are You Waiting For," "Love is a Step Away"

Moore, Tim / *White Shadows* (Asylum, 1977) 8 tracks "In the Middle," "Love Overnight," "It's Your Life," "Dolorosa," "I Got Lost Tonight," "The Devil Inside My Heart," "Little Bo's Peep Show," "To Cry for Love"

Morgan, Jaye P. / *Jaye P. Morgan* (Candor,1976) 4 tracks "Keepin' it to Myself," "Here is Where Your Love Belongs," "It's Been So Long," "Let's Get Together"

Moyet, Alison / *Raindancing* (Epic, 1986) 4 tracks "Weak in the Presence of

Beauty," "You Got Me Wrong," "Without You," "Is this Love?"

Murph the Surf [film soundtrack] (Motown, 1975) No track-specific credits; percussion only

N

N.S.P. / *2-nen-me No Tobira* (Canyon, 1976) 5 tracks "Haru wo Mitsuketa," "Rizumu mo Yoroshiku," "Kimi wo Yuuwaku," "Soup in the Morning," "Oshitaoshitai"

Nakajima, Fumiaki / *Girl Like You* (Hoshizora, 1992) 2 tracks Tracks 3 and 8 (titles in Japanese)

Nakamura, Masatoshi / *Across The Universe* (Columbia, 1988) 8 tracks Tracks 2,4,5,6,7,8,9,10 (titles in Japanese)

Neville, Ivan / *If My Ancestors Could See Me Now* (Polygram, 1988) 9 tracks "Sun," "Primitive Man" (percussion), "Not Just Another Girl," "Falling Out of Love," "Out in the Streets," "Never Should Have Told Me," "Up to You," "Another Day's Gone By," "After All That Time"

Newman, Randy / *Trouble in Paradise* (Warner Bros., 1983) 10 tracks "I Love L.A.," "Christmas in Cape Town," "The Blues," "Mikey's," "My Life is Good," "Miami," "Take Me Back," "There's a Party at My House," "I'm Different," "Song for the Dead"

Newman, Randy / *Land of Dreams* (Reprise, 1988) 4 tracks. For these 4 tracks both Jeff and John Robinson are listed: "Four Eyes," "Something Special," "Red Bandana," "I Want You to Hurt Like I Do"

NewSong / *Living Proof* (DaySpring/Word, 1991) No track-specific credits; only drummer listed, but others on drum programming. Jeff also credited for "miscellaneous percussion and extraneous noise"

Newton, Juice / *Juice Newton & Silver Spur* (RCA, 1975) 1 track "Catwillow River"

Newton, Juice / *Well Kept Secret* (Capitol, 1978) 2 tracks. Tracks unidentified

Newton-John, Olivia / *Making a Good Thing Better* (EMI, 1977) 10 tracks "Making a Good Thing Better," "Slow Dancing," "Ring of Fire," "Coolin' Down," "Sad Songs," "You Won't See Me Cry," "So Easy to Begin," "I Think I'll Say Goodbye," "Don't Ask a Friend," "If Love is Real"

Nougaro / *Pacifique* (1989) 2 tracks "Pacifique," "Kine"

Nunn, Terri — see *Sing* [film soundtrack]

O

Oda, Kazumasa / *K. Oda* (Fun House, 1986) 8 tracks. Note: May be same as album titled *Oh Yeah!*; titles translated from Japanese "Let Me Listen to the Love," "Two of Us in Winter," "Stay the Sadness," "1985," "Nights Fade Away," "Believe Me," "See You in the Sea Tomorrow," "This Sky is Too High"

O'Day, Alan / *Appetizers* (Pacific, 1977) 10 tracks "Soldier of Fortune," "Satisfied," "Started Out Dancing, Ended Up Making Love," "Gifts," "Slot Machine," "Undercover Angel," "Do Me Wrong But Do Me," "Catch My Breath," "Angie Baby," "Caress Me Pretty Music"

O'Day, Alan / *Oh Johnny* (Pacific, 1979) No track-specific credits; 1 of 2 drummers (also Mike Baird)

Off Course / *As Close As Possible* (Fun House, 1987) 1 track "Love Everlasting"

Off Limits [film soundtrack] (Varese, 1988) No track-specific credits; 1 of 4 on percussion (also Joe Porcaro, Emil Richards, Michael Fisher)

O'Kane, John / *Solid* (Charisma, 1991) 4 tracks "Second Time Around," "Move Away," "Solid Ground," "Love Cars"

Okumoto, Ryo / *Makin' Rock* (SeeSaw, 1980) 7 tracks "Keep on Rockin'," "Crystal Highway," "Solid Gold," "L.A. Express," "Freedom," "Original View," "Mystery White"

Omura, Kenji / *Kenji Shock* (Alfa, 1978) 6 tracks "Left-Handed Woman," "Better Make it Through Today," "Yumedono," "Shock," "Boston Flight," "The Mase"

Orbison, Roy / *King of Hearts* (Virgin, 1992) 1 track "We'll Take the Night"

Originals / *Communique* (Soul, 1976) No track-specific credits; 1 of 2 drummers (also Alvin Taylor)

Originals / *Down To Love Town* (Soul, 1977) 1 track "Down to Love Town" (with Alvin Taylor)

Or-N-More / *Or-N-More* (EMI, 1991) 4 tracks "Only 2 Hearts," "Half a Heart," "Sail On," "I Need Someone to Talk To"

Ozaki, Ami / *Hot Baby* (Canyon, 1981) 8 tracks "Love is Easy," "Karada ni Nokoru Wine," "Cats Eye," "Kagirinai Nikushimi no Hate Ni," "Angela," "Prism," "Wanderer in Love," "Serenade"

P

Pacific Winds / *Pacific Coast Highway* (Interface[Japan], 1989) No track-specific credits; 1 of 2 drummers (also Mike Baird)

Pack, David / *Anywhere You Go* (Warner Bros., 1985) 1 track "Prove Me Wrong"

Pages / *Pages* (EMI, 1981) 3 tracks "You Need a Hero," "Come on Home," "Automatic"

Palmer, Robert / *Some People Can Do What They Want* (Island, 1976) No track-specific credits; 1 of 3 drummers (also Richie Hayward, Spider Webb)

Parker, Ray Jr. / *After Dark* (Geffen, 1987) No track-specific credits; 1 of 3 drummers (also Carlos Vega, Ollie E. Brown)

Parr, John / *Running the Endless Mile* (Atlantic, 1986) 1 track "Don't Leave Your Mark on Me"

Parton, Dolly / *Dolly, Dolly, Dolly* (RCA, 1980) 10 tracks (entire album)

Patty, Sandi / *Another Time...Another Place* (Word/Epic, 1990) 10 tracks "Unto Us (Isaiah 9)," "Another Time, Another Place," "I Will Rejoice," "Unexpected Friends," "I'll Give You Peace," "For All the World," "Rejoice," "Willing to Wait," "I Lift my Hands," "O Calvary's Lamb"

Patty, Sandi / *Find It On The Wings* (1994) 1 track "Imagine (How God can Sing)" (percussion)

Patton, Robbie / *Do You Wanna Tonight* (1979) No track-specific credits; 1 of 2 drummers (also Ed Greene)

Peck, Danny / *Heart and Soul* (Arista, 1977) 4 tracks "Halo of Fire," "Looking so Hard," "Brother of Mine," "Where is my Heart"

Perry, Phil / *The Heart of the Man* (Manhattan, 1991) 1 track "Good-Bye"

Phillips, Shawn / *Transcendence* (RCA, 1978) 1 track "Lady in Velvet"

Pink Floyd / *The Wall* (Columbia, 1979) 1 track "Mother"

Poco / *Legacy* (RCA, 1989) No track-specific credits; 1 of 3 drummers (also George Grantham [Poco] and Gary Mallaber)

Pointer Sisters / *Energy* (Planet, 1978) 7 tracks "Lay It on the Line," "Hypnotized," "As I Come of Age," "Come and Get Your Love," "Happiness," "Echoes of Love," "Everybody is a Star"

Pointer, June / *June Pointer* (Columbia, 1989) 3 tracks "Why Can't We be Together," "Put Your Dreams Where Your Heart Is," "Love Calling"

Preston, Billy / *The Way I Am* (Motown, 1981) No track-specific credits; 1 of 4 drummers (also Rick Shlosser, James Gadson, Ollie E. Brown)

R

Radioactive / *Ceremony of Innocence* (Marquee/Avalon [Japan], 2001) 8 tracks "Story of Love," "Crimes of Passion," "Waiting for a Miracle," "Ceremony of Innocence," "Liquid," "A Case of Right or Wrong," "Silent Cries," "When You're in Love," "Remember My Conscience" (bonus track on Japanese release, hidden track on European release)

Radioactive / *Taken* (MTM-Music, 2005) 1 track "Stronger than Yesterday"

Raitt, Bonnie / *Home Plate* (Warner Bros., 1975) No track-specific credits; 1 of 2 on percussion (also Joe Porcaro)

Raitt, Bonnie / *Luck of the Draw* (Capitol, 1991) 1 track "Luck of the Draw"

Randall, Elliott / *Elliot Randall's New York* (Kirshner, 1977) 4 tracks "Just a Thought" (with Allan Schwartzberg), "It's Gonna be Great," "I Give Up," "When You got the Music (Part 3)" (with Allan Schwartzberg)

Reddy, Helen / *Music, Music* (Capitol, 1976) 2 tracks "Music, Music," "Music is my Life"

Reddy, Helen / *Ear Candy* (Capitol, 1977) No track-specific credits; 1 of several drummers

Remler, Emily / *This is Me* (Justice, 1990) 2 tracks "Deep in a Trance," "Love Colors"

Rene & Angela / *Rise* (Capitol, 1983) No track-specific credits; 1 of 4 drummers (also Andre Fischer, John Robinson, Ollie Brown)

Richie, Lionel / *Can't Slow Down* (Motown, 1983) 1 track "Running with the Night"

Richie, Lionel / *Louder than Words* (Motown, 1996) 1 track "Climbing"

Ritenour, Lee / *Captain Fingers* (Epic, 1977) 2 tracks "Isn't She Lovely," "Space Glide"

Ritenour, Lee / *Rit* (Elektra, 1981) 2 tracks "Mr. Briefcase," "Good Question"

Ritenour, Lee / *Rit 2* (Elektra, 1982) 1 track "Voices"

Rivera, Danny / *Danny* (1983) 1 of 2 drummers (also Mike Baird)

Roberts, Bruce / *Bruce Roberts* (Elektra, 1977) No track-specific credits; 1 of 2 drummers (also Grady Tate)

Roberts, David / *All Dressed Up* (Elektra, 1982) 10 tracks (entire album)

Rogers, D.J. / *Love, Music and Life* (RCA, 1977) 10 tracks (entire album)

Rogers, D.J. / *On the Road Again* (RCA, 1976) No track-specific credits; 1 of 4 drummers (also Harvey Mason, Paul Mabrey, Rick Calhoun)

Ross, Diana / *Baby It's Me* (Motown, 1977) 5 tracks "Gettin' Ready for Love,"

"You Got It," "Baby it's Me," "Your Love is So Good for Me," "Top of the World"

Ross, Diana / *Ross* (RCA, 1983) 5 tracks "That's How You Start Over," "Love will Make it Right," "You Do It," "Pieces of Ice," "Let's Go Up" (Drums and drum synthesizer)

Russell, Brenda / *Love Life* (A&M, 1981) 8 tracks "Love Life," "Rainbow," "Something I Like to Do," "Lucky," "Sensitive Man," "Deep Dark and Mysterious," "If You Love," "Thank You"

Russell, Brenda / *Two Eyes* (Warner Bros., 1983) 1 track "Hello People" (tambourine)

Russell, Brenda / *Kiss Me with the Wind* (A&M, 1990) 2 tracks "Justice in Truth," "On Your Side"

S

Sager, Carole Bayer / *Too* (Elektra, 1978) 1 track "I Don't Wanna Dance No More"

Sager, Carole Bayer / *Sometimes Late at Night* (Epic, 1981) 6 tracks "I Won't Break," "Tell Her," "You and Me (We Wanted it All)," "Wild Again," "Easy to Love Again," "Stronger than Before"

Sanford & Townsend / *Duo-Glide* (Warner Bros., 1977) 9 tracks "Paradise," "Ain't it So, Love," "Livin's Easy," "Starbrite," "Voodoo," "Mississippi Sunshine," "Eights and Aces," "Sometimes When the Wind Blows," "Eye of my Storm (Oh Woman)"

Satisfaction [film soundtrack] (AJK, 1988) 1 track "(I Can't Get No) Satisfaction" [version 2] (Justine Bateman & the Mystery)

Saunders, Fernando / *Cashmere Dreams* (Grudge, 1989) 2 tracks "Love is Blind," "Let's Talk About It"

Sayer, Leo / *Endless Flight* (Chrysalis, 1976) 3 tracks "When I Need You," "No Business like Love Business," "Magdalena"

Sayer, Leo / *Thunder in my Heart* (Warner Bros., 1977) 6 tracks "Thunder in my Heart," "Easy to Love," "I Want You Back," "World Keeps on Turning," "There isn't Anything," "Everything I've Got" (Drums and drum synthesizer)

Sayer, Leo / *Leo Sayer* (Warner Bros., 1978) 6 tracks "Stormy Weather," "Dancing the Night Away," "La Booga Rooga," "Running to my Freedom," "Frankie Lee," "Don't Look Away"

Sayer, Leo / *World Radio* (Warner Bros., 1982) 10 tracks (entire album)

Scaggs, Boz / *Silk Degrees* (CBS, 1976) 10 tracks (entire album)

Scaggs, Boz / *Down Two Then Left* (CBS, 1977) 10 tracks (entire album) Drums and drum synthesizer

Scaggs, Boz / *Middle Man* (CBS, 1980) 6 tracks "Jojo," "Simone," "You Can Have Me Anytime," "Middle Man," "Angel You," "You Got Some Imagination"

Scaggs, Boz / *Hits!* (Columbia/Legacy, 1980) 7 tracks "Lowdown," "Miss Sun" (not previously released on an album), "Lido Shuffle," "We're All Alone," "Look What You've Done to Me" (not previously released on an album), "Jojo," "You Can Have Me Anytime"

Scaggs, Boz / *Other Roads* (CBS, 1988) 6 tracks "What's Number One," "Right out of my Head," "I Don't Hear You," "Mental Shakedown," "Crimes of Passion," "Cool Running," "The Night of Van Gogh"

Scaggs, Boz — see also *Two of a Kind* [film soundtrack]

Schaffer, Janne / *Earmeal* (CBS, 1978) 9 tracks (entire album)

Schascle / *Haunted by Real Life* (Reprise, 1991) 4 tracks "Restless Sun," "Haunted by Real Life," "Freedom," "Hold Me"

Schmit, Timothy B. / *Playin' It Cool* (Asylum 1984) 3 tracks "Wrong Number," "Take a Good Look Around You," "Tell Me What You Dream"

Schmit, Timothy B. / *Tell Me the Truth* (MCA, 1990) 1 track "Something Sad"

Scialfa, Patti / *Rumble Doll* (Columbia, 1993) 2 tracks "Come Tomorrow," "Talk to Me Like the Rain"

Scott, Marilyn: "God Only Knows"/"Lay Back Daddy" (single) (Big Tree, 1977) 2 tracks

Scott, Tom / *Street Beat* (Columbia, 1979) 6 tracks "Street Beat," "Greed," "Come Closer, Baby," "Heading Home," "Give Me Your Love," "The Shakedown"

Seals & Crofts / *Diamond Girl* (Warner Bros., 1973) 10 tracks. No track-specific credits; 1 of 4 drummers (also Jim Gordon, John Guerin, Harvey Mason, Sr.)

Seals & Crofts / *Unborn Child* (Warner Bros., 1974) 12 tracks (entire album)

Seals and Crofts / *I'll Play for You* (Warner Bros., 1975) 1 track "Golden Rainbow"

Seals & Crofts / *Get Closer* (Warner Bros., 1976) No track-specific credits; 1 of 2 drummers (also Ed Greene)

Sebastian, John / *Welcome Back* (Reprise, 1976) 10 tracks (entire album)

Sgt. Pepper's Lonely Hearts Club Band [film soundtrack] (RSO, 1979) No track-specific credits; 1 of 3 drummers (also Bernard Purdie, David Dowell)

Sharp, Randy / *First in Line* (Nautilus, 1976) 9 tracks (entire album)

Shepard, Vonda / *Vonda Shepard* (Reprise, 1989) 2 tracks "Hold Out," "Baby Don't You Break My Heart Slow"

Shepard, Vonda / *The Radical Light* (Reprise, 1992) 3 tracks "Searchin' My Soul," "100 Tears Away," "Wake Up the House"

Shiratori, Emiko / *Hello* (King, 1991) 2 tracks "Close Your Eyes," "Hello"

Shirley Valentine [film soundtrack] (Silva Screen, 1989)
"The Girl Who Used to be Me" (Patti Austin)

Shot in the Dark / *Shot in the Dark* (RSO, 1981) No track-specific credits; 1 of 3 drummers (also Harry Stinson, Russ Kunkel)

Silveira, Ricardo / *Small World* (Verve, 1992) 2 tracks "Small World," "Haven't We Met"

Simon, Carly — see *The Spy Who Loved Me* [film soundtrack]

Simon, Paul / *Hearts and Bones* (Warner Bros., 1983) 1 track "Train in the Distance"

Simon, Paul / *Negotiations and Love Songs 1971-1986* (Warner Bros., 1988) 1 track "Train in the Distance" (from *Hearts and Bones*, 1983)

Sinclair, Stephen / *A+* (U.A., 1977) No track-specific credits; 1 of 2 drummers (also Ed Greene)

Sing [film soundtrack] (Columbia, 1989) 1 track "Romance (Love Theme)" (Paul Carrack and Terri Nunn)

Sing Like Talking / *Reunion* (Fun House, 1992) 1 track "Stay Gold (Live)"

Snow, Tom / *Taking it All in Stride* (Capitol, 1975) 1 track "Everybody Lives Everybody Dies"

Snow, Tom / *Tom Snow* (Capitol, 1976) 6 tracks "Hurry Boy," "Doin' it All Again," "Rosanna," "Rock & Roll Widow," "Shoestring Destiny," "I'm Only Passin' Through"

Snow, Tom / *Hungry Nights* (Arista, 1982) 2 tracks "Straight for the Heart," "Don't Call it Love"

Sonny & Cher / *Mama was a Rock 'n' Roll Singer* (MCA, 1973) 10 tracks (entire album)

Sonny and Cher / *Live In Las Vegas, Vol. 2* (MCA, 1974) 12 tracks (entire album)

Sorrenti, Alan / *Angeli di Strada* (1982) 1 track "Angeli de Strada (Maybe I Love You)"

Spence, Judson / *Judson Spence* (Atlantic, 1988) 3 tracks "Attitude," "Dance with Me," "Take Your Time" (*bonus track on CD*)

Springsteen, Bruce / *Human Touch* (Columbia, 1992) 12 tracks. All tracks except "With Every Wish" (Kurt Wortman) and "Pony Boy" (no drums)

Springsteen, Bruce / *Tracks* (4 CD set) (Columbia, 1998) 5 tracks "Leavin' Train," "Sad Eyes," "My Lover Man," "When the Lights Go Out," "Trouble in Paradise"

Springsteen, Bruce / *18 Tracks* (Columbia, 1999) 2 tracks "Sad Eyes," "Trouble River"

Springsteen, Bruce — see also Various Artists / *Last Temptation of Elvis*

Spy Who Loved Me, The [film soundtrack] (EMI, 1977) 1 track "Nobody Does it Better" (Carly Simon)

Steely Dan / *Pretzel Logic* (MCA, 1974) 2 tracks "Night by Night," "Parker's Band"

Steely Dan / *Katy Lied* (MCA, 1975) 9 tracks "Black Friday," "Bad Sneakers," "Rose Darling," "Daddy Don't Live in that New York City No More," "Doctor Wu," "Everyone's Gone to the Movies," "Your Gold Teeth II," "Chain Lightning," "Throw Back the Little Ones"

Steely Dan / *Gaucho* (MCA, 1980) 1 track "Gaucho"

Steely Dan / *Gold* (Expanded version) (MCA, 1991) 3 tracks "Chain Lightning," "FM," "Bodhisattva (Live)" (with Jim Hodder)

Steinberg, Dianne / *Universal Child* (ABC, 1977) 1 track "Amazing"

Stewart, Al / *Time Passages* (Arista, 1978) 1 track "Valentina Way"

Stewart, Al / *24 Carrots* (Arista, 1980) No track-specific credits; 1 of 5 drummers (also Russell Kunkel, Mark Sanders, Steve Chapman, Beau Segal)

Stewart, Rod / *Vagabond Heart* (Warner Bros., 1991) 1 track "The Motown Song"

Stigers, Curtis / *Curtis Stigers* (Arista, 1991) 4 tracks "Sleeping with the Lights On," "The Man You're Gonna Fall in Love With," "I Keep Telling Myself," "The Last Time I Said Goodbye"

The Strand / *The Strand* (Island, 1980) 2 tracks "Can't Look Back" (drums), "Just a Little More Time" (percussion), also produced all 10 tracks

Streisand, Barbra / *Streisand Superman* (CBS, 1977) No track-specific credits; 1 of 3 drummers (also Harvey Mason, Ed Greene)

Streisand, Barbra / *Songbird* (CBS, 1978) 4 tracks "Love Breakdown," "Honey Can I Put on Your Clothes," "Songbird," "One More Night"

Streisand, Barbra / *Wet* (CBS, 1979) 2 tracks "Come Rain or Come Shine," "Kiss Me in the Rain"

Streisand, Barbra / *Til I Loved You* (Columbia, 1988) 1 track "Some Good Things Never Last"

Summer, Donna / *Donna Summer* (Casablanca, 1982) 1 track "Protection"

Suzuki, Yoshiyuki / *L.A. Lullaby* (Teichiku, 1981) 9 tracks (entire album)

Syreeta / *The Spell* (Tamla, 1983) 3 tracks "Freddie Um Ready," "Once Love Touches Your Life," "Fall Apart"

T

Taff, Russ / *Walls of Glass* (Myrrh, 1983) 4 tracks "Walls of Glass," "Jeremiah," "Inside Look," "Just Believe"

Taff, Russ / *Russ Taff* (Word, 1987) 1 track "I Still Believe" (hi-hat only)

Tagg, Eric / *Smilin' Memories* (EMI, 1975) 10 tracks "Tell-Tale Eyes," "Love to Love You," "Castle of Loneliness," "Steamboat," "Sandman (Bring me a Dream)," "The Only Thing You Said," "A Fantasy," "After All," "Never had the Feelin'," "Hang On"

Takanaka, Masayoshi / *Brasilian Skies* (Kitty, 1978) No track-specific credits; 1 of 4 drummers (also James Gadson, Shi-Shan Inoe, Wilson Das Neves)

Takeuchi, Mariya / *Miss M* (RCA, 1980) 5 tracks "Sweetest Music," "Every Night," "Morning Glory," "Secret Love," "Heart to Heart"

Tanner, Marc — see Marc Tanner Band

Taupin, Bernie / *He Who Rides the Tiger* (Asylum, 1980) No track-specific credits; 1 of 2 drummers (also Carlos Vega)

Taylor, James "J.T" / *Master of the Game* (MCA, 1989) 1 track "Master of the Game" (Note: Only track featuring a live drummer.)

Taylor, Livingston / *Man's Best Friend* (Epic, 1980) 1 track "Sunshine Girl"

Temptations / *Surface Thrills* (Motown, 1983) 2 tracks "One Man Woman," "Made in America"

Temptations / *Milestone* (1991) 1 track "Get Ready" (tambourine, drums (overdub))

Thomas, Mickey / *As Long as You Love Me* (RCA, 1976) 5 tracks "The Street Only Knew Your Name," "Take Me to Your Lover," "Can You Fool," "Somebody to Love," "Dance it Off"

Three Dog Night / *American Pastime* (ABC, 1976) 1 of 3 drummers (also Micky McMeel, Ed Greene)

Thudpucker, Jimmy & Trudeau, Garry / *Doonesbury's Jimmy Thudpucker and the Walden West Rhythm Section Greatest Hits* (Windsong, 1977) No track-specific credits; 1 of 2 drummers (also Mike Baird)

Torrance, Richard / *Bareback* (Capitol, 1977) 5 tracks "Moonlight Trippin'," "Stay Young," "Lovin' Good," "Tender Memory," "Circle of Confusion"

Toto / *Toto* (Columbia, 1978) 10 tracks

Toto / *Hydra* (Columbia, 1979) 8 tracks

Toto / *Turn Back* (Columbia, 1980) 8 tracks

Toto / *Toto IV* (Columbia, 1982) 10 tracks

Toto / *Isolation* (Columbia, 1984) 10 tracks

Toto / *Fahrenheit* (Columbia, 1986) 10 tracks
(Steve Jordan plays drums on "Lea," Jeff is on percussion)

Toto / *The Seventh One* (Columbia, 1988) 11 tracks

Toto / *Past to Present, 1977-1990* 13 tracks. Includes four previously unreleased tracks: "Love has the Power," "Out of Love," "Can You Hear What I'm Saying," "Animal"

Toto / *Kingdom of Desire* (Relativity, 1992) 12 tracks

Toto / *XX (1977-1997)* (Columbia, 1998) 10 tracks "Goin' Home," "Tale of a Man," "Last Night," "In a Word," "Modern Eyes," "Right Part of Me," "Mrs. Johnson," "Miss Sun," "Love is a Man's World," "On the Run (Live)"

Toto — see also *Dune* [film soundtrack]

Toussaint, Allen / *Motion* (Warner Bros., 1978) 10 tracks (entire album)

Triplets / *Thicker than Water* (Mercury, 1990) 6 tracks "Dancing in the Shadows," "Light a Candle," "So Hard," "Spanish Surrender," "Where Were You When I Needed You," "Reminds Me of You"

Triumvirat / Russian Roulette (Harvest, 1980) 11 tracks (entire album)

Trudeau, Garry — see Thudpucker, Jimmy

Turrentine, Stanley / *Betcha* (Elektra, 1979) 4 tracks "Betcha," "Take Me Home," "Hamlet," "Long Time Gone"

Tutone, Tommy / *National Emotion* (Columbia, 1983) 1 track "National Emotion"

Twenty Mondays / *The Twist Inside* (Spindletop, 1986) 4 tracks "God's Song," "Cracks in the Wall," "The Twist Inside," "Little Girl"

Two of a Kind [film soundtrack] (MCA, 1983) 1 track "The Perfect One" (Boz Scaggs)

V

Various Artists / *12th Annual Battle of the Bands Hollywood Bowl 1971* (Custom Fidelity, 1971) Jeff was invited to play with the production band after his group performed in this event. Unknown if he appears on any tracks included in this 2-record set.

Various Artists / *In Harmony 2* (Columbia, 1981) 1 track "Some Kitties Don't Care" (Kenny Loggins)

Various Artists / "Hands Across America" [single] (EMI, 1986) 1 track

Various Artists / *Last Temptation of Elvis* (Mayking, 1990) 1 track "Viva Las Vegas" (Bruce Springsteen cover done for this charity album)

Vaughan, Sarah / *Songs of the Beatles* (Atlantic, 1981; re-issued on CD) 12 tracks "Get Back," "And I Love Her," "Eleanor Rigby," "Fool on the Hill," "You Never Give Me Your Money," "Come Together," "I Want You (She's so Heavy)," "Blackbird," "Something," "Here There and Everywhere," "The Long and Winding Road," "Hey Jude"

Voudouris, Roger / *On the Heels of Love* (Boardwalk, 1981) 8 tracks (entire album)

W

Walsh, Brock / *Dateline: Tokyo* (Warner Bros., 1983) No track-specific credits; 1 of 3 drummers (also Beau Segal, Mike Botts)

Walsh, Joe / *The Confessor* (Warner Bros., 1985) No track-specific credits; 1 of 5 drummers (also Denny Carmassi, Jim Keltner, Chet McCracken, Rick Marotta)

Wandelmer, Emile / *Lover Cafe* (WEA, 1990) 6 tracks "Lovers Cafe," "Nora," "Charlie," "Vends Pas Ton Blues," "Dame," "Seul"

Ware, Leon / *Leon Ware* (Elektra, 1982) 6 tracks "Slippin' Away," "Lost in Love with You," "Shelter," "Can I Touch You There," "Miracles," "Where are They Now"

Warwick, Dionne / *Friends In Love* (Arista, 1982) 1 track "What is This"

Warwick, Dionne / *Friends* (Arista, 1985) 2 tracks "Whisper in the Dark," "Remember Your Heart"

Watanabe, Misato / *Flower Bed* (Sony, 1989) 1 track "Pineapple Romance"

Watanabe, Misato / *Hello Lovers* (Sony, 1992) 2 tracks "Lovin' You," Japanese title

Watanabe, Sadao / *Front Seat* (Warner Bros., 1989) 4 tracks "Only in My Mind," "Miles Apart," "Any Other Fool," "Takin' Time"

The Waters / *Waters* (Warner Bros., 1977) 7 tracks "I Just Wanna Be the One (In Your Life)," "What am I Doing Wrong," "If There's a Way," "Could it be the Magic," "Party, Party," "We Can Change It," "Peace at Last"

Waters, Roger / *Amused To Death* (Columbia, 1992) 1 track "It's a Miracle"

Waybill, Fee / *Read My Lips* (Capitol, 1984) 1 track "Caribbean Sunsets"

Weaver, Patty / *Patty Weaver* (Warner Bros., 1982) No track-specific credits; 1 of 2 drummers (also Mike Baird)

Webb, Jimmy / *Angel Heart* (Columbia, 1982) 10 tracks (entire album)

Webb, Susan / *Bye Bye Pretty Baby* (Anchor, 1975) No track-specific credits; (also Jim Keltner and Jim Gordon)

Weisberg, Tim / *Outrageous Temptations* (Cypress, 1989) 3 tracks "Outrageous Temptations," "Promise Me," "Margarita"

White Horse / *White Horse* (Capitol, 1977) 5 tracks "It Doesn't Take Much," "Lost and in Trouble," "Can't Stop Loving You (Though I Try)," "Everloving Arms," "Take Me Back"

Williams, David / *Take the Ball and Run* (O.F., 1983) 3 tracks "When Your Dreams Come True," "I Don't Want to Say Goodbye," "She's That Lady"

Williams, David / *Somethin' Special* (1991) 1 track "Tell the World"

Williams, Deniece / *When Love Comes Calling* (CBS, 1979) 5 tracks "When Love Comes Calling," "Why Can't We Fall in Love?," "God Knows," "I Found Love," "Turn Around"

Williams, Jerry [Lynn] / *Gone* (Warner Bros., 1979) 5 tracks "Gone," "Easy on Yourself," "Talk to Me," "Song for my Father," "Getting Stronger"

Williams, Joseph / *I Am Alive* (Kitty (J), 1996) 1 track "I am Alive"

Williams, Paul / *Classics* (1977) 2 tracks "Evergreen (Love Theme from *A Star is Born*)," "With One More Look at You"

Wood, Lauren / *Lauren Wood* (Warner Bros., 1979) No track-specific credits; 1 of 5 drummers (also Alvin Taylor, Jim Keltner, Mike Baird, Rick Shlosser)

Woods, Ren / *Out of the Woods* (1979) No track-specific credits; 1 of 3 drummers (also Ed Greene, James Gadson)

Wright, Gary / *Headin' Home* (Warner Bros., 1979) 1 track "Moonbeams"

Y

Yamamoto, Tatsuhiko / *Next* (Alfa, 1990) 6 tracks "Swinging in the Rain," "Phoenix Islands," "Rain and Pain," "Heroine with No Name," 2 Japanese titles

Yazawa, Eikichi / *P.M. 9* (Warner Bros., 1982) No track-specific credits; 1 of 3 drummers (also Gary Ferguson, Rick Shlosser)

Yazawa, Eikichi / *I am a Model* (Warner Bros., 1983) 9 tracks (entire album)

Young, Paul / *The Crossing* (Columbia, 1993) 6 tracks "Hope in a Hopeless World," "Won't Look Back," "Only Game in Town," "Love Has No Pride," "Half a

Step Away," "Follow On"

Young, Paul / *Tomb of Memories: The CBS Years 1982-1994* (Sony, 2015) 5 tracks. "Hope in a Hopeless World," "Now I Know What Made Otis Blue," "Half a Step Away," "Souls Unknown," "Cold Sweat" (Note: The last two tracks were recorded at the sessions for *The Crossing* in 1992 and not released until this compilation.)

Z

Zevon, Warren / *Excitable Boy* (Asylum, 1978) 1 track "Night Time in the Switching Yard"

Zevon, Warren / *The Envoy* (Asylum, 1982) 5 tracks "The Envoy," "The Overdraft," "The Hula Hula Boys" (+ Tahitian log drums, pule sticks), "Let Nothing Come Between You," "Looking for the Next Best Thing"

Zevon, Warren / *Mr. Bad Example* (Giant, 1991) 9 tracks. All tracks except "Things to Do in Denver When You're Dead" (Jim Keltner)

At Billy Cobham's PASIC 1985 clinic at the Sheraton Universal Hotel, Los Angeles. Front row L to R: Greg Errico, Neal Schon, Jeff Porcaro, unknown, Buddy Miles. (Photo by Rick Malkin)